DEFINING THE HUMANITIES

DEFINING THE HUMANITIES

❧

HOW REDISCOVERING A TRADITION CAN IMPROVE OUR SCHOOLS

❧

WITH A CURRICULUM FOR TODAY'S STUDENTS

Second Edition

/Formerly published as *Education's Great Amnesia: Reconsidering the Humanities from Petrarch to Freud*/

Robert E. Proctor

INDIANA UNIVERSITY PRESS • BLOOMINGTON AND INDIANAPOLIS

This book is a publication of

Indiana University Press
601 North Morton Street
Bloomington, Indiana 47404-3797 USA

www.indiana.edu/~iupress

Telephone orders   800-842-6796
Fax orders   812-855-7931
Orders by e-mail   iuporder@indiana.edu

Originally published by Indiana University Press in 1988 as *Education's Great Amnesia: Reconsidering the Humanities from Petrarch to Freud*

The paper used in this publication meets the minimum requirements of American National Standard for Information Sciences—Permanence of Paper for Printed Library Materials, ANSI Z39.48-1984.

Manufactured in the United States of America

Library of Congress Cataloging-in-Publication Data

Proctor, Robert E., date
Defining the humanities : how rediscovering a tradition can improve our schools : with a curriculum for today's students / Robert E. Proctor. — 2nd ed.
  p.   cm.
Rev. ed. of: Education's great amnesia. c1988.
Includes bibliographical references (p.   ) and index.
ISBN 0-253-33421-7 (cloth : alk. paper). — ISBN 0-253-21219-7 (pbk. : alk. paper)
1. Learning and scholarship—History. 2. Humanities—Study and teaching—United States. 3. Education, Humanistic—United States.
I. Proctor, Robert E., date   . Education's great amnesia.
II. Title.
AZ221.P75   1998
001.3'09—dc21   98-18653

1 2 3 4 5 03 02 01 00 99 98

*For
my mother and brother
and
in memory of my father*

Contents

❧

PREFACE TO THE SECOND EDITION   ix

PREFACE   xix   INTRODUCTION   xxiii

PART ONE
The Birth of the Humanities in the Renaissance

1
The Humanist Transformation of Classical Antiquity
3

2
Petrarch and the Origins of the Humanities
25

3
Cicero in Grief: The Classical Soul Revealed
59

4
Ancient and Modern Categories of Thought
76

PART TWO

The Death of the Humanities in the Modern World

5

Degeneration from Within
87

6

Change from Without
118

PART THREE

Looking Forward

7

Lessons from the Renaissance
146

8

The Relevance of the Ancients
156

9

A Curriculum for Today
170

Epilogue
200

APPENDIX: THE HUMANITIES AND INTERNATIONAL STUDIES   203

NOTES   211   WORKS CITED   222   INDEX   231

PREFACE TO THE SECOND EDITION

This book first appeared in 1988 as *Education's Great Amnesia: Reconsidering the Humanities from Petrarch to Freud, with a Curriculum for Today's Students*. I have renamed this new edition *Defining the Humanities: How Rediscovering a Tradition Can Improve Our Schools* in order to speak more directly to a new generation of readers, for whom the word "amnesia" no longer applies. You can't forget what you never knew. The humanities were once synonymous with "classical education"—the study of the languages and culture of ancient Greece and Rome—and constitute one of the primary educational and cultural traditions of Western civilization. But most people today know the humanities only ahistorically, simply as a group of disciplines, juxtaposed to other groups, such as the sciences, the social sciences, and the arts, and with no particular connection to Western civilization. The problem with this understanding is that its incompleteness robs us of the rich insights that a dialogue with the *tradition* of the humanities provides. Consider a recent book on the decline of the humanities: *What's Happened to the Humanities?* (ed. Alvin Kernan, Princeton: Princeton University Press, 1997). By defining the humanities "historically" as "the old subjects, which in many forms and under a variety of names—the nine muses; the liberal arts; quadrivium and trivium; rhetoric, dialectic, and logic; humane letters—were the major part of Western education for over two millennia" (p. 3), the editor presents a false and confused picture of what the humanities were, and thus precludes at the very outset a full answer to the question asked in the title. The contributors, in fact, are either unaware that the humanities have a history, or do not see the relevance of that history to our discussions today. I do. That's the case I try to make in this book.

Reviewers have accepted without serious criticism the main outlines of the story I tell. My one regret is that I did not mention Giambattista Vico. The title of Mark Lilla's excellent book tells why: *G. B. Vico: The Making of an Anti-Modern* (Cambridge, Mass.: Harvard University Press, 1993). Vico, long before Nietzsche, studied classical antiquity as a way of thinking more clearly about the pitfalls of modernity, especially the limitations of Descartes's attempt to reduce knowledge to clear and distinct ideas. Vico stressed the importance of imagination, especially historical imagination, and metaphor and analogy, as ways of understanding and talking about human existence. But the inclusion of Vico would not change the main point of the story: that within the crucible of the

Renaissance's reappropriation of classical culture, the humanities emerged as a response to a new "modern" experience of the self—our self.

Mention of Vico brings to mind the work of Hans-Georg Gadamer, whose *Truth and Method* (2nd rev. ed., New York: Crossroad, 1991) I had not read when I wrote this book. In an age dominated by what he calls "the ontological prejudice implied in the ideal of scientific objectivity" whereby "science attempts to become certain about entities by methodically organizing its knowledge of the world" (p. 476), Gadamer seeks to provide the philosophical and epistemological underpinnings for another kind of knowledge and experience, the historical (and ultimately aesthetic and moral) knowledge we derive from a conversation with the past. A dialogue across time stands at the heart of the tradition of the humanities. Gadamer's work underscores the importance of this tradition by showing how the process of understanding in general, even in the sciences, is fundamentally historical and "dialogic" in nature.

Another work I was unable to comment upon in the first edition is Bruce A. Kimball's *Orators and Philosophers: A History of the Idea of Liberal Education* (1986; expanded ed., New York: College Entrance Examination Board, 1995). It shares with my own work a desire to put our contemporary debates into an historical context. Kimball is concerned with the history of liberal education, I with the history of the humanities. The two are not the same (see below, pp. 14–16). The Renaissance humanities, however, play a crucial role in the transmission of the liberal arts ideal, thus the story that Kimball tells, if correct, will broaden the context in which we think about the humanities. The story is simple: Cicero lamented that Socrates, in attacking the sophists, had divorced philosophy from oratory, wisdom from eloquence (*De oratore* 3.16.59–61). Kimball interprets the history of liberal education in the West as a competition between the philosopher's search for truth and the orator's desire to shape moral character and create good citizens. According to this scheme, Renaissance humanism marks one of the periods in Western history when the oratorical tradition was dominant. While not disagreeing entirely with this assessment, I would highlight an important difference between Kimball's approach and mine: I see more discontinuities in our cultural inheritance than he does. I argue that the Renaissance humanists profoundly transformed classical culture in the very act of trying to recover it. They preserved the ideal of a liberal arts education, but in a psychological and epistemological context that is modern rather than ancient. The transformation was so complete that it continues to influence our understanding of the ancients, including Kimball's. Furthermore, if my description of the ancient versus the modern experience of self and community is at least partially correct, it suggests that the ideals that Kimball delineates may have changed meaning over time in a very significant way. The fundamental contrast in the liberal arts tradition is thus not between orators and philosophers, but between ancient and modern self-consciousness.

The necessity of coming to terms with breaks in our cultural inheritances is one of the main points of this book, and one that separates my recommendations for the humanities from those who call simply for a return to more structured general education programs. Discussions in the press of Harold Bloom's *The Western Canon: The Books and School of the Ages* (New York: Harcourt Brace & Company, 1994) and David Denby's *Great Books: My Adventures with Homer, Rousseau, Woolf, and Other Indestructible Writers of the Western World* (New York: Simon & Schuster, 1996) point to a renewed interest in Great Books programs, especially among those of the baby-boomer generation who now look back with nostalgia on the more structured curricula they had in college and high school. The Great Books approach is certainly to be preferred to fragmented and incoherent general-education programs. But as I explain more fully below (pp. 192–93), studying the tradition of the humanities is an even better approach to general education because it forces us to think historically, and thus critically, about our cultural inheritance, including Great Books programs themselves.

By thinking critically, however, I do not mean following Gerald Graff's suggestion (in *Beyond the Culture Wars: How Teaching the Conflicts Can Revitalize American Education* [New York: Norton, 1992]) that we embrace the culture wars simply by "teaching the conflicts." The current ones are too narrow. The ground on which the battle between the latest theories of literary and cultural criticism is fought is modern; it assumes a materialistic, secular, and all too often narcissistic experience of life. Thinking occurs best through comparison and contrast. If all you know is the present, you have nothing to compare it to, and thus no way of thinking about it. Cut off from a dialogue with the past, our minds contract and atrophy. We end up living in what Christopher Lasch once called "the windowless room of the present." It is in this room that most of our intellectual conflicts are taking place. If we want to teach real intellectual conflicts, we should juxtapose modern and premodern understandings of the self and of the transcendent. The historical context that Graff himself provides at several points in his book does not extend farther back in time than the last century, when the humanities were already in crisis and the changes leading to our current curricula were well underway.

With all the talk about "multiculturalism" and "diversity" today, I am not surprised that some teachers initially question my insistence on the centrality of classical antiquity in the tradition of the humanities. But that is exactly where an understanding of their history leads. I ask only that we take this history seriously. The humanities, which began in the Renaissance, are synonymous with it to the extent that they are founded on a "prejudice," as Gadamer would put it, in favor of classical culture. In order to understand the moral and spiritual resources this tradition can offer us today, we need to respect this judgement. Doing so will bring great rewards, not the least of which will be the heightened capacity to take other cultures seriously.

How can this be? Thomas Merton once said that he was not interested in discussing other religious traditions with people who did not take seriously their own. At the very time that Merton was studying the Zen Buddhist tradition, he was probing the depths of his own Western monastic tradition of spirituality. I have found that my study of the history of the humanities enables me to engage in a fascinating conversation with neo-Confucian scholars, in part because we are both struggling with what Tu Wei-ming calls "tradition within modernity," with how premodern values and modes of thought can help us understand and perhaps even solve some seemingly intractable "modern" problems, such as those discussed in Part 3 of this book. People who urge us to understand other cultures and civilizations without at the same time seeking to understand our own are asking us to take neither seriously.

The harshest criticism I have ever received for this book occurred during a public discussion when an irate scholar said I was just like Petrarch in rejecting my own time and wanting to live in another age (for Petrarch see below, p. 151). For me, it is not a question of wanting to live at another time in history, but of acknowledging that we can find wisdom in the past. As Nietzsche put it, "I cannot imagine what would be the meaning of classical philology in our own age, if it is not to be untimely—that is, to act against the age, and by so doing, have an effect on the age, and, let us hope, to the benefit of a future age" (quoted in Bernard Williams, *Shame and Necessity* [Berkeley: University of California Press, 1993], p. 4). Furthermore, rather than build a Taj Mahal around the tradition of the humanities, I argue that we have to discover what went wrong with it. My approach has been to look not just for external changes in the economy and society that would account for the demise of the tradition of the humanities in our own time, but to look as well for weaknesses internal to the tradition itself, weaknesses that we must address in reappropriating it today. In short, I stress the importance of coming to terms with the *actual history* of the humanities.

As Leonardo Bruni's letter to Battista di Montefeltro illustrates so graphically (see below, pp. 4–10), at their point of origin in the early Renaissance the humanities constituted a curriculum with a specific, and for the time revolutionary, *content*. When I wrote that the disappearance of this content has created a conceptual vacuum which we avoid confronting by talking instead about the technology and techniques of teaching (see below p. 144), I had primarily my fellow university teachers in mind. I have since learned that the problem of aimless, unfocused curricula exists in an even more serious way at the elementary and secondary levels, because mainstream educational thought in our century has denigrated content, and focused instead on the teaching of skills. E. D. Hirsch, Jr. has described the disastrous effects this philosophy of "educational formalism" (skills divorced from content), combined with Romantic notions of free and "natural" human growth and development, has had on our schools (*Cultural Literary: What Every American Needs to Know* [Boston: Houghton Mifflin, 1987], especially Chapter 5). Hirsch's critique of the ruling ideas entrenched in our educational bureaucracies provides another reason for studying the history of the humanities: it can be a powerful catalyst for sparking a discussion of the specific knowledge our children should be acquiring. I applaud Hirsch's suggestion that at the elementary level parents and teachers insist that their "school clearly state the core of *specific* knowledge that each child in a grade must learn" (see the "General Introduction" to any of his *The Core Knowledge Series* books (New York: Doubleday, 1991ff.). I would go even further by suggesting that parents and teachers at both the elementary and secondary level raise the fundamental question posed by the humanities: What role should classical and Renaissance culture play in our schools? Is it better to teach our students only modern and contemporary culture, or can they learn something from a dialogue with the more distant past?

The experience of parenting in the 1990s makes the content of our children's studies an important issue because consumer capitalism makes it increasingly difficult for us to be the parents we would like to be. In her book *Reviving Ophelia: Saving the Selves of Adolescent Girls* (New York: Ballantine, 1994) Mary Pipher, a psychotherapist working with teenage girls and their parents, argues that those of us who grew up in the fifties and sixties are for the most part totally unprepared to comprehend the effect on our children of the junk values fed them in "the electronic community of rock music, television, videos, and movies" where "[a]dulthood, as presented by the media, implies drinking, spending money, and being sexually active." She goes on to identify a very painful conflict in our culture: "The mass media has the goal of making money from teenagers, while parents have the goal of producing happy, well-adjusted adults" (p. 82). Unless families and schools show our children other ways of understanding the human condition, the media-saturated junk culture risks becoming their primary form of cultural education. Our cultural *traditions*, of which the humanities are an important one, can be antidotes to this poison. But to use our cultural traditions in this way we have to recognize them as such.

I am not suggesting that we study *only* the ancients and their Renaissance and modern interpreters. I say so clearly on page 170, but some people still take the curriculum I propose as the only one I believe college students should study. I would like to see students read Petrarch and Cicero, and make them their lifelong companions. But I would also love to see them read the Bible, and study other world cultures and the modern age itself. The broader their learning the better. The tradition of the humanities cannot and should not be our only guide to adding depth and coherence to the curricula of our schools. But it should be a principal one, for it constitutes one of the richest cultural traditions we inherit.

Not imitation but *emulation* of past greatness should be our goal. We rise to moral, aesthetic, and intellectual heights by learning from and emulating those who are already there. Dante could not have written the *Divine Comedy* without the example of Vergil's *Aeneid*. Michelangelo could not have sculpted the Medici tombs without the examples of Roman and Greek sculptures discovered during his times. The Founding Fathers could have never created the "Republic" of the United States of America without engaging in a dialogue with ancient political theorists and their Renaissance interpreters (see Carl J. Richard, *The Founders and the Classics: Greece, Rome, and the American Enlightenment* [Cambridge, Mass.: Harvard University Press, 1994]).

Some people find it difficult to think of the humanities as a specific educational and cultural *tradition*, but this difficulty often arises precisely from ideas they have inherited, often without knowing it, from the Enlightenment and Romanticism. "Do not the constraints of tradition stifle one's individuality and creativity?" they ask. On the contrary, they expand it, as the examples mentioned in the preceding paragraph prove. As Hirsch puts it, "[c]hildren can express individuality only in relation to the traditions of their society, which they have to learn. The greatest human individuality is developed in response to a tradition, not in response to disorderly, uncertain, and fragmented education. Americans in their teens and twenties who were brought up under individualistic theories are not less conventional than their predecessors, only less literate, less able to express their individuality" (*Cultural Literary*, p. 126). Furthermore, because its past achievements are now far enough removed from us that they no longer intimidate, and thus no longer constitute the kind of impediment to creativity that W. Jackson Bate described so well in *The Burden of the Past and the English Poet* (Cambridge, Mass.: Belknap Press, 1970), we are freer than we have ever been since the Renaissance to reappropriate the classical tradition in new ways.

A year after the first edition of this book appeared, I was appointed Founding Director of Connecticut College's Center for International Studies and the Liberal Arts (CISLA). I directed this program for six years. Then I served for two years as the college's Provost and Dean of the Faculty. I agreed to become CISLA's Founding Director because I believed a dialogue with the ancients and their Renaissance interpreters would give intellectual depth, and a seriousness of moral purpose, to the study of other world cultures. I was right. What I had learned in writing this book helped us to create a highly successful international studies program, which I describe in a new appendix in order to show how combining the Renaissance humanists' goal of achieving moral and historical consciousness with the ancient liberal arts vision of the complementarity of all the disciplines gives us the philosophy of education we need to confront the complex problems of the modern world. This powerful combination of classical and Renaissance pedagogical ideals raises the discussion of contemporary issues to a higher level. It gives a depth, universality, and even longevity to new educational programs that would otherwise remain narrow and specialized, or worse, address serious questions in a trendy and superficial way. What we accomplished in international studies through a serious dialogue with the liberal arts tradition could be achieved in other new areas of the curriculum, such as environmental studies. As the conservation biologist David W. Orr argues, the problems raised by our relationship to nature need moral, and not just scientific and social-scientific, solutions. (Orr makes this point in two books, citing my understanding of notions of virtue in classical antiquity: *Earth in Mind: On Education, Environment, and the Human Prospect* [Washington, DC and Covelo, Calif.: Island Press, 1994], p. 61 and *Ecological Literacy: Education and the Transition to a Postmodern World* [Albany: State University Press of New York, 1992], p. 182.)

As a provost I observed firsthand what I had already guessed while writing this book: that most of the people leading our educational institutions, especially college presidents, independent school heads, and public school superintendents and principals, are trapped in the windowless room of the present. They are under immense pressures from disparate constituencies to show short-term quantifiable results in an increasing number of areas, from admission and graduation statistics to student "learning outcomes," from faculty publications and work loads to revenue streams and fund-raising. Overwhelmed by these and other demands placed on their time, including the task of managing organizations that have to become more bureaucratic in order to comply with increasing government regulations, many administrators turn to the business world for models of how to lead their institutions. As efficient managers or "change agents" they can talk about putting a computer on every desk, or improving student services, but have trouble defining the humanities or the liberal arts, or explaining, in anything but clichés, why these are worth studying. Just over two years ago, the "Annapolis Group," the presidents of many of the country's most selective liberal arts colleges, hired a public relations firm to define "liberal arts education" because they couldn't! Needless to say, neither could the firm. Our educational institutions have thus come to resemble more and more that humorous but also frightening vignette used to describe modernity itself: "Ladies and gentlemen," the pilot says, "I have bad news and good news. The bad news is we're lost. The good news is we're making very good time." There is no quick fix for this problem, but an understanding of the history of the humanities may give some administrators the wisdom and the courage to stop trying to be corporate managers, and start being educators and intellectual leaders.

In any case, the corporate model simply doesn't work. In Chapter 6 I tried to provide a partial explanation for the lack of leadership at the top by pointing to the transition in the modern world from traditional moral authority to rational bureaucratic authority as one of the external socio-economic factors that has contributed to the deterioration of the tradition of the humanities. Nowhere can we observe this transition more clearly than in our colleges and universities (p. 132). My eight years as an administrator have convinced me, however, that this change is not only not inevitable; it is impossible. While financial operations may need to be considered as a business and "managed" as such, and while some economies and efficiencies can be achieved in peripheral activities, our schools can never become for-profit businesses or even "modern" bureaucratic organizations, and remain schools. The people leading our educational institutions need to explain why. They can do so only if they understand the educational traditions we inherit. (For a discussion of profound differences between our schools and corporations even from a purely economic point of view, see Gordon C. Winston, "Why Can't a College Be More Like a Firm?" *Change*, September/October 1997, pp. 33–38, and Adam Yarmolinsky, "Constraints and Opportunities," in *Rethinking Liberal Education*, ed. Nicholas H. Farnham and Adam Yarmolinsky [New York: Oxford University Press, 1996], especially pp. 125–27.)

I know from experience that most administrators don't have time to study. It's a pity they don't, since the people leading an organization should embody the organization's highest values. Finding a balance between the active life and the contemplative life has always been difficult. It is becoming even more difficult in the fast-paced, future-ori-

ented world of contemporary consumer capitalism, where the triad
"customer, competition, and change" has increasingly replaced "wisdom, virtue, and eloquence" as the mantra of educational administrators. In presenting the second edition of this book I thus take my cue
from Petrarch, who understood the needs of busy people. His most
popular book in the Renaissance was the *De remediis utriusque Fortune,*
"Remedies for Fortune Fair and Foul." As he says in the dedication to
Azzo da Correggio, sometime Lord of Parma and Governor of Verona,
Petrarch wrote this book for those who, like Azzo, were burdened with
so many pressing affairs that they had no time to read extensively in
search of wisdom. So Petrarch collected for Azzo and others the fruits
of his own readings. When I finished writing the first edition of this
book almost ten years ago, I envisioned it as a sharing of what I had
learned about the humanities with my fellow teachers. Now I see it as
a broader sharing, not just with teachers, but with administrators, parents, students, with all who believe that the search for wisdom in living
is enhanced by a lifelong dialogue with outstanding writers and artists
across time, and who want to find ways of using our educational institutions to sustain and nourish this kind of humanistic learning. There
is indeed a future for the humanities, but only if we recover their past.

PREFACE

I see now in retrospect that I began this book long before I ever thought of writing it. In the late seventies I was invited to spend a year at the National Humanities Institute at Yale. Fellows at the NHI—there were twenty of us—were under no obligation to do publishable research; we were expected to spend the year thinking and talking about the humanities. In addition, each of us was to prepare an interdisciplinary course in the humanities, which we would take back to our college or university to teach. These were self-directed activities. We were asked as well to think about what was supposed to be the unifying theme for our year: fellows and staff were to meet weekly to discuss "Uses of a Point of View: The Humanities as a National Resource." These discussions were interesting, and at times stimulating. But they were always inconclusive. It soon became clear that each of us had a different idea of what the humanities are, or should be. And since we were unable to agree on how to define the humanities, we were unable to agree on what we were talking about. After several meetings we thus decided that there was no sense in continuing. Drawn from a wide range of colleges and universities, chosen because of our interest in the humanities and prior experience in teaching them, we probably constituted a group of people as deeply involved in the humanities as could then be found. If we were unable to discuss the humanities intelligently with one another, I found myself asking, who could? The more I considered this problem, the more eager I became to study and understand the history of the humanities. If we could no longer say what the humanities are, I thought, perhaps we could at least agree upon what they had been.

Following my year at the NHI, the National Endowment for the Humanities let me use my National Humanities Institute Demonstration Grant to fund not an undergraduate course, but a faculty seminar at Connecticut College on The Birth of the Humanities in Renaissance Florence. I and seven colleagues from different disciplines met regularly throughout the 1979-80 academic year to study and discuss the emergence of the humanities in the Renaissance. Out of our seminar grew an undergraduate course, which we taught together. I learned much both from my colleagues and from our students during these years.

An NEH Fellowship for College Teachers permitted me to spend the 1980-81 academic year in Italy pursuing my research on the origins of the humanities. It was continued support from the National Endowment for the Humanities over a period of several years, then, that enabled me to do much of the research and thinking out of which this book grew.

During my year in Italy, and during several summers thereafter, I often studied at Villa I Tatti, The Harvard University Center for Italian Renaissance Studies, in Florence. There, in the quiet foothills east of the city, I read Petrarch, Bruni, and other early humanists. I am grateful to Villa I Tatti for the hospitality it has extended to me, as a former Fellow, over the years.

I am grateful as well to Connecticut College for lightening my teaching load so that I could finish this book.

There are many people I am happy to thank for helping me along the way. John Gallman, Director of Indiana University Press, asked me to write this book. Richard D. Birdsall, Samuel K. Cohn Jr., Arthur C. Ferrari, Brian E. McConnell, Spencer J. Pack, Donald M. Peppard Jr., and Frank M. Turner read parts of my manuscript and shared with me their own particular knowledge of some of the topics I discuss. Doris Alexander encouraged me to ask big questions. My former student Margaret Fisher read the entire manuscript, and gave me a high school teacher's reaction to it. My colleague Dirk tom Dieck Held, who participated in our Faculty Humanities Seminar, and who was thus aware of my interest in the history of the humanities, not only read the entire manuscript and suggested ways of improving it, but over the years has brought to my attention books and articles on a wide range of topics that added considerably to the scope and depth of my research.

I owe special thanks to two scholars, F. Edward Cranz and Charles Trinkaus, who can now look back on long lives enriched through communion with the tradition of the humanities. Not only have I learned much from their own scholarship, as the pages which follow show, but each of them read and commented on the first draft of this book, and helped me refine and amplify my argument. F. Edward Cranz, in addition, has shared with me over the years his knowledge of the ancients, and, for this book, discussed with me many of my translations of Cicero and other Roman writers.

My greatest debt of gratitude goes to my wife. She gave me the time and the support to write this book. I would like to thank, finally, Larey Anne Lindberg for her careful proofreading.

Unless otherwise stated, in the pages that follow all translations from Latin into English are mine. I have kept in mind the Loeb translations, and D. R. Shackleton Bailey's translations of Cicero's letters. But since my argument often hangs on the precise meaning of specific words and phrases, I have endeavored to translate my sources as literally as good English prose would bear.

The Introduction is a slightly revised version of the seed from which this book grew, my article "What Has Happened to the Humanities?" *Connecticut College Alumni Magazine* 61 (Winter 1983-84): 2-5. Parts of chapter 1 appeared originally in my essay *"Quaedam Particula Perfecti,"* in *Essays in Honor of Craig Hugh Smyth,* ed. Andrew Morrogh et al., vol. 1, pp. 427-36 (Florence: Giunti Barbèra, 1985).

INTRODUCTION

One of the difficulties facing those of us who teach in colleges and universities today is that we are often unable to agree upon what we should teach and why. This is especially true for those disciplines included under the rubric "humanities." No one today knows what the humanities are. The National Endowment for the Humanities doesn't define them; it merely lists the disciplines Congress has empowered it to fund. And while the 1980 report of the Commission on the Humanities, *The Humanities in American Life*, issues a clarion call for everyone to support the humanities, it never tells us what it is we're supposed to support. "Our meetings have confirmed," the report notes, "how difficult it is for any committee to discuss the humanities" (Commission on the Humanities 1980, p. 19). Even *Newsweek*, describing the High School of the Humanities which opened several years ago on the west side of Manhattan, observes that "there is confusion about just what the humanities are," and goes on to quote William Bennett, then chairman of the National Endowment of the Humanities: " 'There is hardly anything that has not been called humanities or humanistic something or other' " (21 November 1983, p. 99).

The phrase "the humanities" warms almost everyone's heart. But why can't we define them? Because the original humanities are dead, and we have found nothing to replace them. The *Oxford English Dictionary* still provides a definition of what the humanities used to be: "Learning or literature concerned with human culture, especially the ancient Latin and Greek classics." It goes on to point out that the word "humanity," in the singular, is still used in Scottish universities to mean "the study of the Latin language and literature." Does this definition of the humanities surprise you? If it does, then you have just experienced the profound change that has taken place in our educational system over the past hundred years. When you mention the humanities today, it is not the Greeks and the Romans that come to mind, but, ironically, science and technology: most people are able to think about the humanities only in terms of their opposites, the sciences. While the sciences limit themselves to studying that which is objective and quantifiable, the humanities, so this line of reasoning goes, have as their proper domain of inquiry the subjective and qualitative dimensions of human life and culture. Physics and chemistry are sciences; ethics and aesthetics are humanities.

But the original humanities were not just a nonscientific or even a "prescientific" way of looking at man; they had a precise content: the *studia humanitatis*, as they were originally called, began in fifteenth-century Italy as a cultural revolution calling for the imitation of classical, as opposed to medieval, Latin, and for the study of Roman, and to a lesser extent Greek, literature, history, and moral philosophy as guides to individual and collective behavior. The humanists named and created the Renaissance: the same passion that led Brunelleschi (1377-1446), Donatello (1386-1466), and later Michelangelo (1475-1564) to Rome to study ancient buildings and statues had already sent Petrarch (1304-74) and his followers searching through the monastery and cathedral libraries of Europe for lost manuscripts of Cicero, Vergil, Livy, and other Roman writers. In the 1400s the humanists founded new secondary schools in Mantua and Ferrara, and from there a new curriculum, later to be called "classical education," spread throughout Europe. Humanist textbooks gradually replaced the old medieval grammar books, and the study of Greek and Roman authors in the original became the foundation of secondary and, to a large extent, university education in the West for the next five centuries.[1]

As Nietzsche (1844-1900) saw, classical education taught "Greek and Roman antiquity as the incarnate categorical imperative of all culture" (Nietzsche 1924, p. 128). This was a powerful ideal. One way of understanding the current "crisis of the humanities" is to see it as the void created at the very center of our curriculum by the disappearance of the Greeks and Romans. We have simply found no unifying focus to replace the one they provided. Classical education, by the very dialogue it attempted to establish with an anterior civilization, had a unity of content which we no longer enjoy. And the absence from our classrooms of universally acknowledged "classics"—Homer, Vergil, Cicero, and so forth—explains why it is much easier to say what the original humanities were than to describe what has become of them today. If you want to talk about the original *studia humanitatis*, you can talk about the specific books and authors the humanists studied and emulated; but if you try to discuss the humanities today, chances are you won't talk about specific books and authors at all, but will spend your time debating questions of methodology.

In considering the role which a concern for methodology plays in our educational system today, I find a striking similarity between our own times and the period in which the humanities emerged. The intellectual culture of the great medieval universities of the twelfth and thirteenth centuries was characterized by a fervid interest in the *techniques* of research. One made a career, and a name for himself, at the universities of Paris or Bologna, by showing how well he could apply the formal, syllogistic reasoning of Aristotelian logic and metaphysics to the study of theology or law. But the ability to "play" with Aristotelian syllogisms inevitably became an end in itself. The *studia humanitatis* began, in part, as a revolt against this obsession with the techniques of ratiocination. "Our vanity has turned theology into dialectic," Petrarch complains in one of his letters (*Fam.* X, 5, 8). Today, the accolades and the prestigious careers often go to those who seem most adept in inventing new techniques of analysis and research. In literary studies we have gone from the New Criticism in the 1950s to French structuralism and Russian formalism in the sixties to poststructuralism and deconstructionism in the seventies, and now there are some who speak of "postdeconstructionism."

This obsession with methodology is not limited to the humanities; it affects all the disciplines of modern universities. Consider the vogue for "quantitative reasoning" in the social sciences. Several years ago the Nobel Prize-winning economist Wassily Leontief complained that more and more articles in a prestigious American journal of economics were devoted to the elaboration of internally coherent mathematical models based on little or no empirical data: the ability to put together an econometric model had become an end in itself (Leontief 1982). And a friend who teaches sociology tells me that the journals in his field are full of articles presenting "statistical research and models with quantifiable variables which have lost touch with morally significant issues—which is what the social sciences are really about." The message to the graduate student preparing for a university career is clear: if you want to get ahead and publish quickly, don't waste your time reading and thinking; learn a technique and show how brilliantly you can use it.[2]

This obsession with methodological fads, while it may keep a good number of specialized journals and university presses in business, and may offer some teachers and scholars the only deep intellectual stimulation they can now find in the academic world, simply does not address the problem of what, in terms of substantive *content*, we should be teaching our students, unless we're content to argue, as some are, that the essence of education is exposure to different methodologies and disciplinary perspectives.

The early humanists had an answer to this dilemma. Unhappy with a primarily technical approach to education and to life, they condemned the excessive use of logic, and encouraged instead the study of classical poetry, rhetoric, moral philosophy, and history. In a similar fashion those who decry the deforming limitations of a purely "technological society" today often evoke the humanities as champions of the "human" dimension of life. But here the parallel ends. The original hu-

manists knew what the humanities were; they wrote educational treatises stating explicitly which authors and subjects to study, and which
to avoid. We can do nothing of the sort today.

Not everyone is bothered by this lack of focus in our curriculum;
some see it as a sign of healthy pluralism. But it bothers me. This is
one of the reasons why I took up the study of the origins of the humanities: I hoped to discover why the early humanists were able to create a coherent curriculum, while we are not. But one of the unexpected results
of my research has been to force me to change my understanding of
the original humanities. The humanities, I have come to see, grew out
of a particular and historically unique perception of human existence
which we no longer share today. And this discovery leads me to conclude that we cannot revitalize the humanities today simply by trying
to reinstitutionalize earlier humanistic educational ideals.

Petrarch's early followers Coluccio Salutati (1331-1406) and Leonardo Bruni (1370-1444) chose the term *studia humanitatis* to describe
the new pedagogy they advocated. They borrowed the phrase from Cicero, but Bruni especially gave it a very different meaning from the
one it had in classical antiquity. In addition to denoting a new attitude toward, and a new way of teaching, the Greek and Latin classics,
the phrase, in its Renaissance usage, suggests a radically new meaning
of "humanity" (*humanitas*). The writings of Petrarch show clearly that
by the 1300s, if not before, a sharp break was occurring in Western Europe with ancient Graeco-Roman and more recent medieval conceptions of what it means to be human.

The cosmos (*mundus*), for Cicero, is perfect, and it is divine. A
human being is part of the cosmos, and by contemplating and imitating it, he participates in its perfection (*De natura deorum* II, 14, 38-39;
Cato maior de senectute 21, 77). For Dante, man is a worm born to
become an angelic butterfly which flies home to God (*Purgatorio*
X, 124-26). Despite the profound differences in philosophy and world
outlook which separate them, Cicero and Dante share a sense that the
"center," the goal or final resting place, of a human being lies *outside* of
himself, in the perfect, eternal, and unchanging heavens, which, according to a conception of the universe articulated by Aristotle, begin
above the "circle of the moon." Beneath the moon's sphere lie the earth
and the four elements. This sublunar world is a world of continual
generation and corruption, of ceaseless change and mutability. It was
often described as the realm of "Lady Fortune."[3] Cicero's wise man
escapes the realm of Fortune by rising in contemplation above the circle
of the moon. Dante's Christian pilgrim makes a similar journey,
though with the aid of grace from God. Petrarch, however, prefers not
to contemplate the eternal heavens at all; he tries to find a center and

a resting place *within* himself. In one of his letters he states that he knows, as Cicero said, that our life is a journey toward the heavens, but he believes that one can look down on human miseries and reflect the light of celestial happiness while still standing here below (*Fam.* IV, 2, 5-6).

This was more of a hope, however, than a reality. Petrarch lived in constant fear and anxiety. He kept his gaze on the earth, on Fortune's realm—and found himself overwhelmed by his awareness of change and contingency. The humanities emerge, in part, out of Petrarch's attempt to do what Cicero and Dante would have never conceived of doing: triumph over contingency ("chance," "Fortune") by distancing himself from it in his inner life. Petrarch tried to fill his mind with the biographies of ancient Roman heroes in order to strengthen his own soul by comparing his courage to theirs. That their battles were physical ones while his were, for the most part, psychological, made no difference to Petrarch: he wanted to be able to withstand the blows of adverse Fortune by emulating what he believed was the *inner* strength of his ancient heroes. The Renaissance *studia humanitatis*, as a program of primarily literary studies formulated by Petrarch's followers, contain this ideal of forming, shaping, molding one's inner self through the study of other human lives, especially the ancient Romans. And concomitant with this goal of education as the shaping of character is a conception of an autonomous "personal self," which was a Renaissance creation, and which was foreign to the ancient experience of what it meant to be human, even though Petrarch and his followers believed they had indeed discovered a similar self in the ancients.

Long before the Scientific Revolution, then, long before Galileo mathematized movement and change in the physical universe and discovered, with his telescope, that the world above the circle of the moon was just like the world beneath it, the early humanists, especially Petrarch, had already experienced the psychological consequences of living in a world without rest, stability, permanence, or peace, and had found a refuge, of sorts, in the new "humanities."

Lionel Trilling once used the German word *Bildung* to describe the arduous, at times ordeal-like, shaping and disciplining of the self which the original humanities fostered, and he observed that this concept of education went hand-in-hand with two ideas which until quite recently were prevalent in our culture: the idea of "making a life," and the idea of "making a self": one thought of his life, and of his self, as works of art to be carefully shaped, perfected, and completed (Trilling 1982). Already in the 1400s Leonardo Bruni had written that the new studies "are called the *studia humanitatis* because they perfect and adorn a human being (*homo*)" (Bruni 1947, p. 7). Both the ideal and the practice of consciously shaping one's "self" through the study of (mostly classical) literature, history, and moral philosophy have all but disappeared from our schools. We shall explore why in the course of this study. For now suffice it to say that the *studia humanitatis* arose along with an awareness of a new "personal self"—and that their disappearance is related in part, at least, to a changing experience of the "self."

The Harvard paleontologist Stephen Jay Gould, whose revision of Darwin continues to cause such a stir, has argued that for the human species, biological evolution ceased thousands of years ago: as far as our brain capacities and intellectual abilities are concerned, we are Cro-Magnon man. For Gould, and most anthropologists, human evolution occurs now only at the level of culture (Gleick 1983, p. 64). This view places the responsibility for the future of the human race squarely on our shoulders, and not on Nature. As the history of the rise and decline of the *studia humanitatis* vividly shows, there is no biologically predetermined experience of what it means to be "human"; "humanity" is a cultural and historical experience. The challenge facing us today is to rethink and define what we mean by the word "human," a task which demands, I believe, questioning the usefulness of the concept of an exclusively personal, inward-turning "self."

The tradition of classical education, which began in the Renaissance and flourished in Europe and America until the end of the last century, is gone now. How should we react to the death of this tradition? We can either mourn it and try to hold on to it, or we can see its passing as a liberation and as an opportunity for us to appropriate the past in new ways. I prefer the latter. The challenge facing us now is to question who we are and who we would like to be by reexamining the entire history of the West in light of the death of the original humanities. We need especially to investigate the Renaissance's problematic relationship to classical antiquity and our own increasingly problematic relationship to the Renaissance. I would center this inquiry around the concept of a "personal self," on its absence from the classical experience of the human, on its appearance in the Renaissance, and on the limitations it may impose on human experience today. Ironically, in searching for a new, "post-Renaissance" understanding of the human, we may find that we have no sooner let the Greeks and the Romans slip back into their ancient tombs, than we need to call them forth again—but this time in search of answers to questions Petrarch and the early humanists would never have been able to ask. Let us begin by looking more closely at the birth of the humanities in the Renaissance.

DEFINING THE HUMANITIES

PART ONE

*The Birth of the Humanities
in the Renaissance*

CHAPTER I

THE HUMANIST
TRANSFORMATION OF
CLASSICAL ANTIQUITY

ॐ

Leonardo Bruni's Description of the studia humanitatis

IN THE FIRST HALF of the fifteenth century Leonardo Bruni (1370–1444), a humanist scholar and statesman who became chancellor of the Republic of Florence, wrote two letters in which he describes, with characteristic clarity, a new educational program that was just beginning to be known as the *studia humanitatis*.[1] These letters provide the earliest complete description we have of the humanities as they came into being in the early Renaissance. In a letter urging Niccolò Strozzi, scion of a wealthy and powerful Florentine family, to devote himself fully to the new humanities, Bruni says:

> Let your study be twofold, first in the skill of letters (*litterarum peritia*), not the vulgar and common kind, but one which is more diligent and penetrating, and in this I very much want you to excel; and second in the knowledge of those things which pertain to life and moral character (*mores*). These two are therefore called the humanities (*studia humanitatis*), because they perfect and adorn a human being (*homo*). (Bruni 1947, p. 7)

Bruni goes on to exhort Niccolò to be well read and widely learned, and to know how to illuminate and embellish this knowledge with eloquent words. He advises him to learn not only from philosophers, but also from poets, orators, and historians. Aristotle in particular, he says, will give Niccolò a knowledge of "things"; Cicero will teach him how to excel in "letters." Then, in comparing the humanities to law, Bruni asserts that while the study of civil law may be more marketable (*vendibilius*), in usefulness and in dignity it is surpassed by the humanities, for "the humanities as a whole aim at creating a good man (*vir bonus*), than which nothing more useful (*utilius*) can be imag-

3

ined; but civil law has nothing to do with the creation of a good man" (ibid., p. 8).

In contrasting the study of law with the new humanities, Bruni was probably speaking from personal experience: having come from his hometown of Arezzo to Florence as a young man to study law, he met Coluccio Salutati, then Chancellor of the Republic of Florence, and a much respected man of letters. Salutati introduced Bruni to the new classical studies which Petrarch had begun, and which Salutati and a small circle of intellectuals in Florence were continuing. Bruni quickly abandoned law in favor of these new studies, even though he was later forced to return to it for a short time.[2]

Bruni's letter to Niccolò is brief; he does not describe the actual program of studies he wants Niccolò to follow. But he reminds him that he has dealt with the subject more fully in his treatise *De studiis et litteris*, "On Studies and Letters."

Bruni wrote *De studiis et litteris* in the 1420s for Battista di Montefeltro, wife of the Lord of Pesaro. In his letter to Battista he uses the word *studia*, "studies," rather than the phrase *studia humanitatis*, but his remarks to Niccolò make it clear that the two are synonymous.

He opens his treatise by telling Battista that he wants her to become a learned woman (*femina erudita*). Then he explains what he means by "learning":

> By learning, moreover, I do not mean that ignoble and flustered learning which those who profess theology use, but that legitimate and noble learning which joins skill in letters with an understanding of things. This is the learning one finds in Lactantius, Augustine, and in Jerome, men who were both great theologians and accomplished writers. Today, however, it is disgraceful how little those who profess the science of theology know about letters. (Bruni 1969, p. 6)[3]

Here Bruni makes the same fundamental distinction he made in his letter to Niccolò Strozzi: the humanities combine a skill in writing with a knowledge of things. But now he adds something new. In his letter to Niccolò he had used civil law as a foil to the humanities; here he uses scholastic theology to the same purpose. Bruni censures the scholastic theologians of his day for their ignorance of "letters," that is, for their inability to write well. And since one's literary style reflects one's thinking, it is easy for Bruni to dismiss the poorly written theology of his day as "ignoble and flustered learning." Going back to a much earlier period for his models, Bruni points to Lactantius, Augustine, and Jerome, all Fathers of the Church, as examples of men who were "great theologians and accomplished writers." Implied in this contrast between scholastic and patristic theologians is the former's well-known obsession with formal logic, an obsession, Bruni would argue, which corrupted both their thinking and their writing.

This contrast between the Fathers of the Church and contemporary theologians sets the tone for the first part of Bruni's letter. To devote oneself to these new humanities means studying certain authors and assiduously avoiding all others. Under the category of "sacred books," Bruni tells Battista to read Augustine, Jerome, and Lactantius, and the Greek Fathers Gregory Nazianzen, John Chrysostom, and Basil if she can find them translated into good Latin. Under "secular books" he urges her to read Cicero and Vergil, and then Livy, Sallust, and other poets and writers.

Upon what basis does Bruni decide which authors Battista is to read? From his point of view, the Latin authors he names, whether "sacred" or "secular," have one thing in common: they all wrote good classical Latin. It is classical Latin, not the scholastic Latin of the Middle Ages, that Bruni wants Battista to read and emulate. The standard of classical Latin thus determines, to a large extent, the curriculum of the original humanities. Bruni tells Battista to study diligently the writers he recommends "so that, whenever she has to speak or write about something, she set down no word which she has not found beforehand in one of them" (ibid., p. 8).

Such an injunction throws into sharp relief the fundamental radicalism of the original *studia humanitatis*. By telling Battista to use no word which cannot be found in the works of one of his model Latin writers, the most recent of whom, Augustine, died in 430, Bruni is excising from her education almost a thousand years of Western culture. By Bruni's standards, no book written in Latin after the time of Augustine is worth serious study. This is not to say that Bruni and many other humanists were not troubled by the problem of the relationship of their own writings to those of classical antiquity. With standards of excellence set in the past, the whole question of artistic creativity and originality rests on whether one strives to imitate or emulate a predecessor's style.[4] The humanists themselves were sharply divided on the question of how much freedom one should have in deviating from the style and usage of Cicero and other model Roman writers.[5] But this debate between the "moderns" and the "ancients" always took place within the context of the fundamental orientation of the *studia humanitatis* as enunciated here by Bruni: one's chief cultural interlocutors were to be the great writers of classical antiquity, not those associated with the scholastic culture of the Middle Ages.

From this point of view, nothing better describes the state of the humanities in our own times than the contrast between Bruni's exhortation to Battista and our own discussions of the humanities today. The

humanities, for us, have become a generic ideal; they have no defina-
ble content. The *studia humanitatis*, for Bruni, have a sharply defined content: he is able to tell Battista exactly which authors he believes she
must read in order to acquire learning.

He can also tell her, with the same confidence, what dire things will
happen to her literary talent if she reads bad writers. Since, in the final
analysis, it is we who teach ourselves to write well through our own
hard work, our first concern must be that

> we pass our time reading only those books written by the best and most es-
> teemed authors of the Latin language, and that we therefore avoid works
> which are written poorly and without distinction, as if we were fleeing
> from a kind of ruin and destruction of our natural talents. Reading
> coarsely and ineptly written things impresses its defects on the reader and
> pollutes the mind with similar putrefaction.

And if we can actually harm our natural talents by reading poorly
written works, then we must exercise the same care in selecting what
we read that we do in choosing what we eat:

> It is a matter of food for the soul, with which the mind is fed and nour-
> ished. And just as those who care about their stomachs do not pour just
> any kind of food into them, so one who wants to preserve the integrity
> of his mind will not permit it just any reading whatsoever. We must en-
> deavor, therefore, to read nothing but the best and most universally ap-
> proved works. (Ibid., p. 7)

These are strong words. It is another way of Bruni's urging Battista
not to read anything written in scholastic Latin. In his day this injunction would have entailed more than just not reading works written
after the time of Augustine; it would have meant avoiding whatever
was said or written in the universities, then the major, and in most
cases the exclusive, centers of thought and culture in the West. We
thus see again why the humanities, at least as far as their stated ideals
were concerned, amounted to something of a cultural revolution, for
they set themselves up in clear opposition to the dominant language
and thought of their time.

The original humanities, then, were synonymous with what would
later come to be known as "classical education." This meaning is still
preserved in the etymologies of the words *humanist* and *humanities*. During the course of the fifteenth and sixteenth centuries, the new *studia
humanitatis* enjoyed great success and became institutionalized, both in
the new classical secondary schools, which sprang up first in northern
Italy and then spread throughout Europe, and in the universities. The
word *humanista* (*umanista* in Italian) was coined by fifteenth-century uni-

versity students to designate a teacher of the new *studia humanitatis*, following the precedent of words such as *canonista* and *legista*, the names given to professors of canon and civil law. In the Renaissance the word *humanist* thus had both a more precise and more limited meaning than it does today: a humanist was simply a teacher or scholar of Greek and Latin.[6]

Our phrase "the humanities" came into English in the eighteenth century from *les humanités*, the French rendering of the Latin *studia humanitatis*. It still preserves an echo, albeit increasingly faint, of its original association with the *studia humanitatis*. Both the *American Heritage Dictionary of the English Language* and the *Oxford English Dictionary* give, as one of their definitions of the plural of "humanity," "the study of the classical languages and literature of Greece and Rome," as the former puts it. And the *Oxford English Dictionary* goes on to point out that the word *humanity*, in the singular, is still used in Scottish universities to mean "the study of the Latin language and literature." I do not know exactly when, in common parlance, "the humanities" ceased to mean the classical languages and literature of Greece and Rome. C. H. Grandgent, a former professor of Romance languages at Harvard and best known today for his edition of Dante's *Divine Comedy*, spoke in 1917 of the study of Greek and Latin as "the study of the old humanities" (West 1917, p. 310). And William Riley Parker, a professor of English at Indiana University, gave a paper at Cambridge University in 1968 at the Jubilee Congress of the Modern Humanities Research Association in which he said, bluntly, that he recognized no "modern humanities," only what he called "the classical humanities," the study of Latin and Greek (Parker 1969). I suspect, as we shall see more fully when we look at the deterioration of the tradition of the humanities in the last century, that the phrase "the humanities" had already begun to lose its original meaning in the 1860s, when, according to Parker, the slogan "modern humanities" was adopted to foster the recognition of English and modern foreign languages as new disciplines worthy of inclusion in the university curriculum. In any case, one who reads in chronological order the four national reports on the humanities which have appeared in the United States since the Second World War (Jones 1959; Commission on the Humanities 1964; Commission on the Humanities [Founded 1978] 1980; Bennett 1984) will find a progressive attenuation of the humanities' link to the past, along with growing confusion over what the humanities are, and what they are supposed to accomplish.

We have barely begun our investigation of the origins of the humanities, and already we find ourselves thinking about the humanities in a new way. After all, nothing in our contemporary culture draws our thoughts back to the Greeks and the Romans. But then our contemporary culture, like the humanities themselves, is in a state of disorder and confusion. At the very least, studying the history of the humanities enables us to stand outside this disorder and confusion. Looking at what has become of the humanities today from the vantage point of Bruni's description of the original *studia humanitatis* raises questions concerning our relationship to the Renaissance, and to classical antiquity, which would never arise were we to limit our inquiry, as most of the national reports do, to the current state of the humanities.

It is not the study per se of the literature and culture of ancient Greece and Rome, however, that specifically characterizes the humanities as they emerge in the Renaissance. Education in the West, with the exception of our own time, when we find ourselves deeply confused about our relationship to the past, has always been based upon the study of "classical" texts: the Hellenistic Greeks studied Homer and other "classics" from their past; the Romans studied the Greeks; the Christian Middle Ages studied the Greeks and the Romans. And while the humanists liked to believe that they were engaged in bringing back to life the art and culture of classical antiquity after centuries of oblivion, in the larger sense they were merely continuing a dialogue which had never really ceased. Medieval thinkers, of course, were not interested in the philological accuracy which would become the hallmark of humanist scholarship, and they lacked the humanists' recognition of anachronism, out of which the modern disciplines of history and archaeology arose.[7] Nor did it matter to them that they read Aristotle translated into their own peculiar Latin. But their authorities, in addition to the Bible and the Fathers of the Church, were nonetheless classical: Aristotle for logic, natural science, and metaphysics, Justinian for law, Galen for medicine. What specifically characterizes the humanities in this millenary dialogue with classical antiquity is, first of all, their recognition of a historical distance between themselves and the ancients; and, secondly, the content of their educational program itself: their adoption of classical Latin as a standard of discourse, and their choice of particular disciplines to the exclusion of others. We have already seen what Bruni has to say about the importance of Battista's learning to express herself in good classical Latin; let us now look at the particular disciplines he wants her to study. To use Bruni's terms, we now pass from a discussion of "words" to an analysis of those "things" which pertain to life and moral character.

After telling Battista that he wants her to have such an ardent desire for learning that she disdain no form of instruction, Bruni goes on to say that some disciplines, such as geometry and arithmetic, are not worth spending much time on:

For there are certain disciplines in which just as it is not fitting to be entirely uninstructed, so too there is nothing glorious in ascending to their
heights—for example, geometry and arithmetic, in which, if one were to
continue to consume a great deal of time prying into their subtleties and ob-
scurities, I would pull him up and drag him away. (Bruni 1969, p. 11)

He adds that he would do the same if one were spending too much
time studying astrology, and, though less willingly, given his own interest in it, rhetoric. Here Bruni means rhetoric in its more narrow sense
of the art or specific techniques of public speaking, reserved for the
most part to men.

Bruni wants Battista to devote herself instead to those studies which
pertain either to religion or to the good life (*bene vivendum*). He says little about religious studies (*litterae sacrae*), however, other than to ad-
vise Battista to read the Fathers of the Church, especially Augustine,
and not concern herself too much with the theologians of her own
day. Bruni's real interest, to which he devotes most of his treatise, is
in describing the "secular studies" (*saecularia studia*) he wants Battista
to pursue, by which he means the writings of the ancient Greeks and Romans. He wants Battista first of all to

see what, in these writings which concern the good life, the greatest
minds of the philosophers have handed down, what they say concerning
continence, temperance, modesty, justice, fortitude, and liberality. Nor
let her ignore their opinions concerning happiness (*beata vita*). Is virtue itself sufficient for attaining happiness? Do torments, prison, exile, and poverty prevent one from being happy? And if these befall a happy person,
will they make him miserable? Or do they merely take away happiness,
without making him completely wretched? Does happiness (*felicitas*), moreover, consist in pleasure and in the absence of pain, as Epicurus taught,
or in integrity (*honestas*), as in Zeno, or in the practice of virtue, as in Aristotle? (Ibid., p. 12)

It is questions such as these, Bruni says, that most deserve our reflection, since they are both useful in guiding one's life and "also supply
every discussion with a marvelous richness of expression for both speaking and writing." The humanists, in fact, liked to introduce such questions into their speeches and letters. We see then that Bruni begins his
list of the disciplines he wants Battista to study with moral philosophy. It is the most important of the disciplines that make up the original humanities.

What Bruni says here about the usefulness of "secular studies" is
one of the earliest, and perhaps clearest, statements we have of the
value of the humanities in their guise as studies which have both
moral and literary value. Bruni's statement, in fact, can be seen as a pre-

cursor of the argument still made today that a liberal arts, as opposed to a merely technical or preprofessional, education gives one a kind of learning which both guides his life and enables him to express himself effectively.

In order to enhance what she learns from her study of religion and ancient moral philosophy, Bruni urges Battista to read historians such as Livy, Sallust, Tacitus, Curtius, and Caesar; orators such as Cicero; and poets, especially Homer and Vergil. Again, the emphasis is on how these classical studies can give one both wisdom and eloquence: "The knowledge of previous events," Bruni says, "guides our judgments and deliberations, and the outcomes of previous undertakings either encourage or deter us from a similar venture in the present." And he adds, with one's rhetorical skills in mind, "A wealth of examples, moreover, with which we should frequently illustrate our sayings, will be more conveniently appropriated from no other source than history" (ibid., p. 13). From the orators we can learn not only how to embellish our speech, but how to arouse and quiet the passions of the soul, how to comfort, encourage, incite, and deter. As far as a knowledge of poetry is concerned, Bruni points out how often Aristotle and Plato, Cicero, Seneca, Augustine, Jerome, Lactantius, and Boethius cite poets in their writings.

These then are the specific "secular" disciplines which, Bruni believes, will give one knowledge of those things which pertain to life and moral character: moral philosophy, history, oratory, and poetry. The *studia humanitatis*, as Bruni describes them, thus constitute a specialized, and primarily literary, curriculum; logic, mathematics, natural science, and metaphysics have no place in it. And it is precisely in this form that the humanities were recognized and defined in the Renaissance. Using a library canon composed in his youth by Pope Nicholas V for Cosimo de' Medici, and other Renaissance documents, Paul Oskar Kristeller argued some time ago that the *studia humanitatis* were understood by Renaissance teachers and scholars as a new grouping of traditional disciplines (grammar, rhetoric, history, poetry, and moral philosophy) opposed to other academic disciplines (logic, physics or natural science, and metaphysics) (Kristeller 1979, pp. 98 and 282, n. 60). Later we shall look more closely at the relationship between the humanities and the sciences. For the moment it is important to note that the humanities came into being several centuries before the Scientific Revolution, and that from the beginning they stood in opposition to mathematics and natural science.

The *studia humanitatis*, then, as Bruni describes them in his letters to Niccolò Strozzi and Battista di Montefeltro, were a program of classical studies organized into a group of primarily literary disciplines. To what end?

Bruni says that the new studies to which he is urging Niccolò Strozzi to devote himself are called the "humanities," the *studia humanitatis,* "because they perfect and adorn a human being *(homo)*" (Bruni 1947, p. 7).

Both in his letter to Niccolò Strozzi and in his treatise *On Studies and Letters* for Battista Malatesta, Bruni states that the humanities provide both a skill in language and a knowledge of those things concerning life and morals. How do mastering Cicero's Latin style and reading Aristotle's ethics "perfect" *(perficere)* a man? To answer this question we must determine what, according to Bruni, is perfected, and how. Bruni gives us a preliminary answer at the beginning of his letter to Battista:

> Moved by frequent mention of your wonderful virtues, I have decided to write you, so that I can either congratulate you for that natural talent *(ingenium)*—about which I have already heard so many splendid things— if it has already attained perfection *(perfectio)*, or, if it has not, then certainly to urge you through this letter to attain such perfection. (Bruni 1969, p. 5)

The *studia humanitatis,* then, can perfect one's *ingenium,* or natural talent. How?

In his letters to Niccolò and to Battista, Bruni emphasizes that the *ingenium* can be perfected only through hard work and disciplined study. He tells Niccolò that the letter he has just received from him displays "both an outstanding nature *(natura),* which is the result of your inherited talent *(ingenium),* and also an alert and skillful instruction *(disciplina),* which is the result of study and diligence" (Bruni 1947, p. 7). After he has said to Battista that one who aims at the excellence to which he calls her must attain "an expert, attentive, extensive, and profound mastery of letters *(litterarum peritia)*. . .," he observes that in order to attain this mastery of letters, "both instruction and especially your own hard work and careful effort are necessary" (Bruni 1969, p. 7).

If we probe deeper now, and look at the images Bruni uses to describe what this hard work and disciplined study actually accomplish, we discover something very interesting. In a passage I quoted earlier, Bruni employs the image of nutrition to warn Battista not to read poorly written books:

> Reading coarsely and ineptly written things impresses its defects on the reader and pollutes the mind with similar putrefaction. It is a matter of food for the soul, with which the mind is fed and nourished. And just as those who care about their stomachs do not pour just any kind of food into them, so one who wants to preserve the purity of his mind *(sinceritas animi)* will not permit it just any reading whatsoever. (Ibid.)

In other passages he uses the images of setting up or building (*insti-tuere*),[8] and of shaping or giving form to (*informare*), in telling Battista how to discipline herself and how to learn from good authors. By persistent effort (*diligentia*), he says, "we are molded, and, as it were, set up" (*informamur ac velut instituimur*) (ibid.). He observes, using both images, that of constructing and that of nourishing, that Lactantius is a model of good style, "whose fluency of style and figures of speech can build and nourish very well that native talent of which I have been speaking" (ibid., p. 8). These metaphors show clearly how Bruni envisions this perfection to take place. Through hard work and disciplined study, not only the natural talent (*ingenium*), but also the mind or soul (*animus*), and even the whole person (*informamur, instituimur*) are consciously nourished and shaped.

Now, in the context of Bruni's description of the *studia humanitatis* as those studies which "perfect and adorn a human being," the kind of nourishing and shaping Bruni describes is possible only if one posits the existence of an individual subjectivity which experiences its consciousness as an autonomous center of thought and feeling which it can objectify, act upon, and compare to other such autonomous centers of consciousness. Using interchangeably the terms *ingenium* and *animus*, and the first person plural, passive voice, of *informare* and *instituere*, is thus Bruni's way of describing a unique, autonomous, personal self. Bruni says, in fact, that Battista's natural talents are uniquely hers: "For it is proper that so much intelligence and such singular natural talent (*singulare ingenium*) not be given you in vain, and that it should not be content with mediocrity" (ibid., p. 6). He speaks explicitly of an individual self—entrusted, moreover, with its own perfection—when he tells Niccolò that he can become a most excellent man if he does not "desert himself": "Nor do I have any fear, if you do not desert yourself, that you are not going to turn into a most excellent man" (Bruni 1947, p. 7). What the *studia humanitatis* perfect, then, is what we call a "self," a self which is not only individual but also personal and autonomous.

The notion of a personal self implied in Bruni's description of the *studia humanitatis* is characteristic of Renaissance humanism in general. The perception of one's own soul or character as unique and autonomous, capable of being compared to other unique and autonomous souls, occurs already in Petrarch's works, as in his explanation of why he filled his writings with so many examples (*exempla*) of famous men:

Nothing moves me like the examples of famous men. For it helps the soul to rise up, to test whether there is anything solid, noble, indomitable, and unbroken in it in the face of adverse Fortune, or whether it has lied concerning itself. Except through experience, which is the surest teacher of things, this certainly happens in no better way than if I compare my soul to those whom it wants most to be alike. (*Fam.* VI, 4, 3–4)

The belief that man not only has a personal self, but actually creates it, can be found in Pico della Mirandola's (1463–94) explanation of why God made man neither celestial nor terrestrial: "We have made thee neither of heaven nor of earth, neither mortal nor immortal, so that with freedom of choice and with honor, as though the maker and molder of thyself, thou mayest fashion thyself in whatever shape thou shalt prefer" (Pico della Mirandola 1942, p. 106. Trans. in Cassirer 1948, p. 225).

We can now define the original humanities as a program of education having three distinguishing characteristics: a) the concept of a unique, autonomous, personal self, to be shaped through b) the study of the language and literature of ancient Greece and Rome, c) according to the perspectives of a group of primarily literary academic disciplines.

Of these three interrelated attributes, only the last has remained virtually intact up to the present time. The humanities are now most commonly defined by distinguishing them from other groupings of disciplines, especially the sciences. Definition by academic discipline, in fact, has become the primary, and often the only, way the humanities are now defined. The National Endowment for the Humanities, for example, defines the humanities as "language, both modern and classic, linguistics, literature, history, jurisprudence, philosophy, archaeology, the history, criticism and practice of the arts, and those aspects of the social sciences which have humanistic content and employ humanistic methods" (Public Law, 89th Congress, S.1483, September 29, 1965, Sec. 3a). But it does not define "humanistic content" and "humanistic methods."

Of the other two attributes of the original humanities, the concept of a personal self and the study of classical antiquity, the first continues to characterize our understanding of the human, but the ideal of molding or shaping a self is for the most part absent from contemporary discussions of the humanities. The second attribute has now completely disappeared. In fact, most people today are surprised and baffled to learn that the humanities were once synonymous with classical education.

We shall look at all three characteristics of the original humanities. But let us begin with the one which is most familiar to us. It is precisely the specialized nature of the humanities curriculum that can lead us to see their historical uniqueness. For it is not only the limited and re-

stricted nature of the humanities curriculum that has survived all the
way up to the present; it is this characteristic that most clearly distinguishes the Renaissance use of the phrase *studia humanitatis* from the
meaning it had in ancient Rome. Bruni, we have seen, identified the
term *studia humanitatis* with a specific group of disciplines. Let us look
now at Cicero's use of the term.

The studia humanitatis *according to Cicero*

The term *humanista*, as we have seen, is not classical Latin; it was
coined during the Renaissance. If a Roman of Cicero's time could have
visited Renaissance Italy, he would have been baffled by the term; it
was not part of the Latin language he knew, nor was there any profession in classical antiquity to which the word "humanist" could be applied.[9] The phrase *studia humanitatis*, however, from which the term
humanista was coined, is good classical Latin. Cicero uses it. And it
was from Cicero's writings that the Renaissance humanists borrowed
the phrase to name their new program of education. Coluccio Salutati,
Bruni's mentor, was the first one to do so. He found the phrase *studia
humanitatis* in Cicero's oration *Pro Archia*; he used it for the first time
in his own writings in 1369, and often thereafter.[10] But it was not
until Leonardo Bruni described the *studia humanitatis* in his letter to
Battista di Montefeltro that the phrase received a clear and systematic
definition as a new curriculum.

What did Cicero mean by the words *studia humanitatis*, which can be
translated literally as "studies of humanity"? We can answer this question by turning first to the *Pro Archia* itself.

In 62 B.C. Cicero defended his friend and teacher, the Greek poet
Archias, from the charge that his Roman citizenship was invalid. Cicero won, and Archias remained a Roman citizen. A good part of this rel-
atively short speech concerns the role of culture and learning in society. This topic, stated movingly but succinctly in Cicero's eloquent
Latin, made the *Pro Archia* one of Cicero's most widely read and studied speeches, as its success both within and outside the classroom
down through the ages attests.

Very early in his defense Cicero uses the term *studia humanitatis*. He
says to the jury:

> . . . I would ask you to allow me, speaking as I am on behalf of a first-
> rate poet and a very learned man, before this gathering of learned men of
> letters (*homines litteratissimi*), before this humanity (*humanitas*) of yours,
> and finally before this praetor occupying the tribunal, to speak somewhat

openly of the humanities and letters (*studia humanitatis ac litterarum*), and
to employ a rather new and unusual line of defense to suit the character
of one who, because of his withdrawn and studious life, has never been
dragged into perilous court trials. (2, 3)

Cicero would like to defend Archias, then, by speaking of the *studia
humanitatis*, and he asks the jury's indulgence. Perhaps they would
have taken a certain delight in hearing the words *studia humanitatis*. Cicero had used the phrase the year before in his defense of Lucius
Murena (*Pro Murena* 29, 61), and as we have no record of its having
been used before this time, it is at least possible that Cicero coined it.
He would have merely joined two common words, *studium* and
humanitas.[11]

Cicero begins his speech by stating his own personal debt to
Archias. Looking back to the days of his boyhood, he notes that whatever success he has had as an orator is due to his tutor Archias. The
jury may find this surprising, Cicero says, since Archias's talents have
nothing to do with oratory. But Cicero never limited his studies to oratory. "Indeed," he continues, "all those arts (*artes*), which pertain to humanity (*humanitas*), have a kind of common bond and are held together by a certain affinity" (1, 2). What are the arts that pertain to
humanity, of which oratory is only one?

After stating why it is only fitting that he use whatever talent as a lawyer he has, talent ultimately derived from his boyhood studies with
Archias, to defend his old tutor, Cicero turns to tell the jury something about Archias himself. "For as soon as Archias left his boyhood behind him," he says, "and those arts by which the age of boyhood is
wont to be shaped towards humanity (*ad humanitatem informari*), he
turned to writing . . ." (3, 4). The "arts which pertain to humanity"
then, which are held together by a common bond, are those subjects
or arts by which one is "shaped towards humanity" during boyhood.
In this context, it is clear that the phrase *studia humanitatis* is just another name for these arts. Indeed, the phrases *studia humanitatis* and
artes humanitatis are interchangeable in Cicero's writings. Thus, the humanities are all of those related arts which one studies for the first
time in his youth, and which help him attain *humanitas*. What are
these subjects? Cicero does not say during his brief defense of Archias.

But he does in his treatise *De oratore*. Speaking of learned men who
did not actively participate in public life either because they chose not
to or because they were prevented by circumstances beyond their control, he writes:

> . . . some gave themselves totally to the poets, others to the geometri-
> cians, others to the musicians, while still others, such as dialecticians, pro-

duced for themselves a new study and sport; they consumed all their
time and all their years in those arts, which were invented so that the
minds of boys would be formed into humanity and virtue. (III, 15, 58)

Cicero thus gives poetry, geometry, music, and dialectic as examples
of the arts by which young boys are formed into their humanity.
Later in Book III of the *De oratore* he lists geometry, music, "letters"
(*litterarum cognitio*, in the sense of learning in general,)[12] and poetry as
"those arts in which liberal learning, learning befitting free men
(*liberales doctrinae ac ingenuae*), is contained" (32, 127). And in a letter
of 46 B.C. to Sulpicius Rufus, Cicero speaks of himself as having from
childhood taken pleasure in "every liberal art and branch of learning
(*omnis ars et doctrina liberalis*), especially philosophy" (Cicero 1977, 203,
4, 13–14). These additional passages show that what Cicero calls the
studia humanitatis in the *Pro Archia* are synonymous with the *artes
liberales*, that is, with ancient education as a whole, including what
would later[13] come to be known as the *trivium* and *quadrivium* of the liberal arts.[14]

Cicero's use of the phrase *studia humanitatis* helps us to see what is historically unique about the humanities that came into being in the early
Renaissance. The Renaissance's use of the phrase *studia humanitatis* to denote the specific disciplines of grammar, rhetoric, history, moral philosophy, and poetry constitutes a significant—I'm tempted to say, in antici-
pation of what we are about to discover, a dramatic—narrowing of
the ancient program of education signified by the term *studia humanitatis* in Cicero's writings. Consider this striking example: Bruni warns
Battista not to spend too much time studying geometry and arithmetic. Geometry, however, appears prominently in Cicero's lists of the
subjects by which one is shaped toward *humanitas*. How are we to account for this change? The narrowing of the *studia humanitatis* from all
the branches of ancient learning to the Renaissance disciplines of grammar, rhetoric, history, poetry, and moral philosophy, with the specific exclusion of geometry, is in essence the result of a radical change
in the understanding of what it means to be human, especially in
terms of man's conception of himself and his relationship to the cosmos. We can see this striking difference between the classical and the
Renaissance conception of man by contrasting Bruni's understanding
of human perfection with Cicero's.

Human Perfection: Cicero and Bruni Contrasted

In the second book of the *De natura deorum*, "On the Nature of the
Gods," Cicero presents the Stoic beliefs concerning the universe and

God, with which he was sympathetic (as he says in Book III, 40, 95). In a passage fundamental for understanding his conception of man, he states that everything in the universe, except for the universe itself, has been brought into being for the sake of something else—the cover for the shield, the sheath for the sword, plants for animals, and animals for men. Then he says, "But man was born in order to contemplate and imitate the universe; he is in no way perfect, but is some little part of the perfect" (II, 14, 37). Cicero's assertion that man is born to contemplate and imitate the universe signifies that *the meaning of human life is not to be found in the individual human being, but rather in his or her relationship to the universe.* Let us look at the nature of the universe as Cicero describes it.

By *mundus,* "world," Cicero means the universe, that is, all existing things taken as a whole. The *mundus* is perfect precisely because it contains all that is: "But the universe is perfect (*perfectus*) in every respect, since it embraces all things, nor is there anything that is not within it" (II, 14, 38). Here *perfectus* has its basic meaning of "complete." The whole, since it is all, is by definition perfect or complete. Because man is not the whole, he cannot be perfect or complete. But because he is a part of the whole, he is a part of the perfect.

In chapters 11–14 (#29–39) of Book II of the *De natura deorum* Cicero mentions some of the attributes to be found in parts of the universe which attain their perfection in the whole. He states, for example, that if every being above the most simple ones has some organizing principle or governing part (*principatus*), such as sense and appetite in beasts, and mind in man, then sense and reason must exist in a sharper form and to a greater degree in the universe, because the universe contains the organizing principle of all nature:

> Therefore that in which exists the ruling principle of the whole of nature must be the most excellent of all things, and the most worthy of power and domination over all things. Moreover, we see sensation and reason in the parts of the universe (for there is nothing in the whole universe which is not a part of the universe). In that part, therefore, in which the ruling principle of the universe exists, there must be sensation and reason, and in a sharper and greater form.

He concludes that the universe is wise, excels in the perfection of reason, and on that account is divine:

> Wherefore the universe must be wise, and the nature which holds all things in its embrace must excel in the perfection of reason, and therefore the universe must be a god, and all the force of the universe must be held together by nature, which is divine. (II, 11, 29–30)

In another passage, in which he speaks of the fourth or highest level of being, that to be attributed to the divinity, he speaks of the completion or perfection toward which plants and animals develop, and which arts or crafts, such as painting and building, strive to achieve, and he compares this perfection, which can be thwarted by some outside force, to the utterly unimpeded perfection of the whole universe. Again he concludes that the universe must be intelligent and wise:

> Nor can it be said that in any organized arrangement (*institutio*) of things there is not something final and perfect (*perfectum*). For as in vines or in cattle, unless some force stands in the way, we see nature proceed along a certain path to her final end, and as painting and building and the other arts produce some result when the operation is finished, so too, and even more so, in nature as a whole it is necessary that something be completed and brought to perfection. And indeed many external things can obstruct the bringing to perfection of other natures, but nothing can impede nature as a whole, since it holds together and contains within itself all natures. For this reason there must be that fourth and highest stage which no force can threaten. Now this is the stage where nature as a whole is placed, and since it is such that it is superior to all things, and nothing can impede it, it follows that the universe must be intelligent, and indeed also wise. (II, 13, 35–36)

Cicero uses the Stoic Chrysippus' simile of biological maturation, finally, to argue that virtue, which he defines in De legibus, "Concerning Laws," as "nothing other than nature perfected and brought to its highest development" (I, 8, 25), must exist in the universe because nothing is more complete or perfect than it is. Part of his argument turns on the point that if virtue can sometimes be realized in human nature, which is not perfect, it can be realized all the more easily in the universe, which is perfect and complete:

> Accordingly Chrysippus does well when he teaches us, with the addition of examples, that all things are better in what are perfect and mature, as in a horse than in a foal, in a dog than in a puppy, in a man than in a boy, and that in the same way that which is the best in the whole universe must be in something which is perfect and complete; nothing, however, is more perfect than the universe, nothing is better than virtue. Therefore the universe has its own virtue. Nor, moreover, is human nature perfect, and yet virtue may be realized in man; how much more easily then in the universe! Therefore virtue is in the universe; therefore the universe is wise, and consequently a god. (II, 14, 38–39)

Such then is the universe. To contemplate it is to ponder the perfect *ratio* or reason which orders and governs the totality of reality. To imitate it is to live in congruence with this reason. Contemplating and imitating the universe, moreover, brings one peace, for it frees the soul from the turbulent fears and desires, the sorrows and unrestrained

joys, of contingent human existence. In a beautiful description of the
soul of the wise man (*sapiens*), Cicero speaks of how insignificant
human affairs appear to one who knows the eternity and magnitude of
the universe:

> Therefore the man, whoever he is, who through moderation and con-
> stancy is at rest in his soul and at peace with himself, so that he is neither
> wasted away by troubles, nor broken by fear, nor burns thirsting with de-
> sire for something he longs for, nor is he dissipated by exalting in futile
> joy—he is the wise man whom we seek, he is the blessed man, to whom
> nothing that happens to humans can seem unbearable to the point of cast-
> ing down his soul, or so excessively joyful as to carry it away in elation.
> For what can seem of consequence in human affairs to a man who is ac-
> quainted with all eternity and the vastness of the universe. (*Tusc.* IV, 17, 37)

It is important to note, finally, that just as Cicero says that man is
"quaedam particula perfecti," "some little part of the perfect," and
uses the verbs *contemplare* and *imitare* to describe the particular way in
which man, as opposed to other forms of life, consciously associates
himself to the perfect universe, so too he uses the term *particeps*, "having a share or participating in," to describe man's particular relationship to reason. Just as man is not the whole universe, but part of the universe, so too he is not reason, but participates in reason (see, for
example, *De natura deorum* II, 12, 32 and 13, 36).

Cicero's vision of the ultimate goal of study and learning reflects his
understanding of man and the universe. He says in the *De re publica*
that one of the effects of being "polished" by the *artes humanitatis* is to
be able to look down upon all things human, and to turn one's soul toward the eternal and the divine:

> But what dominion, what magistracy, what kingdom can be more excel-
> lent than for one, looking down upon everything human and considering
> it inferior to wisdom, never to revolve anything in his mind except that
> which is eternal and divine? Such a one is persuaded that while others
> may be called human (*homines*), only those are who are polished by the
> proper arts of humanity (*humanitatis artes*). . . . (I, 17, 28)

Now that we have looked at Cicero's understanding of man and the
universe, we can see clearly the differences between Cicero and Bruni.
*For Cicero, the individual human being is part of the whole; for Bruni, the indi-
vidual becomes the whole.* This profound difference between Cicero's
and Bruni's perception of man leads to equally different visions of the
purpose of education. Bruni's *studia humanitatis* promise self-perfection; Cicero's *artes humanitatis* turn the soul away from the human
and toward the divine. In fact, there is no personal, autonomous

self in Cicero to perfect; an individual's identity is to be found in his relationship to the universe, not to himself. Thus while Bruni chooses metaphors of nourishing and shaping to describe how one perfects an autonomous self, Cicero does not use metaphors at all, but speaks literally of contemplation, imitation, and participation as ways in which one identifies himself with the universe.

We have already seen that for Cicero the phrases *artes* and *studia humanitatis* by no means denote the specific and specialized literary curriculum Bruni describes as the *studia humanitatis*. Now we know why: the studies which enable man to contemplate the whole of reality and which shape him, in his youth, "towards humanity," embrace all the areas of ancient learning. Thus we find that what Cicero calls *litterae* ("letters")—a term which, from the Renaissance on, has come to mean literary culture and erudition—means learning in general and includes the study of nature. "For what is sweeter than leisure devoted to letters (*otium litteratum*)?" Cicero asks in the Fifth Book of the *Tusculan Disputations*. "I mean those letters (*litterae*) through which we come to know the infinity of all things and nature, and, in this actual world of ours, the sky, the lands, and the seas" (36, 105).

The Humanities and Modern Science

We have already seen from Cicero's description of the soul of the wise man that "to know the infinity of all things and nature" is to rise above the human and become one with the eternal and the divine. Such indeed was the highest goal of classical education. And this we see not only from the writings of Cicero. In the fourth century A.D. Claudianus Mamertus had this to say about the famous Roman scholar Marcus Varro:

> For what reason did Marcus Varro with a kind of divine disputation exert his mental powers in his books on music, arithmetic, geometry, and philosophy if not to pull his soul, in the marvelous ways of eternal art, away from the visible to the invisible, from places to where there are no places, from the corporeal to the incorporeal? . . . (Quoted in Fuchs 1962, p. 392)

And Augustine recounts that as a young man in Milan ready to be baptized into the Christian faith, he started to write a series of books—which he never finished—on the seven liberal arts, "desiring, through certain, as it were, sure steps, to arrive at or go towards the incorporeal through the corporeal" (ibid.).

This goal of rising from the corporeal to the incorporeal explains why the study of geometry plays such an important role in ancient writings on learning and education. If man is born to contemplate and imitate the cosmos, what discipline better than geometry leads one to ponder the Eternal Forms, and the Reason and Harmony which order and govern all of reality? Thus we find that in the passage quoted above from the *De re publica* in which Cicero says that only those who are polished by the *artes humanitatis* may be truly called human, he goes on immediately to speak of geometry, singling it out as a sure sign of the kind of learning that bespeaks the presence of human beings:

> . . . it seems to me a fine saying of Plato's, or of someone else's; who, after a storm had thrown him up on an unknown land and a deserted shore, and while his companions were fearful because of their ignorance of the place, observed, they say, certain geometrical figures traced in the sand; and when he saw them, he called out to his companions to be of good cheer, for he had seen indications of men. These he deduced not from the cultivation of the soil, which he saw, but from signs of learning (*doctrina*). (I, 17, 29)

It should be clear by now why classical antiquity knew no intellectual specialization comparable to our own, no dichotomy between the "humanities" and the "sciences." The ancients did not think in these terms. Geometry, for Cicero, is one of the *artes humanitatis*, and "letters" (*litterae*) include the study of nature. The unity of man and the cosmos, the participation of the part in the whole, found its intellectual counterpart in the unity of all the "liberal arts," that is, in the unity of all the disciplines befitting free men. It was mirrored in the affinity, as Cicero puts it in the *Pro Archia*, which holds together "all those arts which pertain to humanity." The fragmented curriculum of modern times, and the dichotomy between the humanities and the sciences, arose out of the dissolution of this ancient unity.

By Bruni's time, the movement of the soul out of matter and toward union with the eternal intelligibles was no longer possible, because people no longer postulated the unity of all being the way the ancients had. The goal of the modern humanities is another kind of unity, an intensive unity of a new inward-turning self, as opposed to the ultimately selfless ancient unity of the individual and the cosmos. Unlike the ancient extensive self, which uses all the arts and branches of learning to participate in the reason and harmony of the universe, the modern intensive self[15] finds of use only those disciplines, such as moral philosophy, history, literature, and rhetoric, which it can personalize. Bruni denigrates the study of geometry and arithmetic because, from his point of view, these subjects have nothing to say about how an individual should live his life, or what he must do in order to find happiness and virtue, now understood as personal states of mind rather than attributes of the cosmos.

Petrarch counseled against the study of nature, and for the same reason. In the 1360s he wrote a little treatise entitled *On His Own Ignorance and That of Many Others*. Petrarch was one of the most famous men in Europe by this time, celebrated for his Italian poetry, for his Latin letters and treatises, and for his knowledge of classical antiquity. Although he had no interest in, and was, in fact, quite critical of, the chief subjects taught in the universities of his time—logic, natural science, law, and metaphysics—and although he promoted his own classical studies as more useful and better for one's soul, Petrarch was nonetheless stung by the charge, made in private by four Venetian friends, but soon on the lips of everyone in the city, that he was a good man but not very learned. In his treatise *On His Own Ignorance and That of Many Others*, he replies to this remark by ridiculing much of what passed for learning and erudition in the university culture of his own time. At a certain point in his treatise he argues that those Aristotelians and scholastics who accused him of having little learning are themselves quite ignorant, because either they know nothing, or what they do know is not worth knowing:

> For letters are instruments of insanity for many, of arrogance for almost everyone, if they do not meet with a good and well-trained mind. Therefore, he has much to tell about wild animals, about birds and fishes: how many hairs there are in the lion's mane; how many feathers in the hawk's tail; with how many arms the cuttlefish clasps a shipwrecked man; that elephants couple from behind and are pregnant for two years; that this docile and vigorous animal, the nearest to man by its intelligence, lives until the end of the second or third century of its life. . . .

He goes on, giving more examples of what then passed for natural science. Much of this lore now seems laughable to us, as it did even then to Petrarch. But the conclusion Petrarch draws concerning this kind of learning goes to the heart of the difference between the humanities and the sciences, for he raises the key question, which still haunts us today, of the relationship between learning and moral goodness. He concludes his humorous exposition of natural history by mentioning the belief "that alone among all the living beings the crocodile moves its upper jaw." Then he says:

> All this is for the greater part wrong, as has become manifest in many similar cases when animals were brought into our part of the world. The facts have certainly not been investigated by those who are quoted as authorities for them; they have been all the more promptly believed or boldly invented, since the animals live so far from us.

So far there is nothing controversial in this statement, for in voicing the need for investigation of the facts and for direct observation, rather than blind acceptance of what the so-called authorities have written, Petrarch presents himself as a precursor of the scientific revolution and as holding values which we all share today. But then he goes on, speaking of the natural scientific lore he has just described:

> And even if they were true, they would not contribute anything whatsoever to the blessed life. What is the use—I beseech you—of knowing the nature of quadrupeds, fowls, fishes, and serpents and not knowing or even neglecting man's nature, the purpose for which we are born, and whence and whereto we travel? (Petrarch 1906, pp. 24–25, trans. in Cassirer 1948, pp. 56–59)

In other words, even if we had an accurate knowledge of the natural world, this knowledge would not make us any happier, or morally better; nor would it contribute to our knowledge of ourselves and of the meaning and purpose of our lives.

Petrarch's characterization of the study of the natural world as morally useless throws a different light on the history of the relationship between the humanities and the sciences. Many people believe that the split between the sciences and the humanities is the result of the power and prestige of science and technology in our own time. This is incorrect. The dichotomy between the humanities and the sciences actually antedates the birth of modern science, for it comes into being with the humanities in the early Renaissance, several centuries before the beginning of the Scientific Revolution. The humanities and the sciences are actually two sides of the same coin; they both have their origin in the loss of the ancient Greek and Roman experience of a fundamental harmony and symmetry between the soul, the State, and the universe. But while the humanities attempt to give meaning and purpose to an individual's life by helping him replace this outer unity with a new inner one, the sciences owe their very existence to the disintegration of the ancient experience of man in the cosmos, to the dichotomy between the individual and the universe, between the knower and the known, between man and nature.

Despite their sharp differences in perspective, the modern humanities and the modern sciences thus inhabit the same universe. In fact, one could even argue that the *studia humanitatis* prepared the way for the Scientific Revolution by providing a program of studies and a philosophy of education which helped people adjust to the dichotomies of a postclassical universe centuries before Galileo and Descartes theorized them.

In sum, we see that the goal of education changed radically in the Renaissance. People turned inward in search of an inner wholeness to substi-

tute for the ancient experience of unity with the cosmos. Out of this inward turning, and the dichotomy it created between the individual
and the universe, arose *both* the humanities and the modern sciences.
And it was this inward turning which led to the creation of a unique autonomous self. The humanities, in essence, come into being as a curriculum for the modern self.

Judged by ancient standards, the curriculum Bruni describes is limited and incomplete, for it excludes the study of mathematics and the
natural world. But judged by the standards of an autonomous inward-
turning self, it encompasses the only disciplines truly capable of shaping and perfecting such a self. Recognition of this contrast leads to
two fundamental questions concerning the birth of the humanities in
the early Renaissance: Why, at this particular moment in the history
of the West, did people begin to turn inward and attempt, as Pico
della Mirandola put it, to become makers and molders of themselves?
And how did the study of classical antiquity, even the mastery of classical Latin, sustain this project of self-fashioning? How, in other words,
could Roman words and deeds help to form, shape, and cultivate a
state of soul which the Romans themselves did not possess?

These are hard questions to answer, for they demand first of all that
we admit that our own sense of self is historically unique and thus not
a standard against which to judge how other peoples and other times experience their humanity; and secondly, having accepted the historical relativity of our own experience of the human, answering these questions requires that we find some vantage point from which we can
actually observe the autonomous self as it comes into being. Fortu-
nately, we have such a historical vantage point in the life and writings
of Petrarch, who became synonymous in the Renaissance with the rediscovery of classical antiquity.

CHAPTER 2

PETRARCH AND THE ORIGINS
OF THE HUMANITIES

❧

THE EARLY HUMANISTS celebrated Petrarch as the founder of the *studia humanitatis*.[1] In a letter of 1372 to Jacopo Pizzinga, Giovanni Boccaccio, Petrarch's friend and contemporary, spoke of the decline of poetry in the ages preceding his own. He said that after Dante

> my teacher, Francesco Petrarca . . . arose to seize the ancient road with such courage in his breast and such ardor in his mind and perspicacity of intellect, that no impediments could stop him, or impassable stretches frighten him. On the contrary, when he had pushed aside the brambles and branches, by which the neglect of mortals is manifest, and had restored with firm rampart the overflowing, half-consumed embankments, he opened the way for himself, and for those who wanted to ascend after him. Thereafter the Heliconian fountain was cleansed of mud and swampy reeds and its waves restored to their pristine clarity. . . . He brought the name of poetry, called back from its hiding place, into the light, he awakened in noble souls the hope that had almost been lost, and showed what many had not believed: that Parnassus and its heights were accessible. Nor is it to be doubted that he inspired many to ascend. (Boccaccio 1928, pp. 195–96)

Boccaccio's image of an unused path overgrown with bushes and brambles is typical of the way the first men of the Renaissance pictured what they saw as the neglect and decay of literary culture in the centuries immediately preceding their own. According to Boccaccio, it was Petrarch who opened this path back to classical poetry. Some thirty years later Leonardo Bruni used the same image to describe how Petrarch brought back the ancient humanities. It was Petrarch who "restored the *studia humanitatis*, which were already extinct, and who opened for us the way whereby we could acquire learning" (Bruni 1952, p. 94). And Rudolph Agricola (1443–85), Erasmus's teacher and one of the men responsible for bringing the new humanities to northern Europe, wrote in his biography of Petrarch that to Petrarch "all the erudition of our century is owed . . .", and called him "the initiator of humane studies" and "the liberator and restorer of the *litterae*" (quoted in Mann 1980, p. 288).

Petrarch would have agreed with these assessments of his historical importance. Shortly before he died, he wrote in a letter to Giovanni Boccaccio, "I certainly do not reject the praise you bestow upon me: that I stimulated many minds both in Italy and perhaps farther away to take up these studies of ours which have been neglected for centuries" (*Sen.* XVII, 2, in Petrarca 1955, p. 1144).

Petrarch's choice of the word "stimulate" (*excitasse*) is replete with meaning for anyone wishing to understand both the motivating force behind his own life's work and the particular kind of influence he had on his followers. For it was above all else a kind of moral inspiration that Petrarch sought in his favorite Latin authors, and it was likewise inspiration and encouragement to follow his example and travel back to the ancients that he gave to those who came after him. "Petrarch was not so much an influence for the Renaissance as a paradigm," Charles Trinkaus writes. "It was a token of the potency of his own life and writings that his humanist successors did not always become cultistic imitators but instead carried his insights farther, knowing they had surpassed him, criticized him, but saw him as a pioneer" (1983, p. 147). In fact, because Petrarch had cleared the path and pointed the way, those who came after him were able to walk more easily along it— perhaps too easily, for all too often, whenever the *studia humanitatis* became institutionalized, they risked degenerating into pure scholarship and professional antiquarianism. But Petrarch, unlike many who later taught and practiced the "humanities" as a career, was not a professional classicist.[2] There was no divorce between his literary studies and his life. His scholarship was so personally motivated that one hesitates to call it scholarship at all, because of the connotations of personal detachment and disinterest associated with that word today. Petrarch was driven to study classical antiquity because he was driven to study himself. He used the writers of ancient Rome, Cicero in particular, and the early Fathers of the Church, especially St. Augustine, to mold and shape his own soul.

The fullest expression of a new cultural movement, of a new way in which men and women begin to experience their humanity, often occurs at the beginning, before the movement has triumphed and the experience has lost its disturbing novelty. This is certainly true of the humanities. It is in Petrarch's life and writings that they achieved their fullest expression. For this reason, Petrarch should be the nucleus even today of any discussion concerning the future of the humanities: from him we can learn why the humanities came into being; how, at their very best, they can help us live our lives; and where they fall short— for Petrarch's life exemplifies the weaknesses as well as the strengths of the humanistic educational ideal.

With the possible exception of Cicero, whose collected letters inspired Petrarch to collect and circulate his own, no one before Petrarch has left us such a complete and detailed record of his own inner life and the world in which he lived. In addition to his Italian sonnets, Petrarch wrote poems, short treatises, several uncompleted books, and many prose letters in Latin. His published letters alone number 574 (Wilkins 1960, p. 5). In his works, and especially in his letters, we can see how Petrarch actually put to use, in the concrete circumstances of his daily life, the classical studies which Boccaccio, Bruni, and other humanists said he initiated.

Life beneath the Circle of the Moon:
Death, Change, and Contingency

We are swept into a dark world of grief, despair, and anxiety as we begin to read the very first words of the *Familiares*, Petrarch's great collection of personal letters. Writing to his good friend Ludwig van Kempen, his beloved "Socrates," in 1350, two years after the onset of the Black Death, Petrarch asks:

> What shall we do now, brother? Look, we have tried everything, and peace we have found nowhere. When can we expect it? The times, they say, have slipped through our fingers; our former hopes are buried with our friends. The year 1348 has left us alone and forlorn, for it has taken from us things which neither the Indian nor the Caspian Sea can restore: the latest losses are irreparable, and any wound which death inflicts is incurable. There is only one consolation: we ourselves shall follow those whom we have sent ahead. How short the wait will be I do not know; this I do know, that it cannot be long. And yet, however short it is, it cannot but be full of distress. (*Fam.* I, 1, 1–2)

"Any wound which death inflicts is incurable." It was the death of so many people he loved that turned the years 1348–1350 into one of the bitterest periods of Petrarch's life. The Black Death carried away Laura, the inspiration of some of his finest sonnets; Cardinal Giovanni Colonna, his dear friend and patron; Franceschino degli Albizzi, a distant relative of whom he had grown increasingly fond; and many more friends and acquaintances. In 1349 Petrarch wrote to Socrates about the terrible loneliness he felt after so many of his friends had died. Almost a year and a half has passed since he and Socrates were last together. Petrarch looks back in grief and horror over what has transpired in that brief period of time:

> I do not ask you to look back a long way. Consider these few days and think of what we were, and what we are. Where now are our dear friends? Where are the beloved faces? Where are the soothing words? Where is the pleasant and cheerful conversation? What thunderbolt has destroyed these things? What earthquake has overturned them? What tempest has pulled them under? What bottomless pit has swallowed them up? We used to be a crowd. Now we are almost alone. We have to form new friendships. But where, and for what reason, since the whole race of men is nearly extinct, and the end of the world, I hope, is near. We are alone, brother, we are—why hide it—truly alone. . . . (*Fam.* VIII, 7, 20–21)

The loss Petrarch felt was enormous, almost incommunicable in its finality. The anguish caused by the deaths from this period of his life was so great that it even changed his literary style. Petrarch describes this change in the letter of 1350 from which we quoted at the beginning of this section. This is the letter he wrote to Socrates to tell him that he had decided to collect his prose letters and dedicate them to him. A rich and valuable letter, it is easy to see why Petrarch chose it as the opening letter of the entire collection, for here he speaks clearly, from the vantage point of middle age, of how he understood the course of his life. Petrarch had recently reread chronologically the letters of former years. "Our sorrows constitute too frequent a theme," he says. But what troubles him most is what he perceives as a change in his style of writing:

> I am ashamed that my life has broken down into effeminacy. Look at what the order of these letters shows: at first my speech was sober and strong—the sign of a healthy mind—so that I was able to console not only myself, but others as well. Then the letters become increasingly weak and subdued, filled with not very manly complaints. These especially I beg you to hide. What might others say, when I myself blush as I reread them? Was I thus a man in my youth in order to become a boy in old age? What a sad and abhorrent perversity. I had in mind either to change the order or to take away from you completely those letters I condemn. But it seemed impossible to deceive you, for you have copies of the tearful letters, and they are all dated.

And now Petrarch attempts to account for this great change:

> A long and grave battle with Fortune wore me out. I resisted while I still had the courage and the heart, and urged others to. But when my foot, and my spirit, began to slip under the force and impetus of the enemy,

that magnificent way of speaking suddenly disappeared, and I descended to those laments which now offend me. Perhaps the pity I felt for my friends will exonerate me for this, for while they remained unharmed, no blow of Fortune made me moan. But then, when almost all of them were swept down in one crash and with the whole world dying besides, it seemed inhuman, rather than courageous, not to be affected. Before this time, whoever heard me go around crying about exile, sickness, court trials, elections, the whirlwinds of the forum? Who heard me bemoan my paternal house, lost property, diminished glory, unpaid debts, absent friends? (*Fam.* I, 1, 38–41)

Grief for friends who had died was thus powerful enough, Petrarch believed, to knock the manly vigor out of his style. But there was another, closely related emotion that tortured him as well: constant fear for the friends who were still alive.

In 1342, while he was living in Parma, Petrarch received news that his close friend, Giacomo Colonna, bishop of the town of Lombez in Gascony, was seriously ill. That night Giacomo appeared to Petrarch in a dream, saying that he had been tired out by the storms of the Pyrenees and was on his way to Rome, never to return to Lombez. In the dream Petrarch insisted on accompanying him, but Giacomo pushed him back. " 'Stop,' he said, 'I do not want you to come with me.' I fixed my eyes on him," Petrarch says, "and saw in his exsanguine pallor that he was dead" (*Fam.* V, 7, 14). Less than a month later Petrarch learned that Giacomo had died on the very day of his dream.

In the letter of consolation he wrote to Giacomo's brother, Cardinal Giovanni Colonna, Petrarch describes vividly what happens to him when letters arrive from friends far away:

> Who can have a brother, or especially friends who are absent, and feel secure, except one who, ignorant of the vicissitudes of human life, does not notice the violence and inconstancy of Fortune. Let others speak for themselves; as far as I am concerned, since I have been here [Parma], I always tremble and turn pale when I receive my letters, and after it has been announced that everyone is well, I still do not throw off my cares: for who can assure me that while these letters have travelled across the Alps and over the sea, some misfortune has not occurred, as is wont to happen in the wink of an eye? (*Fam.* IV, 12, 19–20)

Along with grief and bereavement, then, one of the striking characteristics of Petrarch's inner life is that he lived in constant fear that his friends would die suddenly and without warning. And they did. His letters present a remarkable picture of the actual, and at times historically unique, risks, such as the Black Death, to which human life was exposed in his time, for they are full of descriptions of people who have died unnaturally, before their time—and not just in the plague, but in wars between states and noble families, ambushes in the countryside, sword fights in cities, court intrigues, and in natural calamities such as storms and earthquakes.

Franceschino degli Albizzi was a young relative from Florence of whom Petrarch was very fond. After spending a good part of 1345–47 as Petrarch's guest in Vaucluse, Franceschino traveled on to Paris and then returned to Vaucluse the following year, only to find that Petrarch had gone to Italy. So he set out for Parma to meet him there. But during the voyage he was struck with the plague, and died in Savona, in northern Italy.

When Petrarch learned that Franceschino was on his way to Parma to join him he was filled with joy. He wrote a mutual relative, Giovanni dell'Incisa, how happy he was to learn that Franceschino had already reached Marseilles, "after being tossed about by many misfortunes and dangers on land and at sea, yet safe." Soon, Petrarch says, he will reach Parma, where he plans to keep him for himself, since "friendship is much rarer and more precious than gold; if I thus act avariciously, the value of the thing possessed will in one way or another excuse the hardness of the possessor" (*Fam.* VII, 11, 2, 4).

The shock of learning of Franceschino's death at the very time he was eagerly and joyfully awaiting his arrival was too much for Petrarch to bear. He begins a second letter to Giovanni dell'Incisa with a virulent denunciation of the human condition:

> Ah, what is this? What do I hear? O deceitful hope, O superfluous cares, O transient state of mortals! For man nothing is calm, nothing is stable, nothing is safe. Here is Fortune's violence. Here are Death's snares. Here are the charms of the fleeting world. Wretched, we are beset on all sides.(*Fam.* VII, 12, 1)

The following year, 1349, another tragedy occurred in Petrarch's life. This time it was not the plague, but human violence that took another dear friend from him. The loss was equally unexpected, and almost as painful.

Petrarch had for some time thought that he would make his permanent home in Parma. He purchased a house there, and tried to persuade Ludwig van Kempen and two other close friends, Mainardo Accursio and Luca Cristiani, to come live with him. One day Mainardo and Luca chanced to visit him in Parma when Petrarch was away in the Veneto. They spent the night in Petrarch's house and left a note saying they would return. Returning home and finding the note where they had left it in his study, Petrarch wrote Luca, saying that he expected them to keep their promise and visit him now that he was back in Parma. Several days passed. There was no reply. Petrarch then sent a servant off to Florence with a letter for Mainardo. Eight days later, during a violent storm, the servant returned, "drenched in rain and tears." When he entered the room, Petrarch looked up from his writing table, then he caught his breath, and the pen fell out of his hand. Here is the tragic news the servant brought him. Having left Parma, Luca and Mainardo were crossing the Apennines on the road to Florence.

> Simplicius [Mainardo], the best and most innocent of mortals, who may have been riding in front, ran into an ambush. He was attacked immediately, and fell down among the swords of the killers. Olympius [Luca], startled by the noise, dashed into the melee, and single-handedly held his own with drawn sword against ten or more assassins. He gave and received many wounds, and then, spurring his horse, barely escaped alive. The bandits took some, but not all of the spoils from the victim, and ran away so quickly that, wearied by their exertion and by their conscience, they could have easily been captured by the peasants who had gathered at the scene of the assault had not some men, nobles in name only, run down out of the mountains, held the peasants at bay, and taken into their hideouts the nervous band and their bloody spoils. Olympius was seen far off in the forest, still holding his sword. After this, nothing more was heard of him. (*Fam.* VIII, 9, 19–20)

Earlier letters describe other scenes of death. In 1342 Cardinal Giovanni Colonna sent Petrarch to Naples on a diplomatic mission. During his stay there Petrarch wrote Giovanni not only about the missions that had been entrusted to him, but also about his own personal experiences. In two of these letters he tells of human tragedies he happened to witness.

The first letter describes a violent storm which destroyed the port of Naples. It was a little after midnight. Petrarch had just fallen asleep when he was awakened by a terrible crash: the whole building shook. Throughout the night rain and wind, thunder, lightning, and earthquakes ravaged the city. Petrarch and his companions feared for their lives. The following morning, when the terrible storm had subsided, he went down with others to observe what had happened to the port. Here is what he saw:

> When, O God, has anything like this ever been heard of? The oldest sailors say nothing like this ever happened before. There was a sad, horrible shipwreck right in the center of the harbor. The waves were dashing the wretched men against the rocks as they tried to grasp the land nearby with their hands, and broke them apart like so many fragile eggs. The whole shore was covered with still palpitating corpses which were all cut

to pieces: in one the brain, in another the insides were spilling out. And in all of this the screaming of the men and the wailing of the women were so great that they drowned out the roar of the sea and the sky. (*Fam.* V, 5, 12)

Petrarch was so shaken by this experience that he told Giovanni never to command him again to trust his life to the wind and the waves. There was hardly a sea between the two of them, Petrarch observed, on which he had not been shipwrecked. From now on he would travel by land.

The next letter he wrote to Giovanni shows death in yet another form: gratuitous violence. Unaware of what he was about to witness, Petrarch was led to a place outside Naples. The queen and prince consort were there, along with the Neapolitan militia and a packed crowd of common folk. Given the size of the crowd, and the number of prominent people, Petrarch expected that he was about to witness some important event. Suddenly, as if something pleasant had just occurred, loud applause filled the air. Petrarch looked around, just in time to see a very handsome young man fall down at his feet, run through with a sword. It was to a public gladiatorial contest that Petrarch had been led!

I was struck dumb, and I shivered through my whole body. I spurred my horse, and fled the foul and infernal spectacle, damning over and over again my companions' deception, the barbarity of the spectators, and the insanity of the contestants. (*Fam.* V, 6, 5)

Such was the world in which Petrarch lived. Such were the sad events he chose to recollect. It is not surprising, then, to find that Petrarch foresaw the possibility of a violent and untimely death not only for his friends, but for himself as well. In 1350, after so many had died, he was moved to symbolize his own childhood, and his life in general, in terms of the dangerous world in which he lived. In the opening letter to Ludwig van Kempen, Petrarch tells of how his very coming into the world was fraught with peril. "I, conceived in exile, was born in exile, with such suffering for my mother, that not only the midwives, but even the physicians thought for a long time that she had died." Looking back in retrospect, he finds in his perilous birth a symbol for his whole life: "I thus began to be in danger before I was born, and I reached the very threshold of life under the sign of death" (*Fam.* I, 1, 22).

In the same letter Petrarch describes two times in early life when he seemed fated to die. When he was only seven months old, he and the young servant carrying him on horseback fell into the Arno when the horse slipped while crossing the river. "As he struggled to save the burden entrusted to him," Petrarch writes, "he himself almost perished in the violent whirlpool." Seven years later, Petrarch left Pisa with his family and traveled by sea to France; there they were shipwrecked in a storm not far from Marseilles. "I was only a little way from being called back again from the very beginning of my new life," he observes (*Fam.* I, 1, 24).

Why should Petrarch, who would have been forty-six in 1350, have wanted to recall these incidents now, years after they happened? His life, like Ulysses', has been full of wanderings, he tells Ludwig,

> and how many kinds of dangers and fears I have endured while wandering, no one, other than myself, knows better than you. I have wanted to call these things to your mind so that you would remember that I was born amidst dangers, and have grown old among them. . . . (*Fam.* I, 1, 25)

Petrarch must have touched a sensitive chord in many of his contemporaries when he spoke of his life in such terms and described so vividly and so candidly his fears and his anxieties. "Who was more cautious in avoiding dangers?" Coluccio Salutati said of him in his letter to Count Guidi shortly after Petrarch died in 1374 (Salutati 1891, I, p. 178), as if the kind of dangers Petrarch describes in his letters constituted an important part of the subjective experience of life in Petrarch's time.

So far we have seen that two of the strongest emotions Petrarch had to bear were grief and fear, grief for the friends who had died, and fear of death both for himself and for those who were still alive. The therapeutic powers Petrarch found in his study of the ancients must be understood, in part, at least, in terms of these two emotions. Petrarch's devotion to those studies which would come to be known as the "humanities," then, is directly related to the problem of death.

But the problem of death is universal. As Ernest Becker suggests in his book *The Denial of Death*, one way of looking at the human condition is to understand man to be a highly evolved animal cursed with the consciousness that its body is mortal (Becker 1973, pp. 26–27). From this point of view, what distinguishes one human being from another, one historical period from another, is the way in which a person learns to live with this knowledge.

How did Petrarch live with it? Only with great difficulty. And this, it seems, was his cross. For it was not just death per se, not even the death of his friends, that caused Petrarch such deep and searing anguish. Most human beings feel grief and bereavement when people they love die. But how many feel the pain and despair Petrarch experienced? The key to understanding Petrarch's use of Roman literature lies in uncovering another facet of his attitude toward death, one which distinguishes his own personal dilemma, and that of his age, from the grief and anxiety concerning death that accompany all of human history.

If we look again at the letters containing the passages cited earlier concerning the deaths of Petrarch's friends, we see that, in addition to grief and bereavement, Petrarch expresses a deep anguish, an anguish intensified by feelings of anger and protest at what he perceives as the casual, fortuitous, utterly adventitious nature of such deaths. Franceschino degli Albizzi died at the very moment Petrarch was anticipating the joy he would feel when Franceschino arrived. After learning of his death, Petrarch wrote:

> In this matter nothing has hurt me more than not to have foreseen that which not only could happen, but which could not fail to happen: I did not think that he would die. And certainly, if there were any order in this torrent of human affairs, one who was born after me should not have died before me. (*Fam.* VII, 12, 12)

It was thus not just Franceschino's death that overwhelmed Petrarch, but the utter unexpectedness of it.

"For man nothing is calm, nothing is stable, nothing is safe," Petrarch cries out in the letter bemoaning Franceschino's death (*Fam.* VII, 12, 1). Reflecting on the bandits' ambush which took Mainardo Accursio away from him forever, he says in a letter to Ludwig van Kempen:

> And this too, in fact, O my Socrates, Fortune wickedly brought about: that I, who for a whole year had never set foot out of my house, should be away then, so that she [Fortune] could deprive us of seeing one another, and thrust my disoriented friends quickly into the snares of a death prepared for them. (*Fam.* VIII, 9, 11)

The thought that this tragedy could have been avoided, if only Petrarch had been in Parma when Luca and Mainardo came, increased his anguish:

> If they had found me, that hardness of Fortune could have been bent, perhaps, by their delay. Maybe they would have changed their plans, and taken care of the business at home through messengers. Tempted by affection, they would have stayed with me and now—for what prohibits it?— we would all find ourselves together in the quiet we have so long desired. But we were bound by the adamantine chains of fate, and ferocious Fortune saw to it that I was away. (*Fam.* VIII, 9, 12)

Along with the agony the unexpected and fortuitous death of a friend brings him, Petrarch feels anger toward himself, anger arising out of a sense of frustration and disillusionment that no matter how hard he tries, he cannot seem to prepare himself for these unexpected blows of fate. Of Franceschino's death he writes:

So often deceived, so often made sport of, we are unable to shake off the habit of hoping, and a credulity deceived a thousand times over, so great is the sweetness, albeit false, of happiness. How many times have I not said to myself, "O madman, O blind man forgetful of your condition, look here, take note, pay attention, stop, reflect, make a permanent, enduring, indelible sign. Remember this deception and that one. Never hope for anything. Believe nothing of Fortune: she is false, inconstant, capricious, and untrustworthy. First you knew her gentleness and charms, then later her severities. Already tried by this deadly monster, you need no teacher; therefore reflect upon your own examples and be aware of entering into any dealings with her. Despise her when she promises as well as when she denies, scorn her whether she gives or takes away." This I resolved to do, this I set firmly in my mind. But after such a manly resolution, look how womanly, how absurdly I have fallen down again—shall I say laughably, or rather lamentably? Perhaps it is laughable to others, but to me it is utterly pitiful and sad. After the unexpected downfall of so many hopes, I, rash, thoughtless, and ill-advised, persuaded myself to hope again, and to trust in this momentary calm—the calm of a winter's night, as it were—and to wait on the good fortune of tomorrow. (*Fam.* VII, 12, 1–4)

Petrarch's reaction to Franceschino's death was so violent, in fact, that it shocked him into questioning just what kind of person he really was:

Almost never have I scrutinized myself as I have now, and I confess, not without shame, that I find more feeling and less force than I had thought: for I believed—and rightly so, after so much reading and such long experience—that I had become hardened to the blows and injuries of Fortune. Alas, I deceived myself: nothing is softer, nothing more unsinewed, than I am. (*Fam.* VII, 12, 11)

What then specifically characterizes Petrarch's attitude toward death? Behind the spectre of death, for Petrarch, lies the abyss of contingency. The grief and feelings of desolation that swept over him when a friend died, and the anxiety that tortured him as he wondered about his own safety and that of friends who were still alive, were intensified, if not actually caused, by his perception that the events of life happen by chance. More than death itself, Petrarch was haunted by change, unexpected, inexplicable change. "For man nothing is calm, nothing is stable, nothing is safe."

Petrarch's experience of reality, both in his own person and in the world around him, was one of transience, mutability, and incessant motion. It is not without reason that he compared himself to Ulysses: he spent his whole life moving physically from one place to another, and emotionally and intellectually from one project to another, many of which he left unfinished. Even when he settled down in one place for awhile, Petrarch still remained in "actu perpetuo," as he puts it in a letter of 1348 to his brother Gerardo, when he speaks of himself as having been "nourished since my infancy on continual, if not always good (would that it were!) activity" (*Fam.* X, 4, 10). Petrarch's letters, along with his poetry, provide vivid and at times unforgettable descriptions of his careful observation of changes both in his physical appearance and in his state of mind. Other letters document the sense of disorientation he felt when he observed changes in his urban environment. His famous autobiographical letter of 1367 (*Sen.* X, 2, in Petrarca 1955) to his old friend Guido Sette, for example, lists one city and region after another which, dear to Petrarch during his youth, have been utterly transformed, to the point of being almost unrecognizable, by the wars, banditry, civil strife, famine, plague, and economic change and depression that occurred during the course of the fourteenth century. And, as we have seen from the letters we have looked at so far, probably the most painful change of all for Petrarch was the abrupt and irrevocable break in the life-giving bonds of affection and friendship wrought by the untimely deaths of so many of his friends and acquaintances. Petrarch, in sum, perceived constant and unpredictable change not only as the determining condition of the world in which he lived, but also as a fundamental characteristic of his own life as well. Death, sudden and untimely death, became for him the epitome of unpredictable, inscrutable, and inescapable change.

Petrarch was fond of describing himself as a frail bark in a tempest trying desperately to make port. But in setting sail on the vast sea of contingency, he was truly lost, for there was little or nothing in the culture in which he grew up, the culture of the Christian Middle Ages, capable of providing him with a compass, much less an anchor.

A man living in the late Middle Ages was doubtlessly aware of changes in his life, his body, and his environment. But he would have grown up in a religious culture which encouraged him to consider these changes of secondary importance, and to cast his thoughts instead on what was eternal and unchanging: God and his angels; an order of creation in which the earthly hierarchy reflected an eternal, celestial one; and the human soul, directly created by God, with its destiny of eternal happiness or damnation in the life to come.

This emphasis on the eternal and unchanging was reflected in the way Petrarch's world envisioned the structure of the physical universe. From classical antiquity up to the time of Galileo, most people in the West saw the universe as an immobile earth surrounded by nine concentric spheres, beginning with the lowest, the sphere of the Moon, and proceeding up through the spheres of Mercury, Venus, the Sun, Mars, Jupiter, Saturn, the Constellations or Fixed Stars, to the Crystalline Heaven or the Primum Mobile, the swiftest of all the spheres, and the one which imparted motion to all the rest. At the circle of the moon was a great division. Beneath it were the earth and the four elements. This was the realm of birth and death, of corruption and generation, of ceaseless change and mutability arising out of the perpetual combination and re-combination of the four elements. But above the circle of the moon all was pure, eternal, impassible, and unchanging. Here was no motion save the perfect circular motion of the heavenly spheres. And it was here, in the starry heavens above the circle of the moon, that the soul was be-lieved to have its proper abode, for here and here alone could the soul find perfect peace and rest. Cicero gave the classic formulation of this vision of the universe in the *Dream of Scipio,* the Sixth Book of his *De re publica,* in which Scipio Africanus describes the order of the heavens to his adopted grandson Scipio Aemilianus. Having described the higher spheres, the elder Scipio says, "and in the lowest sphere revolves the moon, set on fire by the rays of the sun. But below there is nothing ex-cept that which is mortal and destined to decay, save only the souls given to the human race by the bounty of the gods; above the moon everything is eternal" (17[4], 17).

"The soul of the wise man," Seneca said, "is like the universe (*mundus*) above the moon; it is always calm there" (*Ep.* LIX, 16). Dante's Chris-tian pilgrim rises above the circle of the moon on his way home to God. In this vision of the universe, medieval Christianity preserved the classi-cal unity of physics and philosophy, and the classical ideal of harmony between the cosmos and the soul.

In order to perceive the magnitude of the break Petrarch would make with this vision of the universe, and the effect this break would have upon him, it is important to understand the status of change within such a vision. Whatever change occurred in the limited area beneath the circle of the moon enjoyed little status as an independent and worthwhile ob-ject of observation, for sublunar change was always juxtaposed to, and seen in the larger context of, the eternal and unchanging. For the an-cients, it was in rising above the human, in turning one's gaze away from the earth and toward the contemplation of the eternal and unchanging heavens, that true peace and happiness were to be found.

Petrarch seems to have shared this understanding of the structure of the universe—he could in fact, have had no other. But he was unable to use it in his daily life. In a letter of 1339 he wrote:

Although very intelligent and learned men may think otherwise, human exertion in one way or another can, in this prison of the body, merit and hope for this happiness of which I speak, but it cannot embrace and hold on to it. For it is in this stadium that our life's race is run; the end is where the exertion comes to rest. And we are not alone in this opinion; for what else does Cicero mean when he says that this life is a journey towards heaven? Nevertheless, this mortal life has, now and then, something similar to the eternal life, so that if it is not yet happy—for happiness is only that to which nothing can be added—this mortal life can still look down on human miseries far below it, and, standing below, it can still shine with the light from above. (*Fam* IV, 2, 5–6)

In order to feel the full importance of what Petrarch is saying here in the context of the prevalent beliefs of his time, it is useful to call Dante to mind. Few passages describe so well the radical difference between Dante and Petrarch. They lived roughly at the same time: Petrarch was seventeen when Dante died in 1321. And yet how different were their spiritual lives and the works they left to future generations. Dante, through his art, journeyed to heaven: the *Divine Comedy* ends with a description of Dante's momentary experience of the beatific vision. But Petrarch, through his reading, contemplation, and writing, struggled to "shine with the light from above" while standing down here below. Thus while Dante reserved his greatest efforts of mind and pen for portraying the finish, Petrarch poured all of his emotional and creative energy into surviving the race. *The humanities arose out of Petrarch's attempt to survive the race here below.* We can begin to see why by looking at what the humanities replaced.

Scholastic theology at its best, in the works of Thomas Aquinas, for example, attempted to use the logic and metaphysics of Aristotle to investigate and understand the truths of Christian Revelation.[3] Aristotelian logic and metaphysics, in their concern with what they considered to be universally valid and unchanging categories of thought and being, were admirably suited to an age which looked for the eternal and the unchanging, whether in the social order, the physical universe, or in the world of spirit. This is not to say that scholastic theology had no conception of the contingent. It did. But contingent being was limited to the world of matter beneath the circle of the moon, as we see in Dante's description of the descent of God's light from the nine orders of angels to the elements of the sublunar world (*Par.* XIII/61–66) and in Thomas Aquinas's discussion of contingent beings (*Summa theologica* I, q. 86, a. 3, resp.). The primary concern of medieval theology was always with necessary, not contingent, being, with the eternal peace and happiness to be found with God in paradise, not with the change and mutability of earthly life here below. In concentrating his attention on the change and contingency beneath the circle of the moon, Petrarch was thus left without a coherent intellectual explanation for the purpose and meaning of human life, for there was nothing in the religious culture of his time which would have enabled him to find meaning in all the unexpected and untimely deaths he saw around him without rising above them in contemplation.

By Petrarch's time, moreover, scholastic theology was dominated by the vogue for pure logic and linguistic analysis which had developed in the arts faculties at Paris and Oxford. Scholars became increasingly concerned with discussing the internal signification of sentences and propositions, divorced from their referents in reality. The British philosopher and theologian William of Ockham even went so far as to call into question the ontological status of such important scholastic concepts as "being," "reality," and "essence."[4] In retrospect it is easy to see that this so-called "nominalism" was another sign of the waning interest in metaphysics exemplified in Petrarch's own life,[5] but for Petrarch it represented the degeneration of theology. To a certain extent he was correct. In order to think about God in the categories of the logic and metaphysics of scholastic Aristotelianism, one has to be able to think abstractly, according to the rules of a certain kind of logical analysis. Such ratiocination could easily degenerate into a fascination with the rules themselves, that is, into a narrowly specialized concern for the *technique* of logical and linguistic analysis, quite neglecting the very faith this kind of thinking was meant to illuminate. One of the primary reasons for such a degeneration into narrow specialization was the occasionally vicious competition for positions and prestige that went on among professors in the great medieval universities, and at times between the proponents of the different religious orders themselves.[6] Such a degeneration is doubtlessly what Petrarch had in mind when he complained on several occasions that theologians had become dialecticians (*Fam.* X, 5, 8–9; XVI, 14, 12).[7] By Petrarch's time, the scholastic culture of the Middle Ages was in crisis.

Petrarch's letters suggest that he found the experience of rapid and unpredictable change beneath the circle of the moon so overwhelming that he had to find some way of coming to terms with it in order to go on living. But since he had no way of thinking about contingency per se, he could find no intellectually satisfactory meaning for the experience of change. So it haunted him as an obsession. His study of the Latin classics was the chief means he discovered for controlling this obsession. In sum, if the culture in which Petrarch grew up encouraged him to transcend the unique and the contingent, the world in which he lived, and his own particular sensitivity to it, kept him from doing so. Petrarch was a deeply religious man. But he could not hear the word of God, at least as the scholastics preached it, in human life as he experienced it.[8]

The letters we have cited so far from Petrarch's *Familiares* show how deeply a person's beliefs determine his feelings, how the way in which a person perceives and understands an event influences how he feels about it. Works such as the *Secret (Secretum)*, *On the Life of Solitude (De vita solitaria)*, and *On Monastic Freedom (De otio religioso)* show that Petrarch was indeed searching for new ways of hearing and living the word of God. But whatever Petrarch's religious beliefs may have been, his writings suggest that they were of little or no use to him in his daily emotional life. If his soul was indeed in the constant state of disruption and turmoil he so often describes, it was probably because his intellect could not help him respond to the calamities of his age. It was his inability to "rationalize" the untimely deaths of his friends that made these deaths so bitter.

A deep tension between an apprehension of the contingent and a revolt against it thus flows through Petrarch's writings. It is this tension that animates one of his most moving and anguished descriptions of the plague. Writing to Ludwig van Kempen in 1349 with the expressed purpose of "lamenting this plague without example," as he says in the title of the letter, Petrarch describes the horrors he saw and recounts what happened when he tried to understand them:

> . . . It is the year 1348 of the sixth age which I lament, a year that has stripped not only us of our friends, but the whole world of people; and if it missed anything, look, the following year takes away the rest, and pursues with its deadly sickle whatever survived that storm. When will posterity ever believe that this was a time without a flood or conflagration in the earth or in the heavens, without wars or any other visible disaster, in which not only one part or another of the earth, but almost the entire globe was left without inhabitants? When was anything similar ever seen or heard? In what chronicles has anyone ever read of vacant houses, abandoned cities, desolate farms, fields narrowed by corpses, and a vast and awesome loneliness over all the world? Question the physicians: they are struck dumb. Search out the philosophers: they raise their shoulders and knit their brows, and with a finger to their lips entreat silence. Will you believe these things, posterity, when we who have seen them barely believe them ourselves, and would consider them dreams did we not see them with open eyes, while we were fully awake? And having crossed the city full of funerals only to return home to find it emptied of our children, did we not at least know that those things for which we were weeping were real? (*Fam.* VIII, 7, 11–13)

It is not just the plague itself, but utter ignorance of its causes that makes the spectacle of so many deaths so hard to bear:

> Nor is it fitting to compare these ills with any wars, however great, in which there are many kinds of remedies, the last of which is that men are permitted to die bravely. For to die well is a special consolation for death. Here there is no remedy at all, no consolation; and to the accumula-

tion of disaster is added ignorance of the causes and origins of the evil. (*Ibid.*, 7, 15–16)

Petrarch even arrives at expressing the doubt, which some apparently entertained, that God does not care about man. Although he immediately rejects this explanation for the plague, it is significant that he chose to mention it:

> Is it not true . . . that your clemency, God, exhausted little by little by human crimes, and weighed down by their continual increase, now finally overcome, withdraws, and you, excellent wayfarer, unable to bear any more, throw us behind, and angrily turn the eyes of your mercy away from us? If this be so, then we are paying at the same time not only for our own crimes, but also for those of our fathers—we who are certainly more miserable, if not worse than they. Or perhaps it is true what certain great minds suspect, that God does not care about mortal things. But let this madness be absent from our minds: if you did not care, they would not exist. . . . Certainly you care about us and our affairs, God, but it is for a hidden reason, unknown to us, why we are seen most worthy out of all the ages to be punished so fiercely, by a justice which is not diminished just because it is hidden. For the depth of your judgment is inscrutable and inaccessible to human senses. Thus we are either truly the worst of all, which I would like to deny more than I dare to, or, more truly tried and purged by these present evils, we are being saved for future blessing, or else there is something which we are unable to think at all. (*Ibid.*, 7, 17–19)

Petrarch's inability to make any sense of the plague, or to discover in it the workings of Divine Providence, leads him straightaway to question the meaning and purpose of human existence:

> Overcome by his troubles, Cicero, in a letter to Atticus, asks, "What are we, and for how much longer will we have to worry about these things?" A short, but a good question, unless I am mistaken, and profitable, and pregnant and full of useful thoughts. . . . What are we? I ask. How burdensome, slow, and fragile is our body, how blind, confused, and restless is our soul, how changeable, uncertain, and voluble is our Fortune! How long will we have to worry about these things? Certainly not for very long. Surely what Cicero is saying is nothing more than, "What are we, and for how much longer will we be what we are?" At any rate, by Hercules, not for long, for this existence of ours can even cease between these words, nor if this happened would there be any cause to wonder. You thus ask both questions well, and profoundly, Marcus Tullius. But, I ask you, where have you left the third question—more dangerous in its outcome and more fitting to ask: After we cease to exist, what will become of us? O great and uncertain thing, but neglected! Farewell. (*Ibid.*, 7, 24–26)

These are the words of a man for whom Dante's vision of the universe, and of the place of the individual within it, no longer explains the world he experiences. They are also the words of one who lived before the time of those who believed they had discovered that man makes his own history and can control nature as well. Petrarch is caught between the two.

In finding no satisfactory explanation for the calamities he and his generation lived through, Petrarch had to learn how to live with the confused and anguished state of mind they elicited in him. He turned to reading and writing, and especially to a study of ancient Rome.

The Retreat into the Self: The Therapy of the Word and the Power of Examples

The year before he died, Petrarch wrote a letter to Luca da Penna, then a secretary to the pope at Avignon, replying to Luca's request that he send him copies of any rare works of Cicero's he might possess. Petrarch had none, but he used the occasion to reminisce on the effect Cicero's Latin first had upon him. "From my very childhood," he wrote,

> when all others stood open-mouthed before Prosper or Aesop, I brooded over the books of Cicero, whether by natural instinct or at my father's urging. . . . At that age I could understand nothing, only a certain sweetness and sonority of the words held me, so that whatever else I read, or heard, seemed hoarse and quite dissonant. (*Sen.* XV, [1], in Petrarca 1965, vol. 2, p. 1046)

While still only a child, then, Petrarch was moved by the sounds of words long before he knew what they meant. And by juxtaposing Cicero to "Prosper" and "Aesop," popular medieval Latin textbooks, Petrarch is saying that the sounds that moved him were those of pure classical Latin, not the medieval Latin then taught in the schools.[9]

Petrarch never lost this feeling for the sound of words. It not only made him a great poet, but, more importantly for the history of the humanities, it gave him a clear sense, when he grew older and began to think about the problems of his times, of one way in which he could find consolation for his grief and respite from his anxieties. Writing in midlife to Tommaso da Messina, Petrarch tells how he read aloud in order to lift himself out of melancholy and depression:

> I could not easily say what certain familiar and well-known voices, not only conceived in my heart but brought out by my lips, with which I am wont to arouse my sleeping soul, do for me when I am alone, and how enjoyable it is, moreover, to go back, now and then, over my own

writings, or those of others, and what a weight of bitter and heavy cares I feel lifted from my shoulders through this reading. At times I am helped all the more by my own writings, the more they fit my own languors—writings which the conscious hand of the listless physician applies to himself where he feels the pain to be. And this I could never do unless the words themselves caressed my ears, and moving me to read them over and over again by a certain innate power of sweetness, gradually sank down inside of me, and pierced me there with their hidden points. (*Fam.* I, 9, 11–12)

We know from a passage in the *Secret,* a justly famous little piece of self-analysis Petrarch wrote in the 1340s,[10] that these states of depression were due, in part, at least, to the experience of contingency described above. In a passage reminiscent of the letter which opens the *Familiares,* Petrarch uses an elaborate metaphor drawn from medieval siege warfare to describe how he can be thrown into a state of depression and despair:

As often as Fortune inflicts some wound, I stand firm, undaunted, remembering that often I have walked away the victor after having been seriously knocked down by her. If then she hits me again, I start to stagger for a moment; forced to escape—not in a precipitous flight, but rather with my foot gradually withdrawn—into the fortress of Reason. There, if Fortune presses on me with her army from all sides in order to conquer me, and barrages me with the miseries of the human condition, and with the memory of past toils and the fear of future ones, then at last I groan, battered on all sides. From here arises that oppressive sorrow, as to one surrounded by an innumerable enemy, from whom there appears no escape, no hope of mercy, and no relief, but for whom everything seems threatening. Here the machines are erected, tunnels burrowed underground. Already the towers tremble, the ladders are brought up to the ramparts, the sheds are attached to the walls, and fires run along the floors. Seeing glittering swords everywhere and the threatening face of the enemy, and thinking of approaching destruction, what will he not fear and mourn, when, even if these things should cease, the very loss of liberty is so full of sadness for brave men? (Petrarca 1955, pp. 106, 108)

This is what the contemplation of incessant, unexpected, and meaningless change, especially death, in the finite and unstable world beneath the circle of the moon, did to Petrarch. He felt himself a man besieged. His response to this terrible affliction was literary in the deepest sense: he sought healing from the very *sound* of words.

Through an adept use of words, Petrarch thus became a physician to his own soul. And in healing, or at least soothing, his psychic wounds, he discovered that he could treat those of his body as well. In by far the most popular of his books during the Renaissance, the *De remediis utriusque fortunae,* "On Remedies for Good and Bad Fortune,"

entitled *A Physicke Against Fortune* in its Renaissance English translation,[11] Petrarch says, in the section on pain in the body, that "Words, I
confess, do not heal the body, unless perhaps the enchantments
(*incantationes*) and the incantations (*carmina*) of old women merit some
faith. But words do heal the maladies of souls, the health of which certainly either destroys or mitigates pain in the body" (*De remediis* II,
114, quoted in Trinkaus 1983, p. 162, n. 11). Thus he urged his friend
Giovanni Colonna, who suffered from gout, to do as he did when in
pain, and have a copy of Cicero's *Tusculan Disputations* close at hand
so that he could pick up and read Book Two, "On Bearing Pain," whenever an attack of gout came on (*Fam.* VI, 3, 53).

I have argued that the Renaissance response to the absence of the ancient experience of unity with the cosmos was to turn inward, in
search of an inner unity and personal integration. Such a search led to
the perception of one's "self" as having a kind of inner depth. For Petrarch, the very act of reading gave him a somatic experience of this
depth. He describes himself, as we have seen, as a listless physician feeling his own pain, and he says that the words he read aloud "gradually
sank down inside of me, and pierced me there with their hidden
points." He compares the "mute and superficial pleasure" of possess-
ing gold, silver, gems, purple robes, houses adorned with marble, culti-
vated fields, paintings, and well-caparisoned steeds, with the enjoyment of owning books. "Books," he says, "give us delight down to
the very marrow of our bones . . ." (*Fam.* III, 18, 3). And he tells Boccaccio that he has read Vergil, Horace, Boethius, and Cicero

> not once but thousands of times, nor did I rush (*cucurri*) over but rather
> rested (*incubui*) upon them, and remained in them with all the powers of
> my mind; I ate in the morning what I would digest in the evening, I swal-
> lowed as a boy what I would ruminate upon as a man. These writings
> have entered into me so intimately, and are fixed not only in my mem-
> ory but also in the marrow of my bones, and have so become one with
> my mind (*ingenium*), that even if I were never to read them again, they
> would remain embedded in me, having set their roots in the deepest part
> of my soul. . . . (*Fam.* XXII, 2, 12–13)

Petrarch looked upon reading, then, as a deep, inner experience. He
could feel the words in his body. The healing that came from such reading resulted not from being lifted outside of himself, but rather from
sinking deep down within. And, as he says, the sound of classical
Latin was especially suited to providing this experience.

Moreover, Petrarch wrote, studied, and read not only as a way of finding relief from "bitter and heavy cares"; he sought a kind of moral stimu-

lation as well. Again, no one could move him more than his favorite Latin authors. In the treatise *On His Own Ignorance and That of Many Others*, which, as we have seen, he wrote later in life in order to reply to the accusation of some Venetian friends that he was ignorant of Aristotle, Petrarch explains his love for classical Latin. He has read and knows well the books Aristotle wrote on ethics, he says. He even attended lectures on some of them. But although he has become more learned from reading these works, he has not become a better man. As he puts it, "it is one thing to know, another to love; one thing to understand, another to will." The distinction, prominent in the writings of Petrarch and the early humanists, between being learned as opposed to being good, derives from the distinction between knowing and loving, between the intellect and the will.[12] Aristotle, Petrarch says, "teaches what virtue is . . . but his lesson lacks the words that sting and set afire and urge toward love of virtue and hatred of vice, or, at any rate, does not have enough of such power." The Latin writers, especially Cicero, Seneca, and Horace, have this power,

> for they stamp and drive deep into the heart the sharpest and most ardent stings of speech, by which the lazy are startled, the ailing are kindled, and the sleepy aroused, the sick healed, and the prostrate raised, and those who stick to the ground lifted up to the highest thoughts and to honest desire. Then earthly things become vile; the aspect of vice stirs up an enormous hatred of vicious life; virtue and "the shape, and as it were, the face of honesty" are beheld by the inmost eye "and inspire miraculous love" of wisdom and of themselves, "as Plato says." [Cicero, *De officiis* I, 5, 14] (Cassirer 1948, pp. 103–104, and, for the Latin text, Petrarca 1906, pp. 68–69)

These are strong claims Petrarch is making for the power of the language forged by the Roman writers, and they give us a clear insight into one of the reasons for Petrarch's success in inspiring others to study the classics. The early humanists were attracted to classical Latin, as opposed to medieval or scholastic Latin, which they considered degenerate and barbaric, because they were looking for a language which had rhetorical power, which could arouse or quiet, as the need be, the passions in one's soul. Scholastic Latin was unable to do this. It was not even primarily a written language; it was a technical or "operational" language which evolved out of the oral disputations conducted in the schools.[13] It was an efficient way of testing arguments and propositions. At its best, it helped one think logically; at its worst, it degenerated into artful subtleties and confusing jargon. One can easily experience the difference between the ratiocination scholastic Latin made possible and the powerful music classical Latin could provide, by reading aloud Thomas Aquinas or William of Ockham, followed by Cicero or Seneca.

When Petrarch, Salutati, Bruni, and other humanists such as Erasmus and More ridiculed the scholastics, it was thus not only because scholasticism had degenerated into technical jargon; more importantly, it was because the language, and the kind of thinking this language both grew out of and in turn determined, was incapable of moving one's soul to love virtue and hate vice.

This central issue in the debate between medieval and classical Latin was summarized well by the humanist theologian and rhetorician Lorenzo Valla (c. 1407–1457) in the preface to the Fourth Book of his widely studied work on the Latin language, the *Elegantiae linguae latinae*. Here Valla repeats a theme which runs throughout his writings, and which was already adumbrated by Leonardo Bruni in his letter to Battista Malatesta. Valla says, in essence, that in order to know and love God one must turn away from the writings of scholastic theologians, with their barbarous Latin and obsession with Aristotelian logic and metaphysics, and turn instead to the Old and New Testaments, and to the early Greek and Latin Fathers of the Church, to Jerome and Augustine, the beauty of whose language, along with the absence of metaphysical speculation, will bring us closer to the Divine.[14] Speaking of himself and other humanist theologians who prized "eloquentia" and the beauty of classical Latin, Valla says:

> Others adorn private homes, and they are those who study civil law, canon law, medicine, and philosophy, bringing nothing to the worship of God (*nihil ad rem divinam conferentes*): we adorn the house of God, so that those entering into it are not moved to contempt by physical decay, but rather to worship by the majesty of the place. (Valla 1952, p. 622)

We see then that it was a sensitivity for the sound of words, and the effect of language upon an inner self, that led Petrarch and those who followed him to turn away from the scholastic university culture of their own times, and to look instead to the ancients, especially to the Roman writers, for the healing and inspiration they desired. But the motivating force behind this great turn back to the ancient Romans was not only the beauty of their language; Petrarch found consolation and inspiration in their lives as well.

An examination of the content of Petrarch's reading reveals once again a direct and immediate relationship between his literary studies and his moral life.

In describing the autonomous self that underlies Bruni's understanding of perfection, I quoted a passage from a letter Petrarch wrote to

Giovanni Colonna in the late 1330s or early 1340s in which he says that he compares his soul to the souls of famous men in order to test the strength of his own character. Then he continues: "And so, just as I am grateful to those whom I read who give me the opportunity of experiencing this by citing examples, so I hope that my readers will likewise be grateful to me" (*Fam.* VI, 4, 4).

Petrarch explains at the beginning of this letter that he is writing Giovanni to reply to the criticism some people had made that his writings were overflowing with "examples of illustrious ancients." That Petrarch felt the need to explain his use of *exempla* suggests that it was new or unusual enough to attract attention.

Petrarch goes on to give "examples" of the power of examples. His first is the Roman general Caius Marius (156–86 B.C.), who refused to be strapped down when a surgeon cut the varicose veins out of one of his legs:

> Before Marius, it was customary for everyone who underwent surgery to be tied down, for as it was believed that pain in the body could not be overcome by strength in the soul, people sought the aid of bonds. Marius was the first to be cut without being bound, but after him many were. Why, I ask, unless because the example of such a brave and steadfast man encouraged other souls to imitate him, and, to use the words of his compatriot, his authority had power (*valuit autoritas*)? (*Fam.* VI, 4, 8)

To what use would Petrarch put the thought of Marius' holding his leg steady under the surgeon's knife despite the terrible pain? As he says at the beginning of this letter, he found that he could test the strength of his own soul in the face of adverse Fortune by comparing it to others it would like to resemble. Notice that the comparison here is between "souls," between inner states of mind, not between actions. In another letter Petrarch says that spiritual battles are more bitter than physical ones, that battles between armies are more easy to win than battles within oneself (*Fam.* XII, 2, 6). Petrarch himself was capable of bearing a good deal of physical pain. Once a companion's horse, intent on hurting the horse Petrarch was riding, kicked Petrarch so hard at the point where the knee joins the shin that even those who were somewhat distant could hear the bones crack. The pain was excruciating. But Petrarch bore it (*Fam.* XI, 1, 7–8). It was thus not primarily alleviation from physical pain that Petrarch sought in his reading of Roman history. As in his use of the sounds of words, so too in his use of the examples of famous men, Petrarch was looking for release from pain in his soul, not pain in the body. He could handle the latter; it was the former that gave him trouble. In thinking about Marius, Petrarch would have thought about what he believed must have been Mar-

ius' will power and strength of soul, and he would have tried to measure and test his own inner strength by comparing it to Marius'.
When he broke down and wept upon learning of Franceschino's death,
we can imagine his seeing Marius and other brave Romans rise up to re-
buke him for his unmanly behavior.

When Petrarch read, then, he engaged in a kind of "moral research."[15] He studied the lives of the ancients in order to learn what
kind of soul, what sort of strength of character, he might be able to attain for himself.

This way of using the examples of famous men is an active one: it is
undertaken in order to test, mold, change one's character. In addition,
Petrarch had another, somewhat more passive, use for the fruits of his
reading. In the *Secret*, he tells Augustine why he liked to have ready at
hand examples of famous men:

> Unless I am mistaken, it is a great consolation to be protected by such fa-
> mous companions. I thus confess that I do not disdain the use of such exam-
> ples as a daily aid. For it helps me to have something ready with which
> to console myself not only for those troubles which nature or chance
> have already given me, but for those which they could still give me as
> well. And this I cannot achieve without vigorous reasoning or an illustri-
> ous example. If you were to criticize my fear of thunder . . . I would
> reply that Augustus Caesar had the same sickness. If you were to say that
> I was blind, and if it were true, I would use Appius Caecus, and Homer,
> the prince of poets, as a shield to defend myself; if one-eyed, I would de-
> fend myself with Hannibal, commander of the Carthaginians, or with
> King Philip of Macedonia; if deaf, my shield would be Marcus Crassus,
> if intolerant of heat, Alexander of Macedonia. It would be long to run
> through all of them, but from these examples you can infer the rest.
> (Petrarca 1955, pp. 178, 180)

Here Petrarch uses the examples of other men less for inspiration than
for consolation. He shows how a person can try to console himself for
a specific psychological or physical disability by learning about other
human beings who had the same disability, and who nevertheless managed to attain great fame by achieving something noteworthy in life.

Petrarch's description of how he used the examples of famous men is
useful in two ways: it provides another illustration of how Petrarch's
studies were meant to address the most urgent problems of his daily life,
and it shows how a personal self came into being along with the humanities in the Renaissance. Let us look at this last point more fully.

How is it possible for Petrarch to compare his soul to Caius Marius'? What enables him to empathize with Augustus Caesar's fear of
lightning, or Homer's blindness? These are hard questions to answer,

for we continue to do what Petrarch did: compare ourselves to others, and we do it so naturally that we take it for granted.

Petrarch can use ancient heroes the way he does because he has the same kind of autonomous self Bruni would adumbrate later in his description of the *studia humanitatis*: in order to compare his strength of character to that of an ancient hero, in order to find assurance and consolation by calling to mind the idiosyncratic fears or physical imperfections of a man who achieved fame, Petrarch had to experience his own being as a unique and autonomous self which he could objectify, act upon, and compare to other such autonomous selves. In other words, he had not only to experience his own consciousness as an autonomous center of thought and feeling, he had to believe that others, including the ancients, experienced themselves in this way as well. Petrarch thus had to presume, as most people still do today, that inner consciousness, individual uniqueness, and experiential autonomy are part of human nature.[16] We now know that they are not. Modern anthropology has shown us how unique the "Western self" is in comparison to other cultures. And now we can begin to see, as we try to understand the origins of the humanities, that the autonomous self is a fairly modern creation even for the West.

Our comparison of Bruni's concept of perfection with Cicero's has already shown us one side of this question: the relationship of the individual to the cosmos and to himself. Now Petrarch can show us how this modern self turned classical antiquity into a mirror for its own image: since Petrarch uses ancient Roman sources for his examples of strength of character, we can easily compare his own rendering of a story with the ancients'. We find that when Petrarch retells a famous Roman deed in his own words, a personal self appears where there was none in the original. Let us consider the example of Caius Marius.

Here again is Petrarch's account of Marius:

> Before Marius, it was customary for everyone who underwent surgery to be tied down, for as it was believed that pain in the body could not be overcome by strength in the soul (*animi robor*), people sought the aid of bonds. Marius was the first to be cut without being bound, but after him many were. Why, I ask, unless because the example of such a brave and steadfast man encouraged other souls to imitate him, and, to use the words of his compatriot, his authority had power (*valuit autoritas*)? (*Fam.* VI, 4, 8)

The story comes from Book II of Cicero's *Tusculan Disputations*, one of Petrarch's favorite works. Here is what Cicero says about Marius:

But Caius Marius, a man from the countryside, yet truly a man (*rusticanus vir, sed plane vir*), refused to be bound, as I said above, when he was cut. Nor is it said that anyone before Marius was cut unbound. Why then were others after him? His authority had power (*Valuit auctoritas*).[17] Do you not therefore see that harm (*malum*) is a question of opinion (*opinio*), not of nature? And yet Marius himself showed that the bite of pain was sharp, for he did not offer the other leg. In this way he bore his pain as a man (*vir*), and as a human being (*homo*) did not want to bear greater pain unless it were necessary.

Everything, therefore, lies in this, that you master yourself. But I have shown now what self-mastery is. And this reflection (*cogitatio*) on what most befits patience, fortitude, and greatness of soul, not only curbs the soul, but even, in a certain way, makes the pain milder. (22, 53)

In Petrarch's account, Marius stands out as an autonomous individual because Petrarch sees the issue of whether or not he could hold out his leg and let a surgeon cut into it as an inner struggle between pain in the body and strength in the soul. For Petrarch, Marius' deed demonstrated that he had strength of soul, and that by strength of soul he, and others after him, could overcome pain in the body. Petrarch thus refers to Marius as "a most brave and steadfast man" (*vir constantissimus atque fortissimus*).

In Cicero's account, Marius does not stand out with anywhere near the same autonomy he assumes in Petrarch's. Nor, in Cicero's account, does Marius have an inner dimension: Cicero does not use the phrase "strength of soul" (*animi robor*) in describing what Marius did, nor does he speak of Marius as "a most brave and steadfast man." These are additions Petrarch has made to the story. The attributes by which Cicero identifies Marius, and states the meaning of his action, move in a direction opposite from Petrarch's account, away from the personal and the individual. It is precisely these elements that Petrarch leaves out when he retells the story of Marius. Let us look at them.

In Cicero's account, the concrete, historical individual named Caius Marius has less importance than the social, moral, and ontological categories he exemplifies: Marius, Cicero says, is a man from the countryside (the social distinction between *urbanus*, from the city of Rome, and *rusticus*, was an important one in Cicero's time[18]). But he was nonetheless a true "man" (*vir*), for he refused to be strapped down when a surgeon cut the "varicose veins" out of his leg (as Cicero tells us earlier in Book II, 15, 35). Nevertheless, as a "human being" (*homo*), he felt the pain and did not offer the other leg.

Petrarch, who believes that it was Marius' *animi robor*, "strength of soul," that enabled him to hold his leg steady as the surgeon cut into it, leaves this contrast between Marius as *vir* and Marius as *homo* out of his account. But the contrast is a crucial one for Cicero. As Cicero explains it, the real cause of Marius' act was not Marius, but the attributes of *vir* and *homo* he exemplified: Marius bore the pain "as a man," but "as a human being," he did not want to bear any more pain than was necessary. It may be difficult for us today to apprehend fully the fundamental importance of *vir* and *homo* in this passage, but we can get a glimpse of it by realizing that when we read Cicero's account we cannot think about Caius Marius without the universal and transpersonal categories of *vir* and *homo* entering into our thoughts at the same time.

Why this should be so becomes clearer when we remember that Cicero's description of Marius occurs in the broader context of a philosophical investigation in Book II of the *Tusculan Disputations* of how men can learn to bear pain, that is, of how a *homo* can become a *vir*. Cicero uses the example of a surgeon's cutting the varicose veins out of Marius' leg to illustrate the essentially Stoic teaching that the capacity to bear pain in a manly way depends on opinion (*opinio*), not on nature. Shakespeare's line "There is nothing either good or bad, but thinking makes it so," expresses the letter, if not the spirit, of the point Cicero is trying to make here—which is also the main point of the *Tusculan Disputations* as a whole: that the good is essentially knowledge of the good; and that all moral perversions and psychic turmoil spring from *prava opinio*, which can be variously translated as "bad judgment," "false opinion," "deformed" or "perverse imagination"; happiness, in turn, can be achieved only when *recta ratio*, "right reason," which includes a knowledge of the good, rules over the lower passions of the soul.

The experience of reading Cicero's account of Marius thus exemplifies its own conclusion: the sentences with which Cicero finishes his discussion of Marius take our thoughts away from Marius and lead us to the contemplation of universal, transpersonal virtues—patience, fortitude, and greatness of soul. Petrarch, on the other hand, tells the Marius story in such a way that our gaze rests firmly on Marius.

The sentences which obviously caught Petrarch's eye, "Nor is it said that anyone before Marius was cut unbound. Why then were others after him? His authority had power," appear almost parenthetical in the context of the entire passage. They are certainly not an essential part of what Cicero is trying to say. And if we ask what *Valuit auctoritas* could signify in this context, we find a meaning which contrasts sharply with the one Petrarch will give it. *Vir*, for Cicero, is above all else a social and moral norm. Much of what Roman society held most dear is contained in that word. Cicero says that the word *virtus* comes from *vir* and that the essence of a "man" (*vir*) is fortitude, understood primarily as contempt for pain and for death (*Tusc.* II, 18, 43). In other words, the Roman *vir* is a transpersonal and normative concept. Marius does not create *vir*; he merely exemplifies it. What Marius did was to show another way of being a true Roman. If others after Marius underwent surgery without being strapped down, it was not just because Caius Marius had done so, but because Roman society made fortitude its cardinal virtue and rewarded with praise, glory, and fame acts of courage and mastery of one's lower passions. The particular communal values of ancient Rome conferred on Marius' deed the *auctoritas* of an example which others might then be challenged to emulate.

It is not surprising that when we ask how Petrarch used his knowledge of ancient Rome in his own life, we see that what he was unable to use, and what he leaves out of his writings, was the unbreakable bond between the individual and society in ancient Rome, where individualized expression and experience were possible only through a social framework. When he took the example of Marius from Book II of the *Tusculan Disputations*, Petrarch left Marius' social being behind and endowed him instead with a new autonomous inner self. He found in him a "strength of soul" which Cicero does not mention in his account. The person of Marius and the struggle within his soul take on an inspirational power in Petrarch's account far removed from Cicero's, where *vir, virtus,* and behind them ancient Rome itself, are the real actors on the stage of human pain and suffering.

Petrarch's transformation of ancient heroes from manifestations of collective and normative categories of being into autonomous selves is even clearer in his description of the Decii, father, son, and grandson.

After speaking of Marius, Petrarch, in his letter to Giovanni Colanna, goes on to give the Decii as another example of the power of examples. Here is how he tells their story:

> In the war with the Latins, near Veseris, the consul Decius devoted himself (*se devovit*)[19] for the victory of his legions and the Roman people—a thing easier said than done, to seek death voluntarily in order to gain victory for others. Yet so efficacious and so powerful was his example (*exemplum*) that in the war against the Samnites and the Gauls, his son Decius, a consul himself, arose as the imitator of his father, and invoking his father's name, fearlessly went off to meet his death, which he had learned from his father to disdain for the safety of his citizens. Imitating both of them in the Tarentine War against Pyrrhus, the grandson, the third victim, finally, in the same family, even if not in the dress of consul, nevertheless fell with equal valor of soul and with the same piety for the republic. (*Fam.* VI, 4, 9)

According to Petrarch's account, it was the example of Publius Decius which inspired his son to sacrifice his life in battle. And it was the examples of both the father and the son that moved the grandson to imitate them. In Petrarch's account it is thus the Decii themselves, father, son, and grandson, who hold our attention.

Petrarch's sources tell it differently. Two major differences, not dissimilar from those we have already noted in the case of Caius Marius, stand out between Petrarch's account of the Decii, and their story as Cicero, Seneca, and Valerius Maximus tell it.

First of all, Petrarch has the son imitating the father, and the grandson imitating both of them. Petrarch's sources, however, do not speak of the imitation or emulation of one human being by another, but rather of the imitation or emulation of a deed, or a virtue. In the *De divinatione*, Cicero says that it was P. Decius' deed (*eius factum*) that defeated the Latins, and that his son desired, not to be like the father, but to have the same glorious death:

> . . . when he was consul, he devoted himself (*devovit se*), and rushed full-armed into the Latins' battle-line. By this death of his the Latins were overcome and brought down. So glorious was his death that his son longed for the same. (I, 24, 51)

In *De finibus* Cicero says that if what Decius had done (*eius factum*) had not been justly praised, neither his son nor his grandson would have imitated it:

> And had not his death been justly praised, his son would not have imitated it during his fourth consulship, nor would the latter's son, pursuing as consul the war against Pyrrhus, have fallen in battle and offered himself as the third successive victim for the republic from his family. (II, 19, 61)

In *Cato maior de senectute* Cicero says that it was by P. Decius' deed (*eius factum*) that some men judged that there is something (such as a noble death) desirable in itself:

> Fabricius knew the same Decius, and so did Coruncanius. They judged, both from their own lives, and from Decius' deed, that there is something naturally beautiful and excellent which is sought for its own sake, and which the best person, holding pleasure in contempt and disdain, will pursue. (XIII, 43)

In one of his letters (*Ep.* LXVII, 9), Seneca says that Decius' son sought to rival his father's virtue (*paternae virtutis aemulus*). And Valerius Maximus writes that P. Decius "would have been the sole exemplar of such a commander had he not begot a son who matched his courage" (*Factorum ac doctorum memorabilium libri IX*, V, 6, 6).

We see then that just as Cicero concludes his description of Marius' feat of self-mastery by inviting us to turn our minds to patience, fortitude, and greatness of soul, so too in Cicero's, Seneca's, and Valerius Maximus' accounts of the Decii, the son and grandson are inspired not by thinking about Publius Decius, but by thinking about a glorious death, about virtue, and about courage, of which the person of Publius Decius is only an instrument. It is the noble death itself, and not the person who dies, that inspires others to give their lives for their country.

Petrarch's transformation of the heroes of classical antiquity into personal selves capable of being moved by other personal selves stands out clearly in the difference between Seneca's characterization of Publius Decius' son as *paternae virtutis aemulus*, "emulator of his father's virtue," and Petrarch's *patris imitator*, "imitator of his father." While for Seneca it was his father's virtue, for Petrarch it was the very person of his father that moved his son to die for the fatherland. Furthermore, Petrarch adds to his account a phrase found in none of his sources, a phrase which highlights the shift in perspective we find in Petrarch from the deed or virtue to the person: Petrarch says that P. Decius' son rode off to his death "invoking the name of his father" (*nomine patris vocans*). A Roman soldier would not have "personalized" his death in this manner.

The second difference between Petrarch's retelling of the story of the Decii and the originals lies in the lessons to be drawn from their heroic deaths. From the accounts of Marius and the Decii, Petrarch draws the lesson that human beings can learn about themselves and gain strength of character by pondering what other human beings have done. But his sources draw entirely different lessons.

Just as in his *Tusculan Disputations* Cicero used Caius Marius to illustrate the philosophical proposition that the ability to bear pain in a manly way springs not from nature, but from the way one thinks, so too the story of the Decii, as Cicero, Seneca, and Valerius Maximus tell it, leads us to think about something other than the Decii themselves. In the *Tusculan Disputations* Cicero says that the deaths of the Decii prove that death is not to be feared:

> If death indeed had been feared . . . the elder Decius, fighting it out with the Latins, his son with the Etruscans, his grandson with Pyrrhus, would not have flung themselves against the weapons of the enemy. . . . (I, 37, 89)

In the *De divinatione*, Cicero has P. Decius' death illustrate the power of dreams. In the war against the Samnites,

> . . . when he went too boldly into the dangers of battle and was advised to be more cautious, he replied, as is recorded in the Annals, that it had ap-

peared to him in a dream that while in the midst of the enemy, he would die with the greatest glory. And that time unharmed he freed the army from investment; three years later, however, when he was consul, he devoted himself, and rushed full-armed into the Latins' battle-line. (I, 24, 51)

In *De finibus* Cicero uses P. Decius' death to disprove Epicurus' doctrine of pleasure, at least as he interprets it:

. . . when he (P. Decius) had devoted himself and, giving free rein to his horse, was charging headlong into the center of the Latins' battle-line, was he thinking about one or other of his pleasures? Where would he enjoy it, or when? For he knew he must die in a moment, and sought death with more ardent zeal than Epicurus believes one should seek pleasure. (II, 19, 61)

For Seneca, Decius' death shows that a noble death is desirable in itself:

Decius devoted himself for the republic; spurring his horse on, he rushed headlong into the midst of the enemy, seeking death. The other Decius after him, emulating his father's virtue, pronouncing the solemn and already household words, rushed into the thickest part of the battle-line, concerned only that his sacrifice bring favorable omens, and regarding a good death a thing to be desired. Do you doubt then that the best thing is to die worthy of being remembered, and in performing some work of virtue? (*Ep.* LXVII, 9)

And for Valerius Maximus, finally, the story of the Decii illustrates piety toward the State. He concludes his account with this query:

It is thus hard to decide whether the community of Rome found the Decii more useful when it had them as leaders or when it lost them, since their life kept Rome from being conquered, their death permitted Rome to conquer. (V, 6, 6)

Petrarch's ancient sources say nothing about the Decii as autonomous individuals. Even today, thousands of years later, thoughts of Rome come into our minds when we listen to Cicero, Seneca, and Valerius Maximus tell of the Decii. In order to limit our attention to the Decii themselves, Petrarch must do what he did with Marius: remove them from the communal unity of Roman society and consciousness—outside of which, for the ancient writers, they have no identity, and without which their deaths have no meaning—and read into them a personal self, with its own inner unity. Petrarch brings about this transformation by adding another phrase which is found in none of his sources. Speaking of Decius' vow to die for the State, Petrarch writes: "a thing easier said than done, to seek your death in order to attain victory for another." With these words he shifts attention away from what Decius did to what he imagines must have gone on inside of him as he was preparing to die; in saying that it is easier said than done to go off to die for the fatherland, Petrarch hints at a struggle within Decius' soul, a struggle of the will, to find the courage to ride off to meet his death. Thus while Cicero, Seneca, and Valerius Maximus direct our thoughts to the ultimate sacrifice of laying down one's life for one's country, Petrarch thinks about how hard it must have been for a man, of his own accord, to choose death—and suddenly we find that we are thinking about Publius Decius as a self turned inward.

Petrarch believed that the inner struggle, the battle with one's own will, was much harder to win than the outer struggle of clashing armies. When he read about Marius and the Decii, he turned their military valor into a kind of psychic valor, and he found inspiration in imagining the battle of the will they must have endured, and finally won, before going off to submit themselves to great pain or death. After Petrarch, it has become difficult to think about Marius and the Decii in any other way.

Now that we have seen how Petrarch gave his ancient heroes a personal self, we can finally solve the paradox we mentioned earlier: if the ancient Romans were so different from people of the Renaissance, why did they play such a fundamental role in the molding and shaping of the Renaissance self?

We know not only from Cicero but from the deeds of the ancient Romans themselves, that the chief Roman virtue was fortitude, especially military valor. The Romans were the greatest warriors of classical antiquity, and their military prowess was due in no small measure to their courage. In comparing Greeks and barbarians to Romans, Cicero says that the barbarians were courageous in battle, but were unable to bear the pain of sickness and disease; the Greeks were good at bearing pain but not very courageous in battle; only the Romans could be both (*Tusc. Disp.* II, 27, 65). Whether this is actually true is beside the point; what matters is that in speaking about self-mastery both in sickness and in battle, Cicero gives expression to the fundamental Roman value of *fortitudo*, courage, self-control.

Where did this courage come from? It came from Rome. As Romans, Marius and the Decii learned to think of themselves as part of a larger whole. Their composure and self-control came from without, not from within. We can see clearly one way in which they learned to do this in Polybius' account of a Roman funeral. Polybius (c. 202–120 B.C.) was a Greek who, as a hostage in Rome and a friend of the most important families, became a keen observer of the character and institutions of the ancient Romans. His account of a Roman funeral vividly illustrates how a young Roman was taught to think of his life as part of a communal order of being. Polybius begins his description with the following observation:

> Not only do Italians in general naturally excel Phoenicians and Africans in bodily strength and psychic braveries, but by their institutions also they do much to foster a spirit of bravery in the young men. A single instance will suffice to indicate the pains taken by the state to turn out men who will be ready to endure everything in order to gain a reputation in their country for valour.

Then he continues:

> Whenever any illustrious man dies, he is carried at his funeral into the forum to the so-called rostra, sometimes conspicuous in an upright posture and more rarely reclined. Here with all the people standing round, a grown-up son, if he has left one who happens to be present, or if not some other relative mounts the rostra and discourses on the successful virtues and achievements of the dead. As a consequence the multitude and not only those who had a part in these achievements, but those also who had none, when the facts are recalled to their minds and brought before their eyes, are moved to such sympathy that the loss seems to be not confined to the mourners, but a public one affecting the whole people. Next after the interment and the performance of the usual ceremonies, they place the image of the departed in the most conspicuous position in the house, enclosed in a wooden shrine. This image is a mask reproducing with remarkable fidelity both the features and the complexion of the deceased. On the occasion of public sacrifices they display these images, and decorate them with much care, and when any distinguished member of the family dies they take them to the funeral, putting them on men who seem to them to bear the closest resemblance to the original in stature and carriage. These representatives wear togas, with a purple border if the deceased was a consul or praetor, whole purple if he was a censor, and embroidered with gold if he had celebrated a triumph or achieved anything similar. They all ride in chariots preceded by the fasces, axes, and other insignia by which the different magistrates are wont to be accompanied according to the respective dignity of the offices of state held by each during his life; and when they arrive at the rostra, they all seat themselves in a row on ivory chairs.

Polybius concludes by remarking on the effect the sight of all these men wearing the masks of the dead had upon the young:

> There could not easily be a more ennobling spectacle for a young man who aspires to fame and virtue. For who would not be inspired by the sight of the images of men renowned for their excellence, all together and as if alive and breathing? What spectacle could be more glorious than this? Besides, he who makes the oration over the man about to be buried, when he has finished speaking of him recounts the successes and exploits of the rest whose images are present, beginning from the most an-

cient. By this means, by this constant renewal of the good report of brave men, the celebrity of those who performed noble deeds is rendered immortal, while at the same time the fame of those who did good service to their country becomes known to the people and a heritage for future generations. (*The Histories* VI, 52–54, Loeb translation slightly revised)

Here we see how the individual, the family, and the State constantly renewed themselves as a community through a celebration and commemoration of past deeds intended to inspire similar heroic deeds in the future. These deeds were inspired by looking outward, not inward. It was the absence of a personal self, an absence of Petrarch's inner questioning and struggle of the will, that enabled the Roman to accomplish the feats of self-control that Petrarch found so inspiring. The very absence of an inner self in the accounts of the deeds of these ancient Roman heroes enabled Petrarch, and still enables us today, to read our own experience of a self back into these men. As far as their "personalities" are concerned, Marius and Decii are blank slates; we can write on them whatever we want. We can read about their actions, and then imagine what we would think, how we would feel, in similar circumstances.

When Petrarch turned inward in an attempt to make his soul strong enough to stand up to the blows of Fortune, he turned to the heroic Romans as his guides and believed that he had found in them an inner life similar to, though doubtlessly more courageous than, his own. We have seen that the Romans had no inner life of this sort. The very courage Petrarch wanted to emulate was in fact selfless. How then did a Roman come to terms with the blows of Fortune? Let us look at Cicero in grief.

CHAPTER 3

CICERO IN GRIEF:

THE CLASSICAL SOUL REVEALED

IN THE MIDDLE of January, 45 B.C., Cicero's beloved daughter Tullia
gave birth to a son. A month later, at Tusculanum, her father's villa
south of Rome, she died. Cicero was overwhelmed with grief. He fled
Tusculanum and took refuge in his close friend Atticus' house in
Rome. There he read every book he could find in Atticus' library on
the alleviation of grief (*Att.* 251:3 [XII. 14]).[1] At the same time he
forced himself to keep up appearances by receiving anyone who came
to see him (*Att.* 281:2 [XII. 40]). But Cicero was suffering too much
to play the role expected of a person of his rank and importance in the
uniquely demanding public life of ancient Rome, structured as it was
around a full calendar of religious feasts and rituals, and held together
by a tight web of patron–client relationships in which one's life tended
to become synonymous with one's social intercourse. Cicero needed
to be alone in order to hide his grief. So he left Rome on March 6,
and fled south to Astura, a lonely little town by the sea. He had a villa
there, and there he remained, struggling to free his soul from the anguish that unsettled it, until the middle of May, when he sensed that
he would finally be able to "conquer" his soul and return to Tusculanum (*Att.* 287:1 [XII. 46]).

Cicero wrote Atticus almost daily from Astura, and he asked
Atticus to write back even when he had nothing to say (*Att.* 259:2
[XII. 12]). It was one of the most painful periods in Cicero's life, and
his correspondence with Atticus seems to have helped him through it.
Yet in his letters, Cicero, unlike Petrarch, never dwells on the pain; he
is much more concerned to let Atticus and his friends know that he is
doing everything in his power to "divert" his mind from it (*Att.* 279:1
[XII. 38a]). Petrarch used the pain of grief, as in the case of Franceschino's death, to probe the peculiarities of his own life and character,
while grief following the death of Beatrice forced Dante, as we know

59

from what he tells us in the *Vita Nuova*, to search for a theological meaning in his love for her.[2] But Cicero experienced the passing of his daughter neither as an occasion for self-examination, nor as an invitation to discover her "meaning" in his life. Both reactions belong to another age.
Cicero strove merely to deal with his grief in the way he believed an
ideal Roman should: rise above it in contemplation and appear not to
be debilitated by it. His letters thus reveal the normative standards of
Roman society concerning the proper restraint and alleviation of sorrow, and what these standards imply concerning the absence, in
Cicero's Rome, of either the conception or the experience of a personal, inward-turning self.

The pain Cicero felt after Tullia died was intense. In his first letter
to Atticus he writes, "But the searing pain still drives on and persists
. . ." (*Att.* 250:1 [XII. 13]). Yet he makes it clear to Atticus that it is
not the pain that concerns him so much as his public role and the social problems which his bereavement might cause him. A new augur
was getting ready to take office in Rome when Cicero left for Astura,
and Cicero would have been duty bound, as a member of the College
of Augurs, to attend the inauguration and banquet. His first letters
from Astura show that although M. Appuleius, the newly-elected
augur, had promised not to make trouble for him, Cicero wanted
some of his friends to sign affidavits legally releasing him from the obligation of attending these ceremonies *morbi causa,* on account of ill-
health. "For since I must avoid social occasions," he writes, "I would
rather appear to do so by law, than because of grief" (*Att.* 250:2 [XII.
13]).

In his dialogue on friendship, *Laelius de amicitia,* written the following
year, Cicero explains why he needed to conceal his grief and excuse himself on the basis of ill-health from attending these ceremonies. Cicero has
Scaevola tell how Laelius bore with moderation the death of his dear
friend Scipio Aemilianus: when Laelius failed to attend the monthly
meeting of the College of Augurs after Scipio died, Scaevola says, it was
because he was ill, not because he was in mourning. To this Laelius adds:

Exactly, Scaevola, and rightly so: for I would not have let myself be
taken away from this duty, which I always fulfilled when I was well, on account of an inconvenience; nor do I believe that it can ever befall a man
of constancy that there be any interruption of his duty. (2, 8)

Cicero must have had his own situation in mind when he wrote
these lines. His search for affidavits attesting ill-health, and this passage from the *De amicitia* imply what Seneca would state explicitly a century later—that mourning was socially unacceptable for Roman men:

Our forefathers have enacted that women should have a year to mourn, not so they should mourn so long, but that they should mourn no longer; for men no period of time is legally prescribed, because no period of mourning is honorable. (*Ep.* LXIII, 13)

That the earliest Romans felt the necessity of limiting, or even proscribing, in the case of men, the public expression of grief shows that the Romans did indeed mourn, did indeed experience powerful emotions. But they hid them. They even had a phrase for it, *in sinu gaudere*, "to rejoice inside the fold of one's toga," that is, to keep one's joy to oneself. The expression derived from the Roman's habit of covering his face with his toga in order to hide the expression of any strong emotion, whether sorrow or joy (see *Tusc.* III, 21, 51), as Plutarch says Caesar did when he covered his face with his toga after Brutus stabbed him. (*Brutus* 17, 3).[3]

After Tullia's death, Cicero's overriding concern was to act in accordance with the traditional values of the Roman community. This was the chief concern of his friends as well. Atticus feared that Cicero's popularity and prestige would be diminished by his mourning (*Att.* 281:2 [XII. 40]). He told Cicero that others were talking about him more harshly than either he or Brutus had done in their letters to him, and he urged Cicero to let his strength of mind (*firmitas animi*) show forth (*Att.* 279:1 [XII. 38a]). Atticus, Brutus, and others, in fact, were critical of the way Cicero had reacted to the death of his daughter, and they exhorted him to dissimulate his bitter suffering (*Att.* 258:1 [XII. 20]). Brutus, it seems, had sent Cicero a "scolding" letter (*Att.* 310:3 [XIII. 6]). It is probably this letter Cicero had in mind when he said to Brutus two years later, in a letter of consolation he wrote him after Brutus' wife Portia ended her life by swallowing hot coals, "When I seemed to you to bear my sufferings more weakly than a man (*vir*) should . . . you reproached me in a letter with words harsher than you were wont to use" (*Ad Brut.* 18:1 [17 (1.9)]).

Cicero's response to this criticism shows how seriously he took it. He assures Atticus that he can indeed control his appearance. Having said, in reply to those who urged him to dissimulate his grief, that he could do no more than spend all his time writing, Cicero adds:

Even if I do this not for the sake of dissimulation (*dissimulatio*), but in order to lighten and heal my soul, nevertheless, if I do myself little good, I certainly do enough to keep up appearances (*simulatio*). (*Att.* 258:1 [XII. 20])

In another letter in which he describes daily writing as a kind of check on and relief from his grief, Cicero goes on to say, "I try everything

to bring my face (*vultum*) itself, if not my soul (*animus*), back to composure, if I can, and in so doing sometimes I feel I am committing a
wrong (*peccare*), sometimes I feel I shall do wrong if I fail to do so"
(*Att.* 251:3 [XII. 14]). If he is forced to come to Rome on business, he
tells Atticus, he will see to it that no one, not even Atticus, notices his
sorrow (*Att.* 262:1 [XII. 23]). A few weeks before he left Astura to return to Tusculanum, Cicero wrote Atticus that "when I come to
Rome I shall be reproached neither on account of my face nor my
speech" (*Att.* 281:3 [XII. 40]).

But Cicero did more than assure Atticus that his face and speech
would show no signs of grief; he tried to make Atticus understand,
and through Atticus his other friends as well, how hard he was struggling not to let his grief cast him down. After telling Atticus, in his
first letter from Astura, that he finds the solitude there less painful
than the crowds of the city, and is able to pursue his studies with no
more difficulty than if he were at home, Cicero says, "None the less
the burning pain presses upon me as before and persists, not, by Hercu-
les, with my indulgence, but as I fight back against it" (*Att.* 250:1
[XII. 13]). Acknowledging that Atticus wants him to recover from his
grief, Cicero cries "but you are my witness that I have not failed myself" (*Att.* 251:3 [XII. 14]).

The traditions and values of Rome, then, of which he was constantly and insistently reminded by his friends and acquaintances after
he fled the city, and which he acknowledged with approval in his own
writings, seem to have been uppermost in Cicero's mind during his bereavement. His repeated concern that Atticus and his friends know
how hard he was fighting against his grief, and that they rest assured
that he could at least hide the signs of his sufferings from his face and
his speech if necessary, show that Cicero in grief turned outward, not inward. He thought about Rome, and of himself as a Roman.[4] The specific way in which he tried to control his grief shows him struggling
to rise above his own personal life.

Having read everything in Atticus' library on the alleviation of sorrow, Cicero found that he was still inconsolable. So he did something
which he believed no one had ever done before:

> I have consoled myself by writing. I shall send you the book as soon as
> the copyists have finished it. I assure you that there is no consolation like
> this. I write all day long, not that I do myself any good, but for the time
> being it holds me back (*impedior*)—not enough (for the power of my
> grief presses upon me), but still I get some relief. . . . (*Att.* 251:3 [XII. 14])

Tullia's death, in fact, occasioned the most productive period of
study and philosophical writing in Cicero's life. In addition to the

book that he refers to above, which may be the lost *Consolatio*, a consolation in the form of a letter which Cicero addressed to himself,[5] Cicero finished the original version of the *Academica* in two books by mid-May, then expanded them to four, while writing the *De finibus*. Then he wrote the *Tusculanae disputationes*, one of Petrarch's favorite books, and by late August seems to have been thinking about the *De natura deorum*.[6] By the end of 44 B.C. he had written, in addition to these works, *De divinatione, De senectute, De amicitia, De fato, Paradoxa Stoicorum, De officiis*, and some rhetorical treatises such as the *Topica* and *De optimo genere oratorum*.

No one would have been more surprised than Cicero to know that many of these works, even more than his orations, would become the basis of the secondary and even university curriculum in Western Europe, and later America, from the time of the Renaissance through the end of the nineteenth century. These works, which were fundamental to the curriculum of the new *studia humanitatis*, Cicero wrote to divert his mind from grief and at the same time to show his friends that he could conquer his feelings, especially in a dignified way. Speaking of his life at Astura, he tells Atticus that "here, by writing all day, I find no relief, but still I get away (*aberro*) from the grief" (*Att.* 278:1 [XII. 38]). In reply to the charge that he was broken in spirit and enfeebled, Cicero writes:

> . . . if those who think I am broken in spirit and enfeebled knew what and how much I have written, I believe that if they are sensitive human beings (*homines*), they would think that I should not be rebuked, or even deserve some praise, either because I have so uplifted myself that I bring a free mind to the writing of difficult things, or because I have chosen that diversion (*aberratio*) from sorrow which is the noblest and most worthy of a learned man. (*Att.* 279:1 [XII. 38a])

To those who urge him to dissimulate his grief, Cicero asks "what more can I do than consume whole days in literary work?" (*Att.* 258:1 [XII. 20]). "It is in fact unbelievable," he tells Atticus, "how much I write, even at night, for I am unable to sleep" (*Att.* 286:2 [XIII. 26]). In reply to demands that he return to Rome, Cicero says that he prefers to stand by his own judgment. Then he adds:

> And yet I go no farther than the most learned men allow me, all of whose writings concerning this matter I have not only read, which in itself was being a brave invalid and taking one's medicine, but have translated them into my own, which certainly was not like a distressed and broken mind. Don't call me away from these remedies back to the crowd, lest I relapse. (*Att.* 260:5 [XII. 21])

How did this intense study and continuous writing actually constitute "remedies" for Cicero's grief? The explanation lies in the meaning of the phrase *animus vacuus* quoted above: "I have so uplifted myself that I bring a free mind (*animus vacuus*) to the writing of difficult things" (*Att.* 279:1 [XII. 38a]). In his *Tusculan Disputations*, one of the works he wrote after Tullia's death, Cicero gives quite a few examples of the special meaning of the word *vacare,* "to be free from," when applied to the soul. The *Tusculan Disputations* consist of four dialogues concerning death, pain, mental anguish, and other "perturbations" of the soul, and a fifth dialogue on happiness. The work derives its title from Cicero's villa in Tusculanum, where he imagines these conversations to have taken place. Toward the beginning of the dialogue of the Fourth Day, "On the Other Perturbations of the Soul," Cicero has his interlocutor state, by way of negation, exactly what the dialogue will set out to prove: "It does not seem to me that a wise man can be free from (*vacare*) all perturbations of the soul." To which Cicero replies: "Certainly yesterday it seemed that a wise man could free himself from mental anguish (*aegritudo*), unless you agreed on the spur of the moment" (IV, 4, 8).

Now, mourning, *maeror,* is a form of *aegritudo*; Cicero defines it as *aegritudo flebilis,* "mental distress which moves to tears" later in Book 4 (IV, 8, 18). What Cicero is pointing out here, and his interlocutor will immediately agree with him, is that he has already demonstrated in the dialogue of the Third Day that a wise man should be able to free himself from *aegritudo*—and if *aegritudo* in general, then certainly from *maeror,* grief and mourning, that specific form of *aegritudo*, sickness of the mind, against which Cicero himself struggled after Tullia died. The whole point of the *Tusculan Disputations*, in fact, is to prove that the *sapiens*, the sage or wise man, is one who has freed his soul from *all* perturbations. Cicero says, for example, that if a wise man keep his mind focused on certain things—and what these are we shall see in a moment—"he will not only free himself from mental distress, but from all other perturbations." He concludes: "A soul empty of these makes men perfectly and completely happy. . . ." (*Tusc.* IV, 17, 38)

What are these "perturbations," and how does a wise man free his soul of them? Cicero says that he follows Pythagoras and Plato in supposing that the soul, *animus,* is divided into two parts, one which "participates in reason" (*rationis particeps*) and one which does not. The former (often identified with the *mens,* "mind" [*Tusc.* III, 5, 10–11]) enjoys tranquility, which Cicero defines as a "peaceful and quiet constancy." But in the other or lower part of the soul are to be found the "turbulent motions" (*motus turbidi*) of anger and desire, motions which are opposed and hostile to reason (*Tusc.* IV, 5, 10). It is these turbulent motions which Cicero calls "perturbations," defining *perturbatio* as "an agitation of the soul (*animi commotio*) averse to right reason, and against nature" (*Tusc.* IV, 6, 11). There are four fundamental perturbations, distinguished according to whether they concern the future or the present: *libido* ("desire"), *laetitia* ("exuberant joy"), *metus* ("fear"), and *aegritudo* ("mental anguish" or "mental distress") (ibid.).

According to Cicero, these turbulent motions in the lower soul arise out of *prava opinio*, distorted or corrupt opinion, a phrase we met in our discussion of Caius Marius. In comparing the maladies of the soul to those of the body, Cicero writes:

> Just as when blood is adulterated or has too much phlegm or bile, sickness and diseases arise in the body, so too the disturbance (*conturbatio*) of corrupt and warring opinions strips the soul of its health and throws it into confusion with disorders (*morbi*). (*Tusc.* IV, 10, 23)

At the end of Book Four he says, summarizing the main point of the first four books of the *Tusculan Disputations*, "Whence it must be understood that all perturbation lies in opinion (*opinio*)" (IV, 37, 79). Whether it be the fear of death, sharp physical pain, sadness or mental anguish, wrath, desire, or ecstatic joy, these are all violent and unsettling movements in one's soul which are due, according to Cicero, exclusively to what one believes concerning the present or the future (*Tusc.* IV, 6, 7). Change your thinking, he says over and over again in the *Tusculan Disputations*, and you can attain peace of soul.

But how does one change his thinking? How can he free himself from false beliefs? Through philosophy, as the ancients understood and practiced it. Philosophy, according to Cicero, enables one to reason his way to the conclusion that whatever seems to be disturbing his peace of soul is in fact an error of judgment or belief and is therefore voluntary:

> But there is one cure for mental distress and the other diseases of the soul: that they are all based on opinion and are voluntary, and are submitted to because it seems right to do so. This error, which is, as it were, the source of all evils, philosophy promises to pull out by the roots. (*Tusc.* IV, 38, 83)

In his dialogue on friendship, Cicero offers a striking example of how one might reason his way out of grief. Before he wrote this work, Cicero had attempted to prove, in Book I of the *Tusculan Disputations*, that death is not an evil and is not to be feared. Now, in *Laelius*

de amicitia, he has Laelius say, concerning the death of his dear friend
Scipio Aemilianus,

> I console myself, and most of all with that solace that I am free from that
> error on account of which people are generally wont to feel anguish at
> the passing of friends. I believe that nothing bad has happened to Scipio;
> if anything has happened, it has happened to me; but to be gravely dis-
> tressed by one's own discomforts is a characteristic of one who loves him-
> self, and not his friend. (2, 10)

In order to free the soul from turbulent motions, however, it is not
enough to uncover the errors in one's reasoning; a person must be
able to rise above these errors, and all that is mortal and human, by contemplating the divine and the eternal. In describing the *sapiens,* the
sage or wise man, Cicero shows how he is free from the four fundamental passions of the lower soul. Then he asks, "For what in human affairs can seem of consequence to a man who is acquainted with all eternity and the vastness of the universe?" (*Tusc.* IV, 17, 37).

The Greeks and the Romans believed in a fundamental congruity between the order of the heavens and the order of the soul. In relying on
philosophical reasoning to exert the mind's control over the turbulent
passions of the lower soul, one is at the same time rising in contemplation above the earth and participating in the peace, harmony, and constancy of the eternal and unchanging heavens. Our investigation of
Cicero's attempt to free himself from grief thus leads us to look at his understanding of the universe and the place of the individual soul within it.

In Book VI of his *De re publica,* Cicero describes a geocentric universe in which an area of ceaseless change and alteration lies beneath
the circle inscribed in the heavens by the revolution of the moon,
while above it all is eternal and unchanging. I quoted this passage earlier in discussing Petrarch's fascination with earthly change and contingency. It is worth looking at it again now in the context of Cicero's
grief. After pointing to the sphere of the sun, Scipio shows his grandson the rest of the heavenly spheres:

> The orbits of Venus, and of Mercury, follow him like companions, and
> in the lowest sphere revolves the moon, set on fire by the rays of the
> sun. But below there is nothing except that which is mortal and destined
> to decay, save only the souls given to the human race by the bounty of
> the gods; above the moon everything is eternal. (VI, 17 [4] 17)

It is through the soul, in its highest part or function, *mens* or *ratio,*
mind or reason, that we are joined to the eternal heavens, and it is the
heavens that make it possible for us to attain peace, harmony, and

order in our earthly lives. The gods put souls into human bodies, Cicero has Cato explain in his dialogue on old age,

> so that there would be beings who would look after the earth, and who, in contemplating the order of the heavens, would imitate it in the measure and constancy of their lives. (*Cato maior de senectute* 21, 77)

We can imitate the order of the heavens because of the special place we occupy in the scheme of things. In chapters 11–14 of Book II of the *De natura deorum*, "On the Nature of the Gods," Cicero presents arguments to prove the Stoic belief, which he shares, that the cosmos is a god, because it is self-sufficient, wise, virtuous, and perfect in reason. Man occupies a special place in the cosmos: born to contemplate and imitate the heavens, "he is by no means perfect, but a little part of the perfect" (II, 14, 37). To say then, as Cicero does in the *Tusculan Disputations*, that the higher soul "participates in reason" (*rationis particeps*), is not a metaphor; *ratio*, reason or mind, exists in the eternal, unchanging, harmonious, and perfectly ordered heavens above the circle of the moon. By contemplating and imitating these heavens we achieve, by exercising our soul's birthright and "participating" in them, something of their order and constancy. To put it in teleological terms, our final resting place lies above and outside of our individual self.

The ancients even saw a symmetry between the cosmos and the body: at the beginning of the *Tusculan Disputations* Cicero cites Plato's understanding that reason is located in the head, wrath in the chest, and desire below the diaphragm so that anger and desire are subservient to reason (I, 10, 20).

The *mens* or *ratio* which Cicero will use in his struggle against grief is thus a force or a power which he will find by looking up at the heavens, and not down into himself. He will find reason also in the earthly city of which he is a part. Just as we have discovered a symmetry between the hierarchies of the soul and those of the cosmos, so too there is another symmetry in Cicero's world in which reason plays a key part: that between mind and society.

A *vir*, a "man," for Cicero, is one whose reason has command over the lower part of his soul:

> A man must see that it (reason) exercises authority over that part of the soul which must obey it. How? you ask. Either as master over slave, commander over soldier, or parent over son. (*Tusc.* II, 21, 48)

Vir, "man," as opposed to *homo*, "human being," it is important to remember, can mean "man" in the special sense of strength and probity of character, consciously acquired and refined through exercise, habit, mental preparation, and reason (*Tusc.* II, 18, 42). It is in fact from the word *vir*, Cicero rightly observes, that the word *virtus* comes. And the virtue which most properly belongs to a man, Cicero says, is fortitude, of which there are two principal characteristics: contempt for death, and contempt for pain (*Tusc.* II, 18, 43).

Now, while it is through the mind, through philosophical contemplation, that one "rises" into true and perfect virtue, the city-state, one's earthly community, stands guard to make sure that all male human beings behave as men. If reason fails to exercise its authority over the lower part of the soul, then the community must step in to act in its stead. Thus the society in which one lives functions, from time to time, as *mens* or *ratio*:

> If that part of the soul, which I have said to be soft, gives itself over to effeminate laments and tears, let it be bound and fettered by the guardianship of friends and relatives; for often we see those controlled by shame (*pudor*) who could not be overcome by any reason. (*Tusc.* II, 21, 48)

Here Cicero links *pudor* and *ratio*. Shame, in fact, was one of the chief ways in which Roman society enforced conformity to the order and harmony of reason. From this point of view, Cicero's friends, Brutus, and others who were concerned about him, acted not as an "alter ego" but as an "altera ratio," "another reason," during the period of his most violent distress. They called him away from the mourning which, by Roman standards, was not only debilitating, but shameful. That this is exactly what they should have done is made clear by the letter Cicero wrote to Brutus two years later to console Brutus for the death of his wife Portia. Cicero opens this brief letter with the words: "I would perform that duty (*officium*) which you performed during my mourning and console you with a letter . . ." (*Ad Brut.* 18:1 [17 (1.9)]). *Officium* is a strong word; it means that which one is obliged to do by religion, by morality, or by law. Atticus, Brutus, and others, like Cicero himself toward Brutus two years later, were duty-bound to shame Cicero, if necessary, into behaving according to the standard of *ratio*, as found in the soul of the wise man, in society (*De officiis* I, 7, 20), and in the heavens above the circle of the moon. Cicero's understanding of his relationship to the cosmos was of a piece, then, with his experience of life in Rome. His writings, moreover, describe a symmetry between the individual and the cosmos, the individual and society, and society and the cosmos, for the same *ratio* governs all three.

The knowledge that friends and relatives have a duty to *shame* a Roman into controlling the expression of pain, and the implication that they were actually able to do so, can help us proceed with caution in our understanding of those frequent passages in Cicero's letters from Astura in which he talks about keeping up appearances by dissimulating his grief and bringing his face back to composure. These are perilous passages for a twentieth-century reader because they so readily evoke in us a cluster of moral judgments centered around concepts of sincerity, authenticity, and personal selfhood which have everything to do with our own, but nothing at all to do with the Roman, experience of the human. One way of avoiding reading our own standards, and our own concept of what it means to be a "person," back into Cicero is to consider the extent to which Roman society and Roman religion expected a *vir* to be an actor, that is, a *persona,* literally a mask.

Speaking of the role which imitating the cosmos plays in the moral life of the Stoic, Hans Jonas writes:

> We are spectators and actors alike of the grand play, but we can be the latter successfully and to our own happiness only if we are the former in an ever more comprehensive sweep—encompassing our own acting itself. (Jonas 1963, p. 247)

In his writings, Cicero implies that it is the audience of a person's actions that helps him to become a *vir.* In Book Two of the *Tusculan Disputations,* "On Bearing Pain," he uses the example of gladiators to illustrate how exercise, habit, and mental preparation enable a man to bear the most grievous wounds:

> . . . look at the gladiators, either ruined men or barbarians, what blows they endure! How those who have been well trained prefer to receive a blow rather than avoid it dishonorably! How often it appears that they want nothing other than to do enough for their master or the people! Even when weakened by wounds, they send word to their masters to find out if they are satisfied with what they have done; for their own part they are willing to die. What even ordinary gladiator has ever uttered a cry of pain, has ever changed his countenance? Who has not only stood, but also fallen dishonorably? Who, when he fell, has drawn in his neck when ordered to receive the stroke of the sword? . . . The spectacle of gladiators is wont to seem cruel and inhuman to some, and I do not know whether it should be as it now is. But when criminals fought it out with swords, perhaps there could have been many schools for the ears, but none for the eyes could have been stronger against pain and death. (*Tusc.* II, 17, 41)

This powerful passage gives some sense of the ideal of *vir* Cicero must have had before his eyes when he entered the lists to take up his battle against grief. And we know that when Antony's assassins overtook Cicero near the coast, he ordered his slaves to set the litter down. Then he leaned forward and held out his neck, just like the gladiator he describes, and waited for the sword to fall.[7]

Ideally, one looks at his own actions the way the public looks at the gladiators', and turns his own consciousness into an audience. "[T]here is no better theater for virtue," Cicero says, "than one's consciousness (*conscientia*)" (*Tusc.* II, 26, 64). In his letter of consolation to Brutus, Cicero even uses the word "stage" (*scaena*) to remind Brutus of his obligations. Referring to the letter Brutus had written him two years earlier to criticize his comportment after Tullia died, Cicero writes, "But at that time I, Brutus, had to serve only duty and nature, now you, as they say, must serve the people and the stage." He goes on to remind Brutus that the eyes of his troops, all the citizens, and almost all the nations, are on him (*Ad Brut.* 18:2 [17 (1.9)]). But the distinction Cicero makes between his own situation after the death of Tullia, and Brutus' now, is really only one of degree: the actor on the stage is implied throughout Cicero's letters from Astura, for he tells Atticus on repeated occasions that he is doing everything he can not to "show" his grief.

These quotations suggest an additional dimension to the concept of *vir*. A "man" is not just a person who has virtue—primarily fortitude—because his reason is firmly in command of his lower soul; he is one who has the strength and self-discipline to act, that is, to appear to others, as if he is perfectly in control of the perturbations of his lower soul. And since the Romans judge a man by his deeds, not by his intentions, there is really no difference, as far as the life of virtue is concerned, between appearance and reality: a person is whatever his deeds make him appear to be. When, in his letter to Brutus, Cicero says that he seemed to Brutus to bear his suffering more weakly than a man should (18:1 [17 (1.9)]), Cicero is saying that a "man" has a role to play, a mask to wear. Moreover, Cicero's letters from Astura, as well as his philosophical writings, show that neither the *vir* nor his audience is in any way interested in exploring what lies behind the mask; if you wear the *persona* of *virtus* you are a "man."

From the point of view of our own times, what is striking in Cicero's writings, especially in his letters and in those works concerned with the life of the soul, is thus the lack of any conception of "sincerity" or "authenticity." I use these terms with Lionel Trilling's book *Sincerity and Authenticity* in mind. Trilling attempts to sketch the history of the modern "self" from approximately the seventeenth century to the present, and in so doing distinguishes between "sincerity," congruence between avowal and actual feeling (Trilling 1972, p. 63), and "authenticity," an attempt to act according to the dictates of a dark, unconscious, irrational self that lies buried deep within us, and which throws into question the very possibility of sincerity. This is not the place to summarize Trilling's rich and insightful observations. Suffice it to say that Trilling traces the evolution of the moral life in the modern period from a preoccupation with "sincerity" in the seventeenth century to a concern for "authenticity" in the twentieth: Shakespeare and Molière are interested in sincerity; Diderot (*Le Neveu de Rameau*) throws it into question; Nietzsche, Freud, and Conrad discover authenticity. Trilling's thesis is useful in helping us to understand the emergence of the humanities, because both concepts, sincerity and authenticity, which express so well the Western experience of the human since the Renaissance, imply a personal self, and posit, though in very different ways, that the "truth" of one's being is somehow to be found *within* this self. Consider Trilling's example of sincerity, Polonius' advice to Laertes:

> . . . to thine own self be true
> And it must follow, as night the day,
> Thou canst not then be false to any man.
> (*Hamlet,* Act 1, Scene 3)

Cicero and his fellow Romans would not have understood this advice. They had no concept of sincerity, and no concept of that without which sincerity is impossible: an autonomous inner self which somehow contains its own unique truth, a truth which it can either hide or express. It is only the modern reader who, projecting his or her own experience of the human back into Cicero's time, can question whether or not Cicero is being insincere in hiding his feelings, or being inauthentic in trying to distract his mind from his grief. The words *dissimulatio*, feigning that not to be which is, and *simulatio*, feigning that to be which is not, words which Cicero uses in discussing the public dimension of his grief, contain none of the moral disapprobation they would come to acquire after the Renaissance. When Cicero writes that Atticus and others have urged him to dissimulate his grief and replies that he is spending all his time writing, which, even if he is not doing it for the sake of dissimulation, at least helps him to "keep up appearances" (*simulatio*) (*Att.* 258:1 [XII. 20]), he is using the words in an approbatory sense—and we know why: the man (*vir*) guided by reason, the man who rises in contemplation above the circle of the moon, the man who is regarded as a *vir* by his community, does not publicly mourn. If there is anything for Cicero to be true to, it is not a personal self, but, as he himself puts it, the reason, constancy, and harmony of the heavens.

When Cicero tells Atticus, then, that he brings an *animus vacuus* to his philosophical studies and writing, he is saying that he has freed his soul from the confused and disturbing movements of the passions, in this case grief. Furthermore, the kind of studies he engaged in during this period, and the books he wrote in order to pull his mind away from the grief, show Cicero trying to do exactly what the wise man with an *animus vacuus* does: contemplate the eternal and the divine. Of course the letters to Atticus from Astura suggest that Cicero was not completely successful in this endeavor: he was unable to diminish the pain; he could only take his mind off of it. But as Cicero wrote in Book II of the *Tusculan Disputations*, although no one has yet attained perfect wisdom, it remains nevertheless a normative ideal, something to strive for:

> Certainly the man in whom there will be perfect wisdom—a man whom we have not yet seen, but how he will be, if only at some time he will be, is set forth in the words of philosophers—he then, or rather that reason, which in him will be perfect and complete, will rule over the lower part as a just parent rules over his upright sons. . . . (II, 22, 51)

Cicero's letters to Atticus following the death of Tullia have let us observe Cicero in the midst of an extreme pain that stripped him bare and showed what really mattered to him. As we have seen, Cicero experienced his being as part of a greater whole. During his struggle with grief, he turned outward, not inward. He fought to keep his thoughts away from himself in relation to his daughter Tullia (whom, perhaps for this very reason, he never mentions in any of the letters from Astura), and on the role which he, like every Roman citizen, would have been expected to play under such circumstances. There is nothing in the letters from Astura, or in any of the treatises he wrote to distract his mind from the grief, to suggest that Cicero ever experienced himself the way Petrarch did, and the way we still do today: as a self-consciously unique and autonomous center of cognition, volition, and feeling—in short, as a "personal self."

At first sight the concept of person that emerges from Cicero's letters and philosophical works bears a striking resemblance to that discovered by anthropologists among non-Western people in our own century. In a well-known article, "'From the Native's Point of View': On the Nature of Anthropological Understanding," Clifford Geertz argues that while the concept of person exists among all social groups, the actual understanding of what constitutes a person varies widely:

> The Western conception of the person as a bounded, unique, more or less integrated motivational and cognitive universe, a dynamic center of awareness, emotion, judgment, and action organized into a distinctive

whole and set contrastively both against other such wholes and against its social and natural background, is, however incorrigible it may seem to us, a rather peculiar idea within the context of the world's cultures. (Geertz 1976, p. 225)

Geertz goes on to describe the Javanese sense of what a person is: a person, for the Javanese, is divided into two completely independent realms—an inside, which "consists of the fuzzy, shifting flow of subjective feeling perceived directly in all its phenomenological immediacy but considered to be, at its roots at least, identical across all individuals, whose individuality it thus effaces," and "an outside," "that part of human life which, in our culture, strict behaviorists limit themselves to studying—external actions, movements, postures, speech—again conceived as in its essence invariant from one individual to the next" (ibid., pp. 226–27).

Geertz concludes his description of the Javanese sense of person by recounting how he saw a young Javanese try to come to terms with his wife's unexpected death:

Only when you have seen, as I have, a young man whose wife—a woman he had in fact raised from childhood and who had been the center of his life—has suddenly and inexplicably died, greeting everyone with a set smile and formal apologies for his wife's absence and trying, by mystical techniques, to flatten out, as he himself put it, the hills and valleys of his emotions into an even, level plain ("That is what you have to do," he said to me, "be smooth inside and out") can you come, in the face of our own notions of the intrinsic honesty of deep feeling and the moral importance of personal sincerity, to take the possibility of such a conception of selfhood seriously and appreciate, however inaccessible it is to you, its own sort of force. (Ibid., pp. 227–28)

Having looked carefully at Cicero's reaction to the death of his daughter Tullia, we can see that the particularly Western conception of personal selfhood which Geertz describes has not been Western forever: Cicero and his contemporaries would not have understood it. The "intrinsic honesty of deep feeling and the moral importance of personal sincerity" are values foreign to a culture which demands of men that they dissimulate strong emotions and strive, in all realms of their lives, to live up to communal standards of fortitude and self-control expressed in the normative concepts of *vir, virtus, ratio,* and *sapientia.* The resemblance between the young Javanese man trying to come to terms with his wife's unexpected death and the portrait Cicero gives of himself following Tullia's death is thus striking. But there is nonetheless an important difference between the Javanese sense of what a person is, and the Roman.

As Geertz describes them, the Javanese have little or no sense of individuality. The Romans do; their literature is peopled with individuals. But individuality, for the Roman mind, is never interiorized, never personalized. When a person is named, in Roman literature, and thus singled out as an individual, it is because of his deeds, never because of his personality.

Separating the two, the deeds and the person performing them, is difficult for us to do because our interest, since Petrarch's time, lies with the person. At the deepest level, once we pass beyond physical appearance and social role, we use the concept of "personality" to describe what makes one person different from another. The *American Heritage Dictionary of the English Language* defines personality as "the dynamic character, self, or psyche that constitutes and animates the individual person and makes his experience of life unique." The Romans had no such concept. Roman heroes have no personalities, no unique inner selves. Cicero tells us nothing about what Marius was thinking as he stretched out his leg for the surgeon. Cicero, Seneca, and Valerius Maximus say nothing about what went through the minds of Publius Decius, and his son and grandson, as they solemnly vowed their lives for Rome, and then went off to meet their deaths. These writers show no interest in their heroes' personal selves because, from a Roman point of view, Marius and the Decii did nothing unique at all; they were merely doing, in circumstances peculiar to them, what every *vir* should do. The motive force of their deeds thus came from without, not from within, from the community, not from the individual. Cicero, Seneca, and Valerius Maximus single out Marius and the Decii for attention in order to praise their deeds, not their persons, and to use these deeds to define and teach virtue. If we still need to know what Marius must have been thinking as the surgeon cut into his leg, or what was in their thoughts as the Decii prepared for death, we would have to say, as Cicero does in the sentences following his description of Marius, that they had "that which befits patience, fortitude, and greatness of soul" in their minds.[8]

A person is named, in Roman literature, and thus individualized, that is, literally, "singled out," solely in order to exemplify virtue (or, sometimes, the lack of it). Consider the picture of warfare Vergil gives us in the *Aeneid*. Vergil depicts war as hand-to-hand combat between individuals, clearly recognized as such by friends and foes alike by the distinctive features of their armor, and sometimes even by their appearance or bearing. But what kind of individuals are these? Certainly not people who have any unique inner life we could ever come to know. During the Trojans' war with Turnus, Lausus sees Aeneas wound and prepare to kill his father, the Etruscan king Mezentius. Lausus rushes

into the fray, and stays the point of Aeneas' sword with his own. As
both men shield themselves from the shower of javelins launched by Turnus' forces to protect Mezentius' withdrawal, Aeneas asks Lausus why
he rushed to his death, letting his love for his father (*pietas*) embolden
him beyond his strength. His anger rising, Aeneas then runs Lausus
through with his sword. But as he watches Lausus die, something happens to Aeneas: Lausus' *pietas* reminds him of his own. Vergil writes:

> But seeing the look
> On the young man's face in death, a face so pale
> As to be awesome, then Anchises' son
> Groaned in profound pity. He held out
> His hand as filial piety, mirrored here,
> Wrung his own heart, and said:
> "O poor young soldier,
> How will Aeneas reward your splendid fight?
> How honor you, in keeping with your nature?
> Keep the arms you loved to use, for I
> Return you to your forebears, ash and shades,
> If this concerns you now. Unlucky boy,
> One consolation for sad death is this:
> You die by the sword-thrust of great Aeneas."
> (X, 821–830, trans. Fitzgerald, 1983)

It is *pietas*, not Lausus, that moves Aeneas to groan in pity after he
has slain him. The Lausus Vergil depicts here in this touching scene
has no personal self. It is the deed that interests Vergil. In dying to
save his father's life, Lausus shows the power of something that utterly transcends his own individuality: the power of *pietas*, the very
same *pietas* Aeneas feels for his own father, the *pietas* that moves every
noble Roman to sacrifice his life for his family and for his country. As
Lausus dies, and Aeneas groans over his body, these two hostile combat-
ants, now slayer and slain, are drawn together into a larger whole:
they are both *pius*.

Hans Jonas has spoken of the relationship of the Many and the One
as the most fundamental problem of ancient ontology.[9] Here, in this
scene from the *Aeneid*, individuality is effaced by the virtue it exemplifies, and the many become one. Lausus does not die alone; human existence, for the Greeks and the Romans, was not unique and isolated.
To be human is to be a part of and to participate in a whole outside of
oneself, whether it be the cosmos, the polis, or the *civitas*. Both the
life of virtue and the individual heroic deed are not only motivated
by, but actually bespeak, this participation.

CHAPTER 4

ANCIENT AND MODERN
CATEGORIES OF THOUGHT

❧

THE ANCIENT EXPERIENCE of the human throws into bold relief the novelty of the Renaissance humanities. For Cicero, the individual is part
of the whole; for Bruni, the individual becomes the whole. Petrarch in
grief turns inward and tries to build for himself a character that can
stand up to the blows of Fortune. Cicero in grief turns outward and
tries to free his soul from unruly passions by rising above the human
through contemplation of the divine and the eternal. Let us now take
a broader overview and try to state, on a more theoretical level, some
of the essential differences between the ancient and the modern experience of the human condition.

In expounding the doctrine of man's "participation" in the cosmos,
Cicero provides a clear and striking example of the way in which classical man experienced his being not as unique, separate, and autonomous, but as part of a larger whole. Here is how Hans Jonas, in his
book *The Gnostic Religion*, describes this relationship:

> Man's relationship to the cosmos is a special case of the part-whole relation-
> ship which is so fundamental a theme in classical thought. Philosophy
> and political science alike had ever anew discussed its problems, which in
> the last analysis led back to the most fundamental problem of ancient ontol-
> ogy, that of the Many and the One. According to classical doctrine, the
> whole is prior to the parts, is better than the parts, and therefore that for
> the sake of which the parts are and wherein they have not only the cause
> but also the meaning of their existence. The living example of such a
> whole had been the classical *polis,* the city-state, whose citizens had a
> share of the whole and could affirm its superior status in the knowledge
> that they the parts, however passing and exchangeable, not only were *depen-
> dent* on the whole *for* their being but also *maintained* that whole *with* their
> being: just as the condition of the whole made a difference to the being
> and possible perfection of the parts, so their conduct made a difference to

the being and perfection of the whole. Thus this whole, making possible first the very life and then the good life of the individual, was at the same time entrusted to the individual's care, and in surpassing and outlasting him was also his supreme achievement. (Jonas 1963, p. 248)

It should thus not surprise us to find that even death itself, which we today regard as the most personal and lonely of all experiences, was for classical man understood as part of a whole.

Carl Kerenyi concludes his study *The Religion of the Greeks and the Romans* with an epilogue on "The Religious Idea of Non-Existence." He quotes Epicurus: "Death is no concern of ours. For when we are present, death is not present, and when death is present, we are not" (Kerenyi 1962, p. 267). Kerenyi argues that "it is not until much later times that we find a special *sense* of 'one's own death'" (ibid.), and he uses Max Scheler's idea of the "death-direction" to make a fundamental distinction between the Greek and Roman idea of non-existence and our own. By "death-direction" Scheler means that in every moment of our lives we experience an increasing difference between two lengths: the future shrinks, and the past grows longer. We sense that we are moving toward death. Kerenyi writes:

> Scheler describes the death-direction from the point of view of a man turned in on himself. For the ancients the corresponding description, although it also included a man's *own* death, would have to be a description not of his inner life, but of the world of men. This is the world which contracts around us in our experience of the death-direction, indeed independently of our actual experience, and which in its relation to ourselves approaches closer and closer to rejection and complete negation. (Ibid., pp. 268–69)

Kerenyi quotes these beautiful, but to the modern mind strangely cold and impersonal, lines from Catullus' poem *Vivamus mea Lesbia* (5), which provide a reminder, in an ancient festive way, of the "death-face of the world":

> *Soles occidere et redire possunt,*
> *Nobis cum semel occidit brevis lux*
> *Nox est perpetua una dormienda.*

> Suns may set and still return,
> When our brief light has set, for us
> There's one perpetual night of sleep. (Ibid., p. 272)

Catullus is looking outward, not inward, as he playfully raises the question of his and Lesbia's non-existence.

Looking at classical antiquity from an epistemological point of view, F. E. Cranz, in a series of unpublished but widely read papers, offers another understanding of how a Greek or a Roman might have experienced his own existence.[1] Citing texts from both the Platonist and Aristotelian traditions of thought, Cranz argues that a person living in the Graeco-Roman world 1) becomes united or joined with the object he knows or senses; 2) feels himself to be a part of a *single* order of being which includes all other beings and of which persons are in the fullest sense parts; and 3) experiences this single world of being as an "aggregate" order in which parts constitute the whole. Within this ancient experience, knowledge and reason achieve a certain "immediacy" and "ultimacy," particularly because the ancients describe knowledge and reason as "vision" in which the "eye of the mind" is united with what it sees.

Here is Aristotle on the conjunction of the knower with what is known:

> In what is without matter, what intellects and what is intellected are the same. . . . Theoretical science and that which is so scienced are the same. . . . Science in act is the same as the thing. (*De anima* III, 4, 430a2 f. and 7, 431a1 f., Cranz, p. 3)

Cranz cites another passage from the *De anima* to illustrate what he calls the ancient experience of an "extensive self," a self which "was in the fullest sense a part of a single realm of being and indeed, potentially identical with it" (p. 2):

> Now in summarizing what has been said about the soul, we say again that the soul is somehow all beings. The beings are either sensible or intelligible, and science is somehow the scienced, and sense the sensibles. (III, 8, 431b20 f., Cranz p. 4)

He observes that "if one starts from the order of beings, one finds that the self is among them; if one starts from the soul one finds that it somehow embraces all beings" (p. 4).

Cranz points to the same experience of an "extensive self," potentially identical with all being, in the Platonist tradition. Plotinus writes:

> For we and the "ours" are led up to being. . . . When we know [the intelligibles] we do not have images or impressions of them . . . but we are them. If we participate in true science, we are [the intelligibles]; we do not take them into us but we are them. (*Ennead* VI, 5, 7, Cranz, p. 4)

Augustine, finally, offers an example of the ancient experience of reason and argument as a kind of vision in which the knower is joined with what he knows: "There is this good and that good. Remove the 'this' and the 'that' and see, if you can, the good itself. Thus you will see God . . . " *(De Trinitate* VIII, 3, 4, Cranz, p. 4). And in *De immortali-tate animae* he says that "[t]he soul cannot see the truth except through some conjunction with it" (I, 6, 10, Cranz, p. 5).

Cicero, we remember, said that man is born to contemplate and imitate the cosmos, and that he is not perfect, "but is some little part of the perfect." Cranz's study of ancient epistemology helps us to see more clearly the full extent to which the ancients conceived of intellection as conscious participation in the whole order of being, a participation which, to use Cranz's terms, carries with it an experience of "immediacy" and "ultimacy" which has been lost in the modern world.

We have spoken of the humanities as an attempt to substitute an inner, personal unity for the ancient unity of the individual and the cosmos. We could also say that the humanities were one attempt in the West to recapture the ancient experience of immediacy and ultimacy, though now as an intense inner experience. In order to see how, let us look now at Cranz's explanation for the breakdown of the ancient categories of thought.

Toward the end of the eleventh century, Anselm of Canterbury (1033–1109), often called the founder of scholasticism, discovered what has come to be known as his "ontological argument" for the existence of God: God is "something than which nothing greater can be cogitated" *(aliquid quo nihil maius cogitari possit) (Proslogion* II, *Opera* I, p. 101). This proof commands assent, Anselm believes, by the sheer fact that the definition of God can be thought and understood. Commenting on his proof for the existence of God in his *Reply of the Editor,* he writes:

> I think that I have shown not by a weak but by a sufficiently necessary argument in the aforesaid book [the *Proslogion*] that in fact there exists something than which nothing greater can be cogitated, nor is this argument weakened by any objection. The meaning *(significatio)* of this phrase has so much force that that itself which is said, of necessity by the very fact that it is understood or cogitated, is both proved in fact to exist, and to be itself whatever we ought to believe of the divine substance. *(Responsio editoris* 10, *Opera* I, pp. 138–139)

Cranz believes that he has found in Anselm's ontological proof for the existence of God a clear indication that the ancient experience of the unity of all being had come to an end. Anselm expressed for the first time, Cranz argues, what we now recognize as Western "reason": an experience of knowing and sensing characterized by a dichotomy between the knower and the known in a world of being now divided into a separate realm of "meanings" and a separate realm of "things." The order of this new divided world, moreover, is "systematic" in the sense that the parts no longer constitute the whole but are only "functions" of it, as, for example, in Galileo's Law of Falling Bodies, where each particular falling body is understood as a function of the law. And while the ancients understood reason as a kind of vision in which one is joined with what he intellects, Anselm's reason rests solely on the coherence of what is said.

But inner coherence is not vision. After this reorientation, the categories of thought and experience, knowledge and reason, lack both immediacy and ultimacy. Anselm acknowledges as much when, having believed that he has reasoned his way to God, he cries out in despair:

> Have you found, my soul, what you sought? . . . For if you have not found your God, how is He that which you have found and which you have intellected [Him to be] with such certain truth and with such true certainty. If you have found Him, why is it that you do not feel *(sentis)* what you have found. Why, Lord God, does my soul not feel You if it has found You? *(Proslogion* XIV, *Opera* I, p. 111)

Cranz argues that after 1100 A.D., European thought has two polarized thrusts. First, there is the triumphant progress of the new reason which first appeared in Anselm's theological speculations and was quickly secularized, and which then constituted the backbone of scholastic theology. This reason led to the new mathematical-mechanical forms of thought typical of and unique to the West: the new science, pointing toward Galileo; the new "economics," pointing toward double-entry bookkeeping; and the new "politics," pointing toward bureaucracy and Machiavelli.

Against this triumphant new movement was another, far more diffuse and fragmented, movement of thought, which, like Anselm's, stressed the lack of immediacy and ultimacy in the new world of "reason," and which tried to find a place for man, and God, elsewhere. This cultural movement, where it related to the ancients, had two characteristics: 1) it recognized that the ancients, in their "vision of the mind," possessed the immediacy and ultimacy that it sought to recapture; but 2) whether or not its protagonists realized it consciously, the reorientation of 1100 A.D. remained irreversible: it was simply impossible to "go back." We thus find the creation of new forms of immediacy and ultimacy which endeavored to recapture the ancient experience of knowing and sensing but which was now, after Anselm and the reorientation of the categories of Western thought, inaccessible in its original form.

Petrarch is one of the examples Cranz uses to illustrate his thesis that when thinkers after Anselm studied the ancients and tried to recapture their experience of immediacy and ultimacy, they ended up doing something totally new. Toward the end of Book I of the *Secret*, Petrarch tells Augustine that he recently put aside his reading of philosophers and poets and read Augustine's *On True Religion (De vera religione)* with great interest. Augustine observes that although the language of his book is that of one who espouses the truths of the Catholic faith, a good part of the book is based upon the teachings of Socrates and Plato. Furthermore, Augustine says, it was a statement of Cicero's that inspired him to begin this book (Petrarca 1955, p. 66): discussing various opinions concerning the existence of the soul after death, Cicero speaks of those who are able to think only in corporeal terms. "For they could see nothing with the mind, but referred everything to the eyes. Indeed, it requires a powerful intellect to call the mind back from the senses, and lead thought away from habit" *(Tusc.* I, 16, 37).

Cranz observes that this program of "seeing with the mind" is central to Petrarch's thought.[2] And yet what Petrarch means by "seeing with the mind" is very different from what Cicero and Augustine meant. Ancient "seeing with the mind," Cranz argues, "was a conjunctive vision of intelligible beings, and Petrarch has no such vision nor, indeed, any such intelligible beings" (Cranz, p. 11). Toward the end of *On True Religion* Augustine writes:

> We are reminded by the things we judge to see that by which we judge, and as we turn from the work of art to the law of the arts, we see with the mind that form *(species)* in comparison with which even those fair things through it are foul. "The invisible things of God from the creation of the world are clearly seen as they are intellected through what has been made" [Romans I, 20]. (LII, 101)

What Augustine "sees" with his mind is something no material eye could see. It is the "law of the arts," an intelligible, not a corporeal, being.

Petrarch's "seeing with the mind," as he describes it in the *Secret,* is quite different. He uses his *imagination* to evoke the immediacy of *sensuously* perceived experience. In a famous passage, Augustine tells Petrarch how to meditate on death in such a way that the experience shakes him to the very core of his being. It is not enough, he tells him, just to hear the word "death" or to remember briefly a death:

> [O]ne must linger longer and with intense meditation run over *(percurrere)* each member of the dying one, as the extremities already grow cold, the middle of the body burns and drips with a distressing sweat, the side throbs, and the life-giving breath slackens with approaching death.

The passage continues for some time as Augustine describes many more details of the body of a dying person. He tells Petrarch to meditate in the same way on the pains of hell. "[A]ll should come before the eyes *(ante oculos venerint),*" he says, "not as feigned but as true, not as possible but as necessarily and inevitably to come and as even now almost present . . . (Petrarca 1955, pp. 54 and 56). Then Petrarch tells Augustine how he immerses himself in such meditations daily, especially at night, "when freed from the cares of day, my mind *(animus)* gathers itself into itself *(se in se ipsum recolligit)*." He tells how he places himself in the posture of a person who is dying, and imagines intensely everything horrible that comes to mind concerning the hour of death "to such an extent that, placed in the agony of dying, I seem to myself at times to see *(conspicere)* Hell and all the evils you tell of . . . " (ibid., p. 58).

When Cicero speaks of "seeing with the mind" in the *Tusculan Disputations,* he is speaking of those things, such as the soul, which cannot be seen with the eyes, that is, which cannot be seen corporeally. A good part of Augustine's treatise *On True Religion* concerns a human being's struggling to pass from the corporeal to the incorporeal, from the experience of matter to a perception of spirit. We have already seen from our study of some of Cicero's writings, moreover, how the individual, in contemplating the heavens, strives to rise above the circle of the moon to become one with the perfect wisdom, virtue, and reason of the universe. In *On True Religion* Augustine takes up as well the ancient problem of the One and the Many, and speaks of how the soul, through grace given to it by God, returns "from many changeables to the one unchangeable" *(a multis mutabilibus ad unum incommutabile) (De vera religione* XII, 24; see also XXI, 41). The contrast between Cicero and Augustine on the one hand, and Petrarch on the other, is sharp and clear: rather than rising above the human when he meditates, Petrarch sinks down deep into himself, and rather than struggling to contemplate spiritual and unchangeable realities, he conjures up the most vividly sensuous and fleshy images he can imagine. In Ciceronian terms, Petrarch embraces the perturbations of the lower soul, rather than trying to rise above them.

In speaking of Petrarch's sensitivity to the sound of words, especially in their therapeutic aspect, we observed how he describes his experience of reading, especially of reading aloud, as a deep inner experience: he says he has read Vergil, Cicero, and other ancient writers so much that their words have penetrated all the way down into the marrow of his bones; and he speaks of the sound of his own words read aloud as sinking down inside of him and piercing him there with their hidden points. In the *Secret,* Petrarch tries to pull his mind together and "center" his thoughts on vivid and terrifying images of physical death. These are some of the ways Petrarch found of retreating within himself and creating an autonomous center there. The contrast with Cicero and Augustine, moreover, shows us something which it would be impossible to see in the West from an exclusively twentieth-century point of view: that Petrarch's sense of self is nourished by an obsession with matter, with the physical and the corporeal, as opposed to the spiritual. As Petrarch himself was able to recognize, it was based upon a vision of reality consciously limited to the world beneath the circle of the moon.

We have already used Petrarch's description of his life, his studies, and his fears to investigate the origins of the *studia humanitatis*. Cranz's thesis concerning the fundamental differences between the ancient and modern categories of thought helps us to see Petrarch in an even fuller light. It is precisely because they show so clearly how and why he revised the ancient categories of thought that Petrarch's writings are the best source we have or will ever have for understanding not only the origins of the modern self, but its very nature. In this respect Petrarch may prove to be more useful to us than Freud. Freud, good scientist that he tried to be, arrived at an understanding of the human psyche which is essentially ahistorical: like the human body itself, the fundamental structure of the human psyche, along with the laws of its operation, remains the same throughout history. This belief has given rise to the academic subdiscipline of "psychohistory," which is based upon the assumption that what we know about human psychology today can help us discover the motivations of human actions in the past. But in reading Petrarch we are led back to the ancients, and in seeking to understand Petrarch's transformation of the ancients, we discover that they thought of their individual lives as part of the whole world of being, while the only whole we can envision lies within. We are thus led to the realization that our own sense of self is historically unique, that it is not biologically determined, but is rather the manifestation of a great change in Western consciousness which may have begun around 1100 A.D., and which received perhaps its richest cultural expression during the Renaissance. The *studia humanitatis* constituted an important part of this cultural expression, for the Renaissance humanities arose as a curriculum for this new experience of the self. Let us now look at what happened to this curriculum, and the concept of the self it implied, in the centuries between the Renaissance and our own time.

PART TWO

---

*The Death of the Humanities
in the Modern World*

CHAPTER 5

DEGENERATION FROM WITHIN

ᕭ

THE HUMANITIES have had a strangely cyclical history. They degenerated in the late Renaissance, came back to life in the early eighteenth century, and have degenerated again in our own time. The deterioration of a tradition is usually due to both internal and external factors, to contradictions and weaknesses within the tradition itself, and to social, economic, and cultural changes in the society of which the tradition constitutes a part. Let us begin by looking at those factors inherent within the humanities themselves.

It is a sign both of our own cultural amnesia, and of the fragmentation and specialization to which the tradition of the humanities has been liable, that the history of this tradition has never been examined as a whole, but only in fragments: the history of classical scholarship, the history of education, the history of classical political ideas, and the historical evolution of Renaissance individualism are all established areas of research. But no one, to my knowledge, has asked how all of these fragments might fit together to form the history of the humanities.

This may be because until our own time no one has felt the need to examine such a history. The reports of all the national commissions on the humanities since the Second World War have tended to see the humanities as coterminous either with the history of mankind, or with the history of Western civilization, usually beginning with ancient Greece. It is only with the so-called "crisis of the humanities" that the question of defining and understanding the humanities historically becomes a relevant and a useful one. And what, in the final analysis, does a historical understanding of this crisis mean? If there is any truth to Hegel's dictum that "the owl of Minerva takes wing at dusk," that is, that one can understand only what has already happened, then certainly the very fact that some of us, at this particular moment in time, feel compelled to understand the *history* of the humanities implies that the tradition of the *studia humanitatis* has "already happened."

Let us now try to understand what happened to this tradition. We can begin by examining the triumph of scholarship, the first—at least from a chronological point of view—factor that contributed to its deterioration.

The Triumph of Scholarship

Any cultural movement that requires learning and scholarship risks degenerating into nothing but scholarship. This is what happened to the Renaissance humanities: at the hands of their professional practitioners they degenerated into philology and antiquarianism.

The history of classical scholarship, at least in its main outlines, has already been told. Sir John Edwin Sandys, *A History of Classical Scholarship* (1967), Rudolf Pfeiffer, *History of Classical Scholarship from 1300 to 1850* (1976), and Ulrich von Wilamowitz-Moellendorff, *History of Classical Scholarship* (1982) are useful studies. Anthony Grafton's recent work on Joseph Scaliger (1983) not only takes us deeply into the life of one of the key figures in this tradition of scholarship, but offers a fascinating picture of the academic debates and scholarly issues involved in the early practice of classical philology. It is not my intention to summarize these books here. I want rather to state what the history of classical scholarship can tell us about the deterioration of the humanities.[1]

The reason for the degeneration of the original humanities into pure scholarship lies in the specific "tools" and skills necessary for establishing a dialogue with classical antiquity. One needs, first of all, the writings of the ancients. Petrarch and his disciples searched the cathedral and monastery libraries of Europe for lost manuscripts of ancient authors. In 1333 in Liège, for example, Petrarch discovered Cicero's speech *Pro Archia*, the speech from which Salutati borrowed the term *studia humanitatis*. Of much greater importance for his own life, in 1345 Petrarch found, in the cathedral library at Verona, a manuscript of Cicero's letters to Atticus, to his brother Quintus, and to Brutus. It was these letters, as we have seen, that inspired Petrarch to collect his own.

But finding a manuscript of a lost work is often only the first step in rediscovering the voices of the past. In copying manuscripts, scribes make mistakes, and sometimes they intentionally change words they have difficulty deciphering or understanding. Textual criticism, which had been practiced in classical antiquity, began again in the West when Petrarch carefully compared two manuscripts of Livy's history of Rome. He studied variant readings, and then emended a number of passages.[2] But it is important to note, in light of what was to come as soon as the study of classical antiquity became institutionalized, that in trying to produce a text as close as possible to the original, Petrarch was not engaging in scholarship merely for the sake of scholarship. Petrarch's study of the text of Livy's history grew out of two writing projects he was then engaged in: *Africa*, a long epic poem in Vergilian hexameters on Scipio Africanus, and a prose work *De viris illustribus*, "Concerning Famous Men," on ancient Roman heroes. Petrarch used Livy for both, and emended the text critically at the same time. Petrarch's study of classical antiquity, moreover, grew out of an attempt to live through the social and religious crises of his own time. Scholarship, for Petrarch, was thus never an end in itself, but only a tool for accomplishing something much more meaningful and important.

What can be said of Petrarch can be said equally well of two other great humanists whose important scholarly activities were subordinated to and directed by their theological and social concerns: Lorenzo Valla (1407–1457) and Desiderius Erasmus (1466?–1536).

By chance, Petrarch's copy of Livy wound up a century later in the hands of Valla, and Valla added his own notes to Petrarch's. Valla continued Petrarch's work of establishing the best text of Livy. It is a sign of his scholarly ability that many of his emendations are still accepted today. Indeed, his work marks a decisive stage in the development of textual criticism during the Renaissance. But Valla, like Petrarch, was not a professional scholar; gaining knowledge of classical antiquity was never an end in itself. Valla engaged in a long struggle against scholastic theology and its use of Aristotelian logic and metaphysics as ways of thinking and speaking about God. Like Bruni before him, he discounted all that had been written about philosophy and theology in the West following the fall of the Roman Empire, and turned his attention instead to the Fathers of the Church and to Scripture itself. Again like Bruni, he mastered Greek in addition to classical Latin. In his *Adnotationes in Novum Testamentum* he compared St. Jerome's Latin version of the New Testament, the famous Vulgate, to the Greek original, and made a list of Jerome's errors of translation. In many ways Valla anticipated the Protestant Reformation, for he wanted to hear the word of God directly, unencumbered by scholastic commentaries and poor translations.[3]

When Erasmus chanced upon a manuscript of Valla's *Adnotationes* in an abbey library near Louvain, he discovered in Valla an important predecessor. Valla's critical notes on Jerome's translation were extremely useful to Erasmus in his own great scholarly work, his edition of the Greek text of the New Testament and his translation of it into Latin.

Like Petrarch, Bruni, and Valla, Erasmus engaged in textual criticism not as an end in itself, but as a way of bringing about what he hoped would be a cultural and religious renovation. Erasmus believed strongly that the spiritual decline of his age was due to a lack of knowledge of God as He appears in the Bible and in the writings of the Fathers of the Church. He ridiculed scholastic theology, just as Valla, Bruni, and Petrarch had done before him, because he believed that spiritual and moral renovation could be achieved only by direct contact with the ancient texts. But these texts would have to be revised, in order to bring them back as close as possible to the original, and such revision would require an improved knowledge of Greek and Latin, and even the study of Hebrew. For Erasmus, then, textual criticism was a direct way of arriving at *veritas evangelica*, the truth of the Gospel. The spiritual corruption of his age, he believed, was related to the corruption of its hallowed texts. By purifying these texts of the errors which had crept into them over the centuries, one could restore them to their simple truth, a truth available to all.

In terms of its influence, Erasmus's greatest work was his edition of the New Testament in its original Greek. The text was sanctioned by the Medici pope Leo X. Luther used it in his revolutionary lecture on Paul's Epistle to the Romans, and as one of the main sources for his German translation of the New Testament.

The greatest humanists, then, studied classical antiquity in order to solve the problems of their own times. But as the *studia humanitatis* became institutionalized in the schools of Europe, and the tools of textual criticism became more refined, the study of the ancients became an end in itself, and the love of classical antiquity was replaced by devotion to the profession of philology.

In a review of Anthony Grafton's *Joseph Scaliger: A Study in the History of Classical Scholarship* (1983), Donald R. Kelley gives a thumbnail sketch of this degeneration. It is worth repeating here because of its brevity and clarity. Kelley points out that the great textual scholars of the generation following Valla's were more expert, but also more narrow and less reflective. Ermolao Barbaro, Filippo Beroaldo, and Angelo Poliziano—who was also an outstanding poet—were essentially grammarians. "They were even more literal- (hence critical- and perhaps historical-) minded than were their rhetorical colleagues," Kelley observes, with Bruni and Valla in mind, "concerned as they were not with their own discourse and its social implications but rather with the correction—the 'emendation' and 'castigation'—of ancient texts, Greek as well as Latin" (Kelley 1985, p. 80).

Kelley observes that while the great sixteenth-century Hellenists such as Guillaume Budé and Erasmus were able to achieve a synthesis of grammar and rhetoric, of intellectual inspiration and textual criticism, this synthesis came to an end as a result of the religious wars of the sixteenth century. Erasmus's scholarship was engagé, as was Luther's. When the smoke cleared around 1560, the new generation of "humanists" who emerged "in the backlash to the defilement and politicization of humanist scholarship" turned away from the big questions that had concerned Petrarch, Bruni, Valla, and Erasmus, and dedicated themselves instead to the preservation of "pure scholarship." Kelley writes:

> Typical of this group, Scaliger, as Grafton points out, tended to avoid contemporary relevance like the plague, at least in his published work (for his conversations were filled with attacks on popery). More than anyone he and his colleagues were responsible for giving antiquarianism (like "grammar") first its good, and then its bad, name. If their books and editions had any socially redeeming value, it was neither apparent nor advertised; and if they had any philosophical significance, it was inadvertent. Not reason or imagination but rather memory was the faculty prized by these men. No wonder their reputations hardly survived that "age of genius" in natural philosophy which many of them lived to see but hardly to appreciate. (Ibid., p. 81)

But this avoidance of contemporary relevance did not last forever. Two centuries later there was a revival of classical studies in Germany. Nietzsche noted that the new era began on 8 April 1777, when Friedrich August Wolf, who later was to write a famous *Prolegomma ad Homerum* destined to have a profound effect on Greek studies, entered the University of Göttingen and insisted on being enrolled as "studiosus philologiae," a student of philology.[4]

While the first revival of classical studies in the Renaissance had been interested primarily in the world of ancient Rome, this new revival was concerned with ancient Greece. It began primarily as a literary and cultural movement, led by men such as Winckelmann (1717–68), Lessing (1729–81), Herder (1744–1803), Goethe (1749–1832), and Wilhelm von Humboldt (1767–1835), who saw in the study of Greek antiquity a means of discovering ideals which could shape and illuminate modern life and art.[5] German "pan-Hellenism" was nourished by a fertile contact between university scholars and artists, writers, and intellectuals who lived outside a strictly academic milieu. Goethe, for example, had a high regard for scholarship; he made good use of his friendship with Friedrich August Wolf and Gottfried Hermann, another great scholar, and at several different times in his life he studied Greek art and literature to the extent he felt necessary for his own creative work and thinking. He even employed a good scholar, Friedrich Wilhelm Riemer, as his assistant. When Wolf, in his book on Homer, argued that there was no Homer because the Homeric epics were in fact the compilation of a succession of miscellaneous lays which had evolved collectively over the centuries, Goethe reacted with hostility, but then changed his mind after discussing the theory with Wolf himself.[6]

In some ways this second revival of classical studies rivals the early Renaissance itself in the extent to which artists, writers, and statesmen used the study of antiquity to address the concerns of the present. This was true not only in Germany, but also in nineteenth-century England, as the example of Matthew Arnold so clearly shows.[7] But this efflorescence of a vital interest in classical antiquity was dead by the time of the First World War, and it was classical scholarship itself that helped to kill it.

Academic philology, especially in the great German universities of the nineteenth century, was deeply affected by perhaps the two most powerful and characteristic intellectual trends of the century: the vast development of historical studies, and the growth of the natural sciences. History, archeology, epigraphy, and the new discipline of comparative linguistics began to take their place alongside of textual criticism in the academic study of antiquity. Philology was now called *Altertumswissenschaft*, "science of the ancient world." No longer interested exclusively in the emendation of ancient texts, scholars such as Ulrich von Wilamowitz-Moellendorff, who graduated four years after Nietzsche from Schulpforta, the most famous classical school in Germany, now tried to understand classical antiquity as a whole and bring this understanding to bear, if need be, in establishing and interpreting a particular text.

This was an admirable goal, but there were several things wrong with the method. First of all, scholarship quickly became separated from literature. In their research and writings, academic philologists began to emulate the natural sciences, especially what appeared to men of the nineteenth century as the marvelous ability of these ascendant sciences to discover concrete "facts." Classical scholars, inspired to give their own profession a veneer of positivistic respectability, went looking for "facts." Soon they began collecting "facts" for their own sake, and ended up judging their work and that of their colleagues by the number of concrete facts they had been able to establish positively. Scholars began to "produce" scholarship. And as the whole of classical antiquity was now a potential source for the discovery of new facts, increased specialization was inevitable.

But what good is it to accumulate mountains of new information about classical antiquity unless this information can be of some use in the present? Nietzsche saw clearly how the humanities in his own time

had degenerated into scholarship, and his observations are as relevant
now as they were a hundred years ago.

In notes for an 1871 course entitled "Introduction to Philology"
(*Einleitung in das Studium der classischen Philologie* [Nietzsche 1920]), Nietzsche listed what he believed were three requirements for becoming a
good philologist: a bent for teaching; a "delight in antiquity" (*Freude
am Alterthum*); and a pure desire for knowledge (ibid., p. 340). Of
the three, Nietzsche treated the second as the most important. He
went on to observe that modern classical education is designed to produce *scholars*, a goal quite different from the purpose of ancient Greek education.[8] For Nietzsche believed that most German philologists of his
time were devoted to the accumulation of facts for their own sake.
They worked hard, but they lacked ideals and, what was worse, love
for the object of their study. In *On the Genealogy of Morals (Zur
Genealogie der Moral)* Nietzsche writes:

> . . . Scholarship today has neither faith in itself nor an ideal beyond itself,
> and wherever it remains passion, love, devotion, suffering, it represents
> not the reverse of the ascetic ideal but its latest and highest form. Does
> this sound odd to you? There are many decent, unassuming, industrious
> scholars among us, who appear quite content with their tiny niche and
> therefore claim, somewhat immodestly, that everybody should be con-
> tent with things as they are these days—and especially in the humanities
> and in science where so much useful work remains to be done. I quite
> agree. I would be the last to try and spoil the pleasure these honest schol-
> ars take in their work, since I like what they are doing. *But the fact that
> men work industriously at their disciplines and are content with their work does
> not prove that scholarship as a whole today has a purpose, an ideal, or a passion-
> ate conviction.* As I remarked earlier, the reverse is true. . . . Scholarship
> today is the refuge for every kind of maladjustment, bland disinterest, self-
> contempt, bad conscience. Its incessant activity only thinly disguises its
> lack of ideals, the want of a great love, its dissatisfaction with a restraint im-
> posed upon it from without. . . . (III, 23, translated in Nietzsche, Sum-
> mer 1963, p. 26. My emphasis)

What Nietzsche is saying here is not too different from what Petrarch
and his early disciple Coluccio Salutati used to say concerning the ped-
antry of scholastic philosophers and theologians: it is better to be
good than learned.

Classical scholarship, Nietzsche believed, could even ruin one's
mind. "On running through the history of classical scholarship, it is
striking how few really gifted men have had a hand in it," he wrote in
his uncompleted book *We Philologists (Wir Philologen)*. "Among the
most famous," he continued, "are several who ruined their minds
with encyclopaedic erudition, and among the most intelligent were

some who could only use their intelligence on microscopic minutiae. It is a sad story. In my opinion no academic field is so poor in talent. It is the intellectually crippled who found a hobby horse in this verbal quibbling" (#51, translated in Nietzsche, Spring 1963, pp. 16–17). And in the same work he quoted with approval the judgment of the great classical scholar Friedrich August Wolf on amateurs in classical studies:

> "If they found themselves naturally endowed with a bent akin to the genius of the ancients or were capable of adapting nimbly to alien modes of thought and conditions of life, they doubtless acquired, even from their partial acquaintance with the best authors, more of the riches of those powerful natures and great models of thought and action than most of those who gave their entire lives to the interpretation of the classics." (#61, translated in Nietzsche, Spring 1963, p. 17)

In a typically vivid image, Nietzsche expressed his great fear: that the philologists, in their busy pursuit of facts, would eventually destroy classical antiquity. In *On the Future of Our Educational Institutions (Über die Zukunft unserer Bildungs-Anstalten)* he writes:

> I should like to take by the hand every talented or talentless man who feels a certain professional inclination urging him on to the study of antiquity, and harangue him as follows: "Young sir, do you know what perils threaten you, with your little stock of school learning, before you become a man in the full sense of the word. Have you heard that, according to Aristotle, it is by no means a tragic death to be slain by a statue? Does that surprise you? Know, then, that for centuries philologists have been trying, with ever-failing strength, to re-erect the fallen statue of Greek antiquity, but without success; for it is a colossus around which single individual men crawl like pygmies. The leverage of the united representatives of modern culture is utilised for the purpose; but it invariably happens that the huge column is scarcely more than lifted from the ground when it falls down again, crushing beneath its weight the luckless wights under it. That, however, may be tolerated, for every being must perish by some means or other; but who is there to guarantee that during all these attempts the statue itself will not break in pieces! *The philologists are being crushed by the Greeks—perhaps we can put up with this—but antiquity itself threatens to be crushed by these philologists!*" (Nietzsche 1924, pp. 80–81. My emphasis)

Nietzsche's own life and work exemplify these remarks. Although he was a brilliant student and became a full professor at Basel when he was only twenty-five, Nietzsche gave up his academic career five years later because his interests were too broad for the kind of narrow, specialized, positivistic scholarship that characterized classical studies at the time. Nietzsche's own work, moreover, contains errors of scholarship. When it appeared in 1872, *The Birth of Tragedy*, which presents Nietzsche's basic understanding of Greek antiquity, was derided by his colleagues for the mistakes in scholarship that it contained. And yet it was this book, and not the academic scholarship of his colleagues, that opened the way for a whole new understanding of Greek thought, culminating in works such as E. R. Dodds' *The Greeks and the Irrational*.[9]

We do not have to agree with Nietzsche's own interpretation of Greek antiquity to see that his criticism of his fellow philologists puts him in the tradition of Petrarch and Erasmus, for whom philology was never an end in itself, but only a means for bringing the ancients more fully to life in the present. Nietzsche went against the grain of *Altertumswissenschaft*, with its "scientific" pretensions, just as Petrarch went against the grain of the scholastic university culture of his own time. In the "Introduction to Philology" Nietzsche urges one to spend time on the real classics, and thus sacrifice the concept of antiquity as a whole in order to concentrate attention on the really creative and important periods of Greek thought. He was asking for judgment and discernment in deciding what to study in the ancient world, judgment and discernment which would be shaped by an attempt to use classical antiquity to address the problems of the present. As Hugh Lloyd-Jones, Regius Professor of Greek at Oxford, remarks, "Wilamowitz asked 'What can we do for philology?'; Nietzsche preferred to ask 'What can philology do for us?' " (1982, p. 178). Lloyd-Jones' observation on Nietzsche's use of the past is worth repeating here:

> In the past, we can find working models of culture and civilisation that may be of value to us when we make our own experiments. The main value of historical scholarship is that it can furnish such models to those who can make profitable use of them. Nietzsche himself was such a one. Ernst Howald rightly says that Nietzsche owed nothing to philology, but much to antiquity. . . . (1982, p. 179)

Nietzsche, of course, was an exception. Philology triumphed, and the study of classical antiquity, the object of the original humanities, became dry and forbidding. Although Nietzsche has for the most part been ignored by professional philologists, his remarks appear to rankle them still, and perhaps rightly so, since they must share some responsibility for the death of the original humanities. In 1963 William Arrowsmith wrote in the introduction to his translation of a substantial selection of Nietzsche's remarks on classics and classicists that "only last year the Press Committee of an American university rejected a translation of Nietzsche's *Wir Philologen* with the argument—doubtless sound—that it would antagonize the profession" (Nietzsche, Summer 1963, p. 5). But not all of the blame for the disappearance of the Greeks and the Romans from our classrooms can be attributed to the degeneration of the humanities into scholarship. Poor, uninspired teaching also had a hand in killing the humanities.

The Institutionalization of
Classical Learning in the Schools

One of the unfortunate, though perhaps inevitable, results of the success of the humanities in the schools was that all too many people ended up teaching Greek and Latin who were either poor teachers or uninspired teachers. Once the humanities became institutionalized and evolved into a pedagogical tradition in their own right, they continued to be taught primarily through the force of inertia, as Henry Sidgwick observed over a century ago (Farrar 1868, p. 81). It became possible for one to teach them merely because that was what one was trained and hired to do. It was no longer necessary, as it had been in the early Renaissance, to explain to oneself, much less to one's students, why classical Greek and Latin were worth learning. Thus the love Petrarch and Erasmus felt for the ancients was often never given a chance to kindle in the breasts of young children, for whom learning Latin was made to be a painful and tearstained ordeal by dull, often eccentric, and at times even sadistic, teachers. Charles Dickens describes poor little Paul Dombey's first dinner at Doctor Blimber's, where he has been sent to school:

> Only once during dinner was there any conversation that included the young gentlemen. It happened at the epoch of the cheese, when the Doctor, having taken a glass of port wine, and hemmed twice or thrice, said:
> "It is remarkable, Mr. Feeder, that the Romans—"
> At the mention of this terrible people, their implacable enemies, every young gentleman fastened his gaze upon the Doctor, with an assumption of the deepest interest. One of the number who happened to be drinking, and who caught the Doctor's eye glaring at him through the side of his tumbler, left off so hastily that he was convulsed for some moments, and in the sequel ruined Doctor Blimber's point. (*Dombey and Son*, chapter 12)

The British critic Cyril Connolly, describing his Georgian boyhood, has this to say of his Latin studies at Eton:

> In Latin Literature I read Horace and Virgil but did not enjoy them till later for Horace, except by Headlam, was not inspiringly taught and Virgil associated with too many punishments and in his moments of beauty with Macnaghten's vatic trances. Although I had learnt Latin all my life I still could not appreciate it without a crib and it was the arrival at the

end of my time of the Loeb translations, sanctioned by the authorities, that put its deeper enjoyment within my grasp. Virgil and Horace, without them, had been too difficult, too tearstained. . . . (Connolly 1948, p. 223)

And in *On the Future of Our Educational Institutions*, Nietzsche has the old philosopher say:

"I may be wrong . . . but I suspect that, owing to the way in which Latin and Greek are now taught in schools, the accurate grasp of these languages, the ability to speak and write them with ease, is lost, and that is something in which my own generation distinguished itself—a generation, indeed, whose few survivors have by this time grown old; whilst, on the other hand, the present teachers seem to impress their pupils with the genetic and historical importance of the subject to such an extent that, at best, their scholars ultimately turn into little Sanskritists, etymological spitfires, or reckless conjecturers; but not one of them can read his Plato or Tacitus with pleasure, as we old folk can. (Nietzsche 1924, p. 83)

The philosopher attributes this decline in teaching to the entrance into the schools of great numbers of uninspired philologists who find in the *technique* of linguistics a way of passing their time in the classroom. " 'Consciously or unconsciously,' " he observes, " 'large numbers of them have concluded that it is hopeless and useless for them to come into direct contact with classical antiquity. . . . This herd has turned with much greater zest to the science of language . . . ,' " which he calls an " 'expanse of virgin soil, where even the most mediocre gifts can be turned to account. . . .' " The philologist who has discovered comparative linguistics

now undertakes to teach the youth of the public schools [that is, the German gymnasiums] something about the ancient writers, although he himself has read them without any particular impression, much less with insight! What a dilemma! *Antiquity has said nothing to him, consequently he has nothing to say about antiquity.* A sudden thought strikes him: why is he a skilled philologist at all! Why did these authors write Latin and Greek! And with a light heart he immediately begins to etymologise with Homer, calling Lithuanian or Ecclesiastical Slavonic, or, above all, the sacred Sanskrit, to his assistance: as if Greek lessons were merely the excuse for a general introduction to the study of languages, and as if Homer were lacking in only one respect, namely, not being written in pre-Indogermanic. (Nietzsche 1924, pp. 81–82. My emphasis)

It takes no great leap of the imagination to update the relevance of these remarks by substituting "literary theory" for "the study of languages."

Across the channel, Dickens was by no means alone in his criticism of the way in which school children were taught about the Greeks and the Romans. Victorian England, slow to catch on to *Altertumswissen-schaft*, had no Nietzsche, but it did have some people who were able to state clearly what they thought was wrong with classical educa- tion.[10] They attacked both the hegemony Greek and Latin held in the schools, and the way they were taught. In 1867 F. W. Farrar, Assistant- Master at Harrow and afterward Dean of Canterbury, edited nine *Es- says on a Liberal Education*. It is a book well worth looking at for anyone interested in understanding the ancestry of much of what we think and say about the liberal arts and the humanities today. Writing at a time of ongoing public debate in England concerning the reform of teach- ing in schools and universities, the authors argue that literature and natu- ral science should form the basis of contemporary British education, and that literature should include modern as well as ancient classics. Since the essayists propose that the kind of training of the mind for- merly thought to be obtainable only through the study of Greek and Latin could just as easily, and perhaps even more effectively, be accom- plished by studying modern literature, John William Adamson, in his history *English Education: 1789–1902*, calls this book "one of the earli- est works to assert the possibility of a modern humanism . . ." (Adamson 1964). Now, over a century later, we can see that this so- called "modern humanism" is actually a misnomer, since the original humanities simply died, and nothing replaced them. But this does not detract from the importance of what these British reformers had to say about the deterioration of classical studies in their own times. In his essay "The Teaching of English," J. W. Hales describes what it was like to learn Latin in his time:

> Now, if we introduce a boy to the study of language by putting into his hands a Latin grammar and bidding him master the declensions, how will the case stand with him? How does the case stand with him? What wretched drudgery those early schooldays are! Is it one of the "penalties of Adam" that they should be so? Is it altogether boys' fault that their ele- mentary tutors find them so recalcitrant? Is it wholly through the dulness of their nature that they do not love the Conjugations at first sight, or con- ceive a passionate attachment for the Irregular verbs? What a queer thing their nature would be if it did kindle in them either flame! At all events, it does not. And the ordinary boy's early life is spent in a war of indepen- dence against his Primer. What is the genitive case of the Third Declen- sion to him, or he to it? Then, for the teacher, is the work more inspirit- ing for him? Can his enthusiasm relieve and dissipate the direful tedium? Can he brighten these lack-lustre exercises?
> "Pater ipse colendi
> Haud facilem esse viam voluit."

"Through me you pass into the city of woe," might well be inscribed over the doorway of the lower departments of our classical schools. "All hope abandon, ye who enter here." (Farrar 1868, pp. 302–303)

That many of our high school and college students still go through the same tearful drudgery in learning modern foreign languages, and even their own native English, that Hales imputes to the study of Latin, in no way weakens his criticism of the way Latin was being taught in England a century ago. But it does suggest that the high hopes he and his fellow essayists had of inspiring in students the love of *literature* by beginning their literary education with their native tongue of English, and then teaching a modern language such as French or German alongside of Latin, have not been realized. The schools and universities had certainly taken all the life out of the original humanities by Hales's time, but the "modern humanism" Adamson speaks of was stillborn. Later we shall look at some reasons why modern languages and literatures were unable to fill the vacuum left by the departure of the Greeks and the Romans. But for the present let us be clear about what killed the original humanities.

The Equation of the Classics with Training for the Mind

A sign of how tenuous any life-giving dialogue with classical antiquity had become within the English educational establishment of the last century can be found in a remark Henry Sidgwick reports in his essay, in the same volume, on "The Theory of Classical Education." An advocate of classical education, a certain Mr. Clark, had said, "It is a strong recommendation to any subject to affirm that it is dry and distasteful" (Farrar 1868, p. 137). Sidgwick comments:

> I cannot help thinking that there is some confusion here between "dry" and "hard." No doubt the faculties both of mind and body must be kept a sufficient time in strong tension in order to grow to their full strength: but we find in the development of the body that this tension can be longest and most healthily maintained, by means of exercises that are sought with avidity.

And then he muses in a footnote:

> It is curious, in contemplating English school life as a whole, to reflect how thoroughly we believe in natural exercises for the body, and artificial exercises for the mind. (Farrar 1868, pp. 137–38)

But it was not just the English who were taken with the educational philosophy of "mental discipline." Sidgwick quotes the following passage in French from Cournot's *De l'Instruction publique*, in which it is argued that the grammatical and literary study of a language "forms the whole man":

> Nothing lends itself better to the gradual and methodical development of all the intellectual faculties from childhood to adolescence than the grammatical and literary study of a language. The study exercises the memory, discernment, taste, judgment in all forms, logical or non-logical, that is to say, subject or not to classifications, to deductions and to precise rules. It forms the whole man.

> (Rien ne se prête mieux que l'étude grammaticale et littéraire d'une langue au développement graduel et méthodique de toutes les facultés intellectuelles de l'enfance et de l'adolescence. Cette étude exerce la mémoire, la sagacité, le goût, le jugement sous toutes les formes, logiques ou non logiques, c'est-à-dire, soumises ou non à des classifications, à des déductions et à des règles précises. Elle forme l'homme tout entier." [Farrar 1868, pp. 113–14])

The idea of mental discipline was related to the "faculty psychology" which enjoyed great popularity during the nineteenth century. The soul or mind, it was believed, was made up of independent faculties, that is, specific capabilities or talents, such as reason, memory, judgment, and observation. The goal of education was to sharpen and perfect these capabilities by exercising them strenuously. One of the attractive aspects of faculty psychology for educationalists was that it enabled them to talk about the form education should have while avoiding the more difficult question of its specific content. As Adamson points out in his history of English education, like the earlier Clarendon Commission, the Tauton Commission on secondary education, which reported its findings in 1867,

> was prone to value a branch of knowledge from the standpoint of its real or supposed power to "train the mind" rather than by the positive worth of its content. . . . A meticulous emphasis upon mental discipline, when wedded to a psychology of more or less independent "faculties" . . . was not calculated to assist the discussion of educational values; and it was just this psychology with precisely that emphasis which was in fashion in the 'sixties' and for a generation later amongst those who theorized about the curriculum. (Adamson 1964, pp. 260–61)

Exactly the same kind of thinking and talking about education were going on across the Atlantic. Laurence R. Veysey, in his *The Emergence of the American University* (1965), writes:

> Mental and moral discipline was the purpose which lay behind a fixed, four-year course of study in college. Such a course should be well marked with hurdles (like any demanding racetrack) and should be designed by ex-

pert interpreters of faculty psychology. In the mid-nineteenth century an argument sprang up within the ranks of orthodox educators over whether the sole purpose of college was training for mental and moral power or whether the accumulation of knowledge ("the furnishing of the mind") also had some legitimate place. Yale's Noah Porter usually took the more conservative path when he came to this fork in the road. "The college course," he asserted, "is preeminently designed to give power to acquire and to think, rather than to impart special knowledge or special discipline." This meant that the curriculum must inevitably demand hard work in abstract subjects. William F. Allen, later the mentor of Frederick Jackson Turner at Wisconsin, declared: "The student who has acquired the habit of never letting go a puzzling problem—say a rare Greek verb—until he has analyzed its every element, and understands every point of its etymology, has the habit of mind which will enable him to follow out a legal subtlety with the same accuracy." (Veysey 1965, pp. 23–24)[11]

What the defenders of classical education did not seem to realize was that by reducing the value of the study of Greek and Latin to the mental discipline it provided, they were laying the groundwork for undercutting the very hegemony which these two subjects then enjoyed in the schools. For the argument that the goal of liberal education is to train the mind to reason and think makes it impossible to single out any subject for special consideration, since one can find arguments to show that almost any activity—playing chess, for example—and not just those currently taught as part of the liberal arts curriculum, exercises some faculty of the mind. It was thus easy for nineteenth-century educationalists, such as those who contributed to Farrar's *Essays on a Liberal Education*, to argue, as Henry Sidgwick does in his essay, that the study of the natural sciences as well as the study of languages exercises the reason and the memory, develops "habits of accuracy and quickness," and trains and stimulates the important faculty of judgment (Farrar 1868, pp. 125–26).

If these arguments in favor of mental discipline seem familiar, it is because they still provide a fundamental part of every college's arsenal of arguments in support of a liberal arts education. We can open just about any college catalogue today with the certainty of finding some statement about how such an education trains the mind by teaching young men and women to think accurately and reason critically.

The cult of mental discipline, along with classical philology and uninspired, often sadistic, teaching, was another sign that by the nineteenth century the professional humanists, those who taught and did research in the languages and cultures of Graeco-Roman antiquity, had ceased to find any contemporary relevance and inspiration in their teaching and research. Others of course did. The shaping minds of the nineteenth century—one thinks of Hegel, Marx, Nietzsche, and Freud—

were all classically educated and thought about the present in terms of their understanding of classical man and society. But they were not part of the "humanistic" educational establishment, and it was here, in the schools, that the humanities' life-giving dialogue with classical antiquity degenerated.

In arguing that one striking sign of the deterioration of this tradition in the last century was the use of the idea of "mental discipline" by advocates of classical education, I have in mind the fact that the original *studia humanitatis* began as an explicit attempt to offer something more than training of the mind. After all, the public disputations and syllogistic reasoning which constituted the basic *technique* of teaching and research in medieval universities are examples of mental "training" which have never since been equaled in our educational institutions. Nothing exercised the reason and the memory more, developed more readily habits of accuracy, quickness, and mental agility, than the "mental gymnastics" adolescents at the universities of Paris and Bologna were put through in the thirteenth and fourteenth centuries. And it was precisely the hollowness of these gymnastics, their concern with form and their lack of a substantive content that one could use in his daily moral life, that the humanists, from Petrarch up through Erasmus and More, attacked continually. Writing about a man who had taught logic all of his life and was still teaching it in old age, as if it were the most important of the disciplines, Petrarch says:

> I know how much the Stoics . . . attribute to it. I know it is one of the liberal arts, and a stepping-stone for those who are pressing upwards to higher things. It is not useless armor for those who walk through philosophers' thickets. It arouses the intellect, marks off the path to truth, and shows how to avoid fallacies. Finally, if nothing else, it makes people quick and witty.

Today we say that a liberal arts education stimulates the mind and exercises the critical intelligence.

But Petrarch believed that education should do more. He continues:

> But where it is honorable to pass through, it is not praiseworthy to remain. On the contrary, the traveller who, because the road is pleasant, forgets the goal he has set for himself, is of unsound mind. The traveller's praise lies in having passed quickly through many things, and never having stopped short of the end of the journey. And who among us is not a traveller? We all, for a brief and hostile time, as during a rainy day in winter, make a long and difficult journey. Dialectic can be a part of this journey, but surely not the goal. And it can be the part of this journey we make in the morning, not in the evening. (*Fam.* I, 7, 13–14)

The goal Petrarch is talking about in the context of the journey of one's life is, of course, heaven and the salvation of one's soul. But we have also seen that Petrarch had another goal in mind: the molding and shaping of an inner self, a refuge from the blows of Fortune, an inner center of peace and harmony within the change and mutability of life beneath the circle of the moon. Logic or dialectic, "mental discipline," could not shape such a self. Only the study of the ancients could. And this leads us to the fourth factor in the internal deterioration of the tradition of the humanities: the attempt to substitute the study of the modern languages and literatures for the ancient ones.

The Ascendancy of Modern Language and Literature

At the same time as the humanities were becoming institutionalized in secondary schools and universities, the concept of the self and the humanities' relationship to it were changing. By the late eighteenth and early nineteenth century, proponents of classical education, especially in Germany, gave theoretical formulation to the goal of the original humanities—the shaping and cultivation of one's own unique, individual, autonomous self—which is broader, more explicit, and more self-conscious than any statement on education one can find in Renaissance humanist treatises.

As we have seen, in eighteenth-century Germany there was a revival of the study of classical antiquity. Artists and intellectuals turned to what they believed was the beauty, harmony, and perfection of ancient Greece in search of models to inspire their own art and thinking, and standards and ideas to illuminate the present moment in time. But while this classical revival was in no way as extensive as the earlier Italian one, its influence on educational ideals throughout Europe and America was immense. It led to a revival of the teaching and practice of classical philology in the universities, and to the reform and extension of classical education in the secondary schools. All the great German thinkers of the nineteenth century received classical educations. Marx wrote his Ph.D. thesis on the philosophy of Democritus and Epicurus, and Nietzsche began his career as a professor of classical philology at the University of Basel. But the most important figure as far as the history of the humanities is concerned is Wilhelm von Humboldt (1767–1835). Extremely well-educated, a successful diplomat, and, later in life the author of highly regarded studies on linguistics, as Minister of Education in Prussia (1809–10) Humboldt reformed the Prussian secondary school, the *gymnasium*, and helped to found the University of Berlin. He encouraged research on classical antiquity at the university and the teaching of Greek at the secondary level. His work inspired others outside of Germany. In England, advocates of serious classical scholarship, such as Mark Pattison, turned to the University of Berlin for inspiration. Reformers of secondary education, such as Matthew Arnold, looked to Humboldt's *gymnasium* as a model. Humboldt himself, it is interesting to note, had never been to school, having as a child been privately tutored, and spent only a short time at the university.

Humboldt's writings contain as clear an expression as can be found of education as the forming or shaping (*Bildung*) of the individual self through the study of classical antiquity, in this case the Greeks. Humboldt begins his work *The Limits of State Action (Ideen zu einem Versuch die Grenzen der Wirksamkeit des Staats zu bestimmen)*—which, incidentally, provided John Stuart Mill with the epigraph for his essay *On Liberty*—with the statement:

> The true end of Man, or that which is prescribed by the eternal and immutable dictates of reason, and not suggested by the vague and transient desires, is the highest and most harmonious development [*Bildung*] of his powers to a complete and consistent whole. (1969, p. 16)

The ancient Greeks provide the ideal model for this full and harmonious development of each individual's powers. In his essay *The Eighteenth Century (Das achtzehnte Jahrhundert)* he says:

> The sensitive lover of antiquity . . . admires with joyous wonder the Greeks for harmonious development of all their powers, for the noble freedom of their whole disposition, for the distance they kept between themselves and all menial tasks, for their distinguished indolence and their high esteem of the inner man [*inner Mensch*]. . . . (1963, p. 78)

The Greeks, in short, provide the autonomous self with an ideal of inner *perfection*. In his *History of the Fall and Decline of the Greek City States (Geschichte des Verfalls und Unterganges der griechischen Freistaaten)*, Humboldt writes:

> . . . in the Greeks alone we find the ideal of that which we ourselves should like to be and produce. . . . [T]he Greeks touch just that point in us which is the ultimate goal of all our own strivings. . . . They attract us because they heighten our independence and relate themselves to us only in the idea of ultimate perfection of which they are an undeniable model, permitting us to work toward it ourselves, although in different ways and by a different route. (1963, pp. 79 and 81)[12]

Matthew Arnold (1822–88) called Wilhelm von Humboldt "one of the most beautiful souls that have ever existed," and observed that Hum-

boldt "used to say that one's business in life was first to perfect oneself by all the means in one's power" (1966, p. 126). The quote is
from Arnold's *Culture and Anarchy*, first published in book form in
1869. This work has had an immense afterglow. It continues to be
quoted today—usually in the single phrase "the best that has been
thought and known in the world"—by those intent on defending
what they believe is the tradition of humanistic learning and teaching.
William Bennett builds his definition of the humanities around it in
the recent NEH report on the humanities in education, "To Reclaim
a Legacy" (Bennett 1984). And in fact, in the justly influential work
that *Culture and Anarchy* has become, Arnold achieved the clearest and
most powerful expression in the English-speaking world of the ideal
of humanistic education as the perfecting and shaping of one's self.
But what everyone who quotes Arnold in defense of the humanities
seems to forget is that Arnold, as Humboldt before him, tended to emphasize the role which studying the ancient Greeks can play in perfecting the inner self. This certainly is the message of *Culture and Anarchy*.
"[C]ulture," Arnold writes,

> places human perfection in an *internal* condition, in the growth and pre-
> dominance of our humanity proper, as distinguished from our animality.
> It places it in the ever-increasing efficacy and in the general harmonious ex-
> pansion of those gifts of thought and feeling which make the peculiar dig-
> nity, wealth, and happiness of human nature. (1966, p. 47)

Or more succinctly: culture, Arnold says, "simply means trying to perfect oneself and one's mind as part of oneself . . ." (ibid. p. 82).

This perfection is "a harmonious perfection . . . in which the characters of beauty and intelligence are both present. . . ." Beauty and intelligence, "sweetness and light," Arnold calls them, immortalizing a
phrase of Jonathan Swift's. In the same passage, he goes on to say that
it is in the ancient Greeks that we can find this true perfection, this sweetness and light: "The immense spiritual significance of the Greeks is
due to their having been inspired by this central idea of the essential character of human perfection . . ." (ibid. pp. 53–54).

The shaping of the self did not disappear with the decline of Greek
and Latin in the last century. As an ideal, it was carried over into our
own century, both in the general argument that a liberal arts education not only trains the mind but helps to form or shape "values"; and
in the more specific one that the study of literature has a "humanizing," even "moralizing," effect upon the student. Again, Henry
Sidgwick, a century ago, gave clear expression to arguments still repeated today. After contesting the hegemony which Greek and Latin
then enjoyed in the schools, Sidgwick turns, in his essay on "The The-

ory of Classical Education," to his own recommendations. He believes, first of all, that what he calls the "historical study of literature" will have the greatest utility in the intellectual life of his own age. "Such a course," he writes, ". . . would naturally contain a much larger modern than ancient element: it would be felt in framing it more imperatively necessary to represent French, German, and English thought of recent centuries, than to introduce us to any of the older influences that combined to determine our immediate intellectual antecedents" (Farrar 1868, p. 103). Sidgwick, in short, wants what we today call "contemporary relevance." Moreover, while he recommends the study of English, French, and German, from a purely intellectual point of view any language will do as long as it leads to the study of literature. He states that

> . . . we must remember that it is a point of capital importance that instruction in any language should be carried to the point at which it really throws open a literature: while it is not a point of capital importance that any particular literature should be so thrown open. (Ibid. p. 130)

Why is the study of *literature* so important? Here is the claim Sidgwick makes for it:

> Let us demand . . . that all boys, whatever be their special bent and destination, be really taught literature: so that as far as is possible, they may learn to enjoy intelligently poetry and eloquence; that their interest in history may be awakened, stimulated, guided; that their views and sympathies may be enlarged and expanded by apprehending noble, subtle, and profound thoughts, refined and lofty feelings: that some comprehension of the varied development of human nature may ever abide with them, the source and essence of a truly humanizing culture. Thus in the prosecution of their special study or function, while their energy will be even stimulated, their views and aims will be more intelligent, more central; and therefore their work, if less absorbing, not less effective. (Farrar 1868, pp. 129–30)

This passage contains an interesting mixture of two arguments. While Sidgwick has not left the idea of mental training behind, in speaking of a "truly humanizing culture" he has added to it faint echoes of the idea of *Bildung*, of the forming and perfecting of an inner self, as we find this idea expressed in Humboldt and Arnold. Lionel Trilling argues that while there are differences between Arnold's conception of what literature might do for the health of the State and Sidgwick's, the two are in much accord: "taken together, they constitute the rationale of our own modern theory of general education and they provide what is probably the strongest of all justifications that can be offered for making English literature a school or university subject" (Trilling 1965, p. 211).

Trilling goes on to say that in advocating the study of English literature we must make reference to what we call "the whole man." He observes that the study of literature has been traditionally felt to be
uniquely effective

> in opening the mind and illuminating it, in purging the mind of preju-
> dices and received ideas, in making the mind free and active. The classic de-
> fense of literary study holds that, from the effect which the study of litera-
> ture has upon the private sentiments of a student, there results, or can be
> made to result, an improvement in the intelligence, and especially the intel-
> ligence as it touches the moral life. (Trilling 1965, p. 212)

Trilling has been an eloquent spokesperson for exactly the kind of literary study he describes here. I have found some of his writings very
useful in thinking about the humanities and am deeply in sympathy
with an education which has as its highest object "the intelligence as it
touches the moral life." But I must use this eloquent description of
the value of literary study to demonstrate something which I am sure
Trilling never intended it to show: why the humanities have died in
our own time.

In speaking about the effect that the study of literature has upon "the private sentiments of the student," Trilling is talking
about what I have called the "personal self." The argument Trilling
gives voice to is one which Sidgwick makes, and to which Arnold
gives the classic formulation in *Culture and Anarchy*: that the proper cultivation of the personal or "private" self can have a salutary effect upon
the "public" self and its participation in the general life of the nation.
The threat to society in his own time, as Arnold saw it, was anarchy, anarchy stemming from the disorder resulting from the clash of social
classes and beliefs, all narrow, all influenced in one way or another by
what he saw as the pervasive materialism of his age. Arnold's remedy begins with the individual self: by means of "culture" (Humboldt's
Bildung), a person can transcend what Arnold calls his "ordinary self,"
and move onward to attain his "best self." And since everyone's "best
self" will see reality as it really is, and share in the same lofty values
and ideals, society, as the aggregate of all of these perfected selves,
will pass out of the state of anarchy and become one harmonious
whole.

Although he gave the most memorable expression to this vision of
the role of culture and education in the life of the nation, Arnold was
not alone in holding it. Trilling, in fact, quotes this passage from
Sidgwick's essay:

> . . . if the middleclass Englishman (as he is continually told) is narrow, un-
> refined, conventional, ignorant of what is really good and really evil in

human life; if (as an uncompromising writer says) "he is the tool of big-otry, the echo of stereotyped opinions, the victim of class prejudices, the great stumbling-block in the way of a general diffusion of higher cultiva-tion in this country"—it is not because these persons have had a literary ed-ucation, which their "invincible brutality" has rendered inefficacious: it is because the education has not been (to them) literary: their minds have been simply put through various unmeaning linguistic exercises. (Farrar 1868, p. 129)

But there is a profound difference between Arnold and Sidgwick, and Trilling does not see it. Culture, for Arnold, is "*a study of perfec-tion*" (Arnold 1966, p. 45). It "simply means trying to perfect oneself, and one's mind as part of oneself," and as such it "brings us light" (ibid., p. 82). Where does this culture, this light, come from? From the Greeks. Sidgwick thinks otherwise. He believes that any literary edu-cation will be effective as long as the students are drawn to a true experi-ence of literature, and not burdened down by meaningless linguistic ex-ercises. That the study of English literature will become the chief means for attaining a literary education is due merely to the fact that in England, and in America, English is the student's native language. But this is not the argument Arnold is making. The whole point of *Cul-ture and Anarchy* is to argue that all the English classes, and especially the philistine middle classes, need to study the Greeks in order to at-tain the harmonious development of all their spiritual faculties, and thus counteract the narrow and the one-sided development of the reli-gious, moralistic aspects of their being. In Arnold's terminology, it is a question of using "Hellenism" to balance "Hebraism."

In placing the Greeks at the center of his ideal of culture, Arnold is thus very much in the tradition of the Renaissance *studia humanitatis*, which combined a pedagogy of "self-cultivation" with a clear sense that such cultivation could best be accomplished by emulating the Greeks and the Romans. What Sidgwick and Trilling have done, is to separate the goal of perfecting the inner self from the Greeks and the Ro-mans as the unique standards against which this perfecting can be mea-sured. In fact, Sidgwick and Trilling provide no models, no standards at all for the attainment of "a truly humanizing culture," for "the im-provement of the intelligence . . . as it touches the moral life," other than the generic study of literature, especially English literature.

The rationale for the study of English literature which Trilling pre-sents as the one commonly invoked today is thus, for all the power it still may hold over us, not of one piece, but rather a composite of sev-eral strands of our intellectual heritage: faculty psychology, *Bildung*, and the concept of a personal self.

This is what remains today of the Renaissance *studia humanitatis*: a personal self, and the literary cultivation of that self. But the Greeks and the Romans are gone. We have bits and pieces of the original form, but we have lost its content. And yet perhaps Sidgwick and Trilling are right: if the study of Greek and Roman literature could once form and shape a self, why cannot the study of modern literature do the same?

Here I want to give an answer which I suspect Arnold himself might not have understood, but which Trilling, who opens his last work, *Sincerity and Authenticity*, with the words, "Now and then it is possible to observe the moral life in the process of revising itself . . . ," would have, especially if his own studies of this moral life had proceeded farther back in time than Shakespeare and the English Renaissance: the harmonious perfection which Arnold and Humboldt found in the Greeks, the inner courage and wholeness Petrarch found in the Romans, came from the fact that these peoples looked outward, not inward, for the meaning of their lives. They had individuality, to be sure, but, unlike post-Renaissance man, they had no "personality." They had a self, but it was an extensive, not an intensive self. They experienced their individual lives as *parts* of a greater whole, the whole of the cosmos, the whole of the *polis*, the whole of the *civitas*. The harmonious perfection one finds in the Greeks, the moral wholeness and integrity one finds in the Romans, come not from any ancient *Bildung,* any arduous cultivation of an inner center, but from the contemplation and imitation of the heavens, from an experience, to use Cranz's terms, of the immediacy and ultimacy of the ground of being. As Cicero put it, man is not perfect, but is "some little part of the perfect," *quaedam particula perfecti.* By participating in perfection, the ancient Greeks and the Romans were able to do deeds and create works of art and literature which the humanists in the Renaissance and the eighteenth- and nineteenth-century neo-Hellenists could easily take as standards for their own *inner* perfecting.

In a moment we will look at the question of whether or not it was indeed ever possible to perfect a unique, autonomous, inner self. But accepting, for the sake of argument, that such an enterprise could be successfully undertaken, I want to argue that this shaping cannot be accomplished without models to *emulate,* and that the Greeks and the Romans are the only such models capable of such emulation. The reason is clear: from the Renaissance on, our literature knows nothing but personal selves. And the personal self, in all its glorious autonomy—which is also a form of isolation from both the cosmos and society—is too little, too weak, too "self-centered"—too imperfect in short, to inspire another human being to self-perfection. We can learn a great deal about our selves and our experience of the human by reading and re-reading *Hamlet*. But if our goal is Bruni's or Arnold's "perfecting" of a self, there is nothing in *Hamlet* to emulate. And it is not just a question of irreconcilable conflicts. Sophocles' characters had conflicts. But they were not inner conflicts; they were built into the very structure of being. Although it may have been inscrutable to them, Sophocles' tragic heroes believed in an objective moral order in the universe, an order upheld by the gods.[13] It seems almost too trite to repeat that Shakespeare's characters retain such a deep interest for us because their conflicts, like our own, are in the final analysis inner conflicts. They have unique, autonomous selves the way we do. But it is for this reason that they could never form the basis of a "humanistic" educational program: one can ponder, study, even brood over, the image in a mirror; but he can never emulate it.

Adamson is thus wrong when he says in his *English Education: 1789–1902* that the *Essays on a Liberal Education* "assert the possibility of a modern humanism, the possibility of extracting from modern studies, and especially from modern literature, much which was commonly thought to be derivable from the study of Greek and Latin alone" (Adamson 1964, p. 310). Or rather, to be more precise, he is correct in reporting what Farrar's volume asserted, but the assertion was wrong. There is something to be derived from the study of classical antiquity which no modern literature can provide: an experience of the human as participating in the whole world of being. There can thus be no such thing as a "modern humanism" divorced from what the humanities originally were: the study of the Greeks and the Romans as models for individual and collective behavior.

A further reason for the decline of the humanities, then, along with the degeneration of classical studies into philology, the institutionalization of Greek and Latin in the schools, and the interest in the form of the curriculum ("mental discipline") as opposed to its content, was the attempt, on the whole quite successful, to equate modern language and literature, especially English literature, with the kind of "culture" Matthew Arnold believed the Greeks could provide. By the late nineteenth century, the goal of the Renaissance humanities, that of creating or perfecting a personal self, had thus been divorced from the original content of the humanities, the study of Greek and Latin language and literature, and, along with mental discipline, had become the major argument for a liberal arts education in general.

But this is not the end of the story. Now even the goal of the Renaissance humanities has all but vanished.

Lionel Trilling, in a lucid essay he wrote over a decade ago on

"The Uncertain Future of the Humanistic Educational Ideal," pointed out that we can see the decline of the humanistic ideal of *Bildung* by observing

> the fate of an idea that once was salient in Western culture: the idea of "making a life," by which was meant conceiving human existence, one's own or another's, as if it were a work of art upon which one might pass judgment, assessing it by established criteria. This idea of a conceived and executed life is a very old one and was in force until relatively recently; we regard it as characteristic of the Victorian age, but it of course lasted longer than that. It was what virtually all novels used to be about: how you were born, reared, and shaped, and then how you took over and managed for yourself as best you could. And cognate with the idea of making a life, a nicely proportioned one, with a beginning, a middle, and an end, was the idea of making a self, a good self. (Trilling 1982, pp. 174–75)

As we have seen, the idea of making a unique, autonomous, inner self, lies at the heart of the original *studia humanitatis* as they come into being in the early Renaissance.

Trilling believes that "[t]his desire to fashion, to shape, a self and a life has all but gone from a contemporary culture whose emphasis, paradoxically enough, is so much on self" (1982, p. 175). This is not entirely correct. The image of one's life as a narrative and the desire to mold one's life into a particular shape or form can still be found in cultural discourse today—often, interestingly enough, in the writings of those, such as feminists, who actively struggle to become conscious of their lives and shape them in new ways. Phyllis Rose, for example, in the prologue to *Parallel Lives: Five Victorian Marriages*, writes:

> I believe, first of all, that living is an act of creativity and that, at certain moments of our lives, our creative imaginations are more conspicuously demanded than at others. At certain moments, the need to decide upon the story of our own lives becomes particularly pressing—when we choose a mate, for example, or embark upon a career. . . . There is a kind of arranging and telling and choosing of detail—of narration, in short—which we must do so that one day will prepare for the next day, one week prepare for the next week. . . . To the extent that we impose some narrative form onto our lives, each of us in the ordinary process of living is a fitful novelist, and the biographer is a literary critic. (Rose 1983, pp. 5–6)

The archetype for the kind of "novelist" Rose is talking about might well be Ghismonda, the famous heroine of the First Tale of the Fourth Day of Boccaccio's *Decameron*. Ghismonda fashions her own self, and if not her life, at least her death, by pouring poison into the gold cup containing her lover's heart, which her father has sent her after having him murdered, and drinking it, thereby asserting her own creative will in the face of the kind of adverse Fortune that so haunted the early Renaissance. But the story of Ghismonda serves as a standard against which to measure how weak the metaphor of making one's life, even among those who are trying to do just that, has become today. The metaphor lives on, and Phyllis Rose and others make inspiring and sensible use of it. But Trilling is right in suggesting that the image of one's life as a narrative is now given nowhere near the credence it had not so long ago. This is certainly apparent within our schools today. Most arguments now made in favor of the "practical" value of studying literature are closer to the old "mental discipline" than to *Bildung*. Proponents of modern literary theory and criticism, for example, when pressed to explain the value of "close reading," usually reply that learning to "deconstruct" a text is marvelous exercise for the mind.

Why does the old humanistic ideal of making one's self have so little force today? Trilling believes it is because people now want to envision their lives as a multiplicity of options, and that this ideal works against the earlier one of shaping a particular life and a particular self, with all the limitations such a "narrative" implies:

> . . . if you set yourself to shaping a self, a life, you limit yourself to that self and that life. You preclude any other kind of selfhood remaining available to you. You close out other options, other possibilities which might have been yours. Such limitation, once acceptable, now goes against the cultural grain—it is almost as if the fluidity of the contemporary world demands an analogous limitlessness in our personal perspective. (1982, p. 175)

It has become a cliché to speak about the "rapid change" characteristic of life in the late twentieth century, and doubtless social mobility, economic dislocation, and the commercialization of "life styles" make it difficult for people to shape their material lives, and psychologically unattractive for them to think of their "selves" as coherent narratives in which the preceding chapters in some ways determine those that follow. How could people ever embark on radical career changes, or enjoy "mid-life crisis," if they thought of their lives the way the Victorians did?

But while the social factors Trilling alludes to have doubtlessly contributed to the demise of the humanistic educational ideal in our own time, the question of what has happened to this ideal is also related to important changes within the tradition itself. For example, if, as I have argued, the emulation of the ancients and the perfecting of a self are inseparable, the goal of perfecting a self was fated to lose its power once people tried to emulate the inward-turning and individualistic protagonists of modern literature. But even this is not the whole story. At the heart of the demise of the tradition of the humanities lies the instability of the very concept of a personal self.

The Belief in an Unconscious Self

As we have seen, beginning in Germany in the late eighteenth century and extending all the way up to the Victorian period in England, proponents of classical education, such as Wilhelm von Humboldt and Matthew Arnold, spoke explicitly of the goal of classical education as the shaping and perfecting of a personal self. At the same time, however, philosophers and writers, especially in France, were beginning to portray what they perceived as the elusive and ultimately problematical nature of the self. Continued inspection of the self would ultimately contribute to the demise of classical education, for it would render the whole humanistic educational enterprise questionable by replacing the "cultivation" of the self through the study of classical antiquity with the "analysis" of the self by means of the new science of psychoanalysis. It was thus in the early nineteenth century, during the final consolidation of classical education, in both theory and practice, that the highest goal of this education, the cultivation of the self, began to be undermined.

It is worth considering the main point of Lionel Trilling's *Sincerity and Authenticity:* that the moral life, the life of the self, changes over time, and that by our own time our understanding of the "self," and our hopes of being "true" to it, of living "authentic" lives, lives springing from our deepest self and not conditioned by those around us, have become problematic. As stages in the self's growing self-consciousness and deepening alienation from its social role, Trilling discusses Diderot's *Rameau's Nephew*; Hegel's use of this work in his chapter on "Spirit in Self-Estrangement" in *The Phenomenology of the Mind*; Conrad's *The Heart of Darkness*; and Freud's theory of psychoanalysis. Unlike people of an earlier age, whose selves were integrated and whole because the individual and society were one, Rameau's nephew lives with the consciousness that his social self is not his true self. Social being is nothing but impersonation. The nephew tries to rise above this unhappy condition, and the moral quandries it engenders, through art, through his own virtuoso impersonations. Hegel had this aspect of the nephew's character in mind when he argued that the self's estrangement from its former integrated self, and with it the disintegration of one's consciousness, are necessary steps in the self's attainment of real freedom and autonomy. Conrad added another dimension to our understanding of the self's conflict with society by describing a dark and secret self that calls into question the very possibility of civilization. In many respects, this is the self that Freud tried to probe through psychoanalysis.

Having looked at the origins of the humanities in the Renaissance, we can see that Freud's theory of psychoanalysis now stands out, in retrospect, as the final and in some ways as the inevitable result of the belief that at the center of every human being lies a unique inner self. But Freud's work represents as well a striking example of the deterioration to which the tradition of the humanities has been liable, for the concept of psychoanalysis effectively undercuts the Renaissance belief that this inner self can be consciously molded and shaped. The original *studia humanitatis* held out the promise that through a careful study of certain ancient writers one could create an inner unity to substitute for the ancient unity of the individual and the cosmos. One can try to fashion his own soul, however, only as long as he believes there is something there to fashion. But what happens when he tries to understand what it is that is being fashioned? The concept of a unique, individual, autonomous self becomes problematic when it leads to the realization that one can never really know his true "self." This is exactly where Freud's discovery of the "unconscious" leads: consciousness of a self becomes consciousness of that which is unconscious. It is one thing for Shakespeare to have Polonius tell his son Laertes "to thine own self be true"; it is another for Freud to write, in the radical revision he made in 1919 of his theory of the unconscious, that "[t]here is something in the ego which is also unconscious, which behaves exactly like the repressed—that is, which produces powerful effects without being itself conscious and which requires special work before it is made conscious" (quoted in Trilling 1972, p. 147).

"Which requires special work before it is made conscious." Freud's theory of the unconscious has not only complicated our understanding of the inner world by dividing it up into the id, ego, and superego; it has given us the idea that important aspects of the self remain not only unconscious, but actively hostile to being brought into consciousness. This way of thinking about one's inner life renders the humanistic educational ideal obsolete: if our real self is partly unconscious, and actively hostile to being brought into consciousness, it is not something we can perfect or shape. Personal authenticity in our own time thus has nothing to do with education as the conscious attempt to impose an order on our thoughts and feelings. It is concerned rather with attempting to live in harmony with partially unconscious energies and desires.

In order to fathom the depths within, psychoanalysis employs certain techniques which, like the concept of the unconscious self, completely undercut the old humanistic ideal of *Bildung*. Having rejected as regressive the old humanistic program of consciously forming and shaping a moral character on the basis of external models, Freud put in its stead a technique of self-analysis notable for its tolerance of ambivalence and fluidity of commitment. In words reminiscent of Trilling's remarks on how the desire to keep one's "options" open throughout life has undermined the old humanistic educational ideal, Philip Rieff observes in his book *The Triumph of the Therapeutic: Uses of Faith after Freud* that

> if the analytic therapy has been effective, the therapeutic learns to keep in touch with the options around which the conduct of his life might be organized; ideally, all options ought to be kept alive because, theoretically, all are equally advisable—or inadvisable, in given personal circumstances. . . . Life is individual. Well-being is a delicate personal achievement. . . . (Rieff 1966, p. 50)

To achieve this well-being through psychotherapy demands a kind of "scientific" detachment from and ambivalence toward—not to mention suspicion of—one's "self," and its desires and fantasies, for which the old humanistic ideal of *Bildung*, of self-cultivation, could be seen as even harmful:

> The analytic capacity demands a rare skill: to entertain multiple perspectives upon oneself, and even upon beloved others. A high level of control is necessary in order to shift from one perspective to another, so to soften the demands upon oneself in all the major situations of life—love, parenthood, friendship, work, and citizenship. *Such conscious fluidity of commitment* is not easily acquired. (Ibid., p. 51. My emphasis)

Psychoanalysis is in some ways an attempt to live in a time when most of the ideals of previous ages have lost their force. Compared to the standards of molding and shaping one's self which we traced from Petrarch and Bruni to Humboldt and Arnold, modern psychoanalysis amounts to settling for much less: a modicum of mental stability based upon tolerance of ambiguities and fluidity of commitment, without a concern, so characteristic of the original *studia humanitatis*, for the attainment of virtue and moral goodness. "A man can be made healthier without being made better—rather morally worse," Rieff observes. "Not the good life but better living is the therapeutic stan-

dard" (p. 58). It is precisely in this cautious settling for less, in an age be-
reft of moral ideals, that Freud's attraction lies:

> Freud appeals to us because his wisdom is so cautious. Surely he is not to
> be blamed for living at a time when the inherited aspirations of the
> Greek, Christian, and Humanist past had gone stale, when both Athens
> and Jerusalem, not to mention Paris, Oxford, and the Italian Renaissance
> cities, have become tourist spots rather than shrines of pilgrims in search
> of spiritual knowledge. With no place to go for lessons in the conduct of
> contemporary life, every man must learn, as Freud teaches, to make him-
> self at home in his own grim and gay little Vienna. (Rieff 1966, p. 59)

Not everyone, of course, is a Freudian. The point of Rieff's book is
to show how those who inherited Freud's legacy—Jung, Adler, Reich,
and D. H. Lawrence—attempted to go beyond Freud's cautious, resigned, and morally neutral attempt to analyze the inner world. These
men wanted to turn psychoanalysis into a new religion capable of substituting new moral certainties and commitments for stale and dying
ones. Rieff believes, in fact, that we are in the midst of a profound cultural revolution, out of which will emerge a new type of man:

> Americans no longer model themselves after the Christians or the
> Greeks. Nor are they such economic men as Europeans believe them to
> be. The political man of the Greeks, the religious man of the Hebrews
> and Christians, the enlightened economic man of eighteenth-century Eu-
> rope . . . has been superseded by a new model for the conduct of life. Psy-
> chological man is, I suggest, more native to American culture than the Puri-
> tan sources of that culture would indicate. (Ibid., p. 58)

Rieff exaggerates, of course: other "faiths" continue to vie for the
American's allegiance. But Rieff is certainly correct in arguing that
Freud invented a new doctrine of prudence, a new—albeit much more
cautious—wisdom for Western man in the twentieth century, to replace the wisdom of the ancients. The concept of the "unconscious,"
moreover, has become such a part of the intellectual culture of our
times that it probably influences to some degree our understanding of
ourselves, whether we make self-analysis our life's vocation or not.[14]

In our own time, then, the techniques of psychotherapy have come
to replace, at least provisionally, the traditional pedagogy of the humanities. But while Freud's theory of psychoanalysis can be understood as
a reaction to the deterioration of the humanities in the last century, as
an attempt to live without the ideals and models of the past, it must
also be seen, in the broad sweep of Western history, as the culmination of a development which begins with the emergence of the *studia
humanitatis* in the Renaissance: the belief that every human being is an au-

tonomous individual, for whom happiness is to be sought in the cultivation of one's own unique inner self. From this point of view, psychoanalysis is nothing but the analysis of this self shorn of the classical models that once gave it form. Therapy has replaced emulation, analysis has replaced *Bildung*, but the goal remains surprisingly the same: the achievement, as Rieff puts it, of "what Freud considered the most difficult of all personal accomplishments: a genuinely stable character in an unstable time" (p. 57).

CHAPTER 6

CHANGE FROM WITHOUT

❧

WE HAVE SEEN NOW how the humanities, as a cultural tradition carried on primarily by scholars and teachers, were liable to the particular kinds of degeneration—lifeless scholarship and uninspired teaching—which come from the institutionalization and professionalization of learning. The very success of classical education contributed to its demise. People who had no use for the ancients in their own lives embarked upon careers in classical education and scholarship. In their hands, the Greeks and the Romans lost any real relevance for the present and became dry and difficult objects of teaching and research. Those who had no love for the ancients, but who chose nevertheless to study and teach them, downplayed the importance of the study of Greek and Latin for their own sake, and justified it as a form of mental gymnastics, or as a subspecialization of comparative linguistics, or as a way of adding more knowledge to *Altertumswissenschaft*. It is thus quite understandable that those for whom the ancients did have something important to say, such as Nietzsche, might choose to leave the profession of classical philology entirely, while those who wanted to reform education felt it was necessary to break the hegemony of Greek and Latin in the schools, and attain the ideal of the original Renaissance humanities, the shaping and cultivation of the inner self, through the study of modern subjects, especially one's own native language and literature. In this climate psychoanalysis pushed the inward thrust of the Renaissance self, now shorn of its communion with the ancients, as far as it would go, and turned the analysis of the self, not its cultivation, into one's life project.

These then were some of the major factors internal to the tradition of the humanities which led to its ultimate degeneration and decay. But the humanities did not decay in a vacuum. We must not forget that there were some very practical, what we today would call "career-oriented," reasons for the initial success of the humanities in schools throughout Western Europe, and that their later decline was due in part to changes in career patterns, especially among the ruling classes. Let us look now at some of these changes.

The Rise of the Vernacular and the Growth of Contemporary Knowledge

In attacking the hegemony of classical studies in the British educational system, the essayists in Farrar's *Essays on a Liberal Education* provide an insight not only into why the teaching and study of Greek and Latin lost its preeminence, but also why it kept it for so long. Sidgwick writes: "It is true that these literatures [Greek and Latin] are no longer supposed to contain all knowledge; even their claim to give the best teaching in mental, ethical, and political philosophy, the last relic of their old prestige, is rapidly passing away . . ." (Farrar 1868, pp. 103–104). Hales, in arguing for the study of English, says that in the "linguistic dispensation which seems dawning, no language is called common or unclean. Latin can no longer stand aloof from the languages of modern literatures as if they were inferior things, of suspicious contact. That old exclusive *régime* is gone by for ever . . ." (Farrar 1868, p. 295).

"That old exclusive *régime*" was based on several factors. From the time of the Roman Empire all the way up into the modern period, Latin was the learned language of Europe. It took the rise of the nation states and centuries of growth of the vernacular literatures before English, French, Italian, German, and Spanish replaced Latin as languages of higher learning. Dante wrote the *Divine Comedy* in Italian, rather than Latin, so that it would have a larger audience. But Petrarch, concerned to establish his fame in the ages to come, chose to write what he considered his most important works, such as his unfinished epic poem *Africa,* in Latin rather than in Italian: he could not be certain Italian would always be read in the future; he assumed Latin would. It is interesting in this regard to read what John Dryden wrote in the dedication to his 1679 version of Shakespeare's *Troilus and Cressida:*

> How barbarously we yet write and speak . . . I am sufficiently sensible in my own English. For I am often put to a stand in considering whether what I write be the idiom of the tongue, or false grammar, and nonsense couched beneath that specious name of *Anglicism*; and have no other way to clear my doubts but by translating my English into Latin, and thereby trying what sense the words will bear in a more stable language. (Quoted in Hartman 1980, p. 234)

Dryden describes what he perceived as the awkwardness and instability of English as a literary language compared to Latin. English, of course, eventually attained the same "certainty of words and purity of phrase" Dryden felt that Italian and French had already achieved, and no one in our own age would consider, much less be capable of, translating his English into Latin in order to check his writing. But we tend to forget how recent is the full acceptance of English as a literary language worthy of study and teaching. As late as 1867, Hales found it necessary to assert that Latin could no longer look down on the vernacular literatures as inferior things.

In a sense, the study of Latin contributed to the rise of the modern languages. One of the ultimate aims of rhetorical training in Greek and Latin, first in Italy, then throughout the rest of Renaissance Europe, was to enable preachers and rulers to improve their vernacular style, to give their as yet unsystematized native speech precision, amplitude, grace, and power. German grammar, for example, is a creation of Renaissance scholars, desirous to model their own unformed language on classical Latin. One external reason for the demise of the original humanities, perhaps the most obvious reason, was thus the growth of the vernacular languages as effective tools of learning and discourse.

Sidgwick gives another reason: Latin and Greek literature can no longer be supposed to contain all knowledge. That Sidgwick felt compelled to state this fact shows once again how comparatively recent the demise of classical studies has been. And Sidgwick is not talking just about modern scientific knowledge; he calls into question the hegemony of the ancients in the study of psychology, ethics, and politics. Later we shall look at the question of whether or not the new "knowledge" Sidgwick has in mind was really an advance over the old. But for the present it is enough to observe that a recognition of modern, contemporary sources of knowledge was another factor contributing to the decline of the original humanities.

The replacement of Latin by the vernacular languages and the growth of new kinds and sources of knowledge are not, however, the only external explanations for the demise of the humanistic educational program. There are even more profound ones. Today one of the major arguments both for and against—depending on one's point of view—the humanities, and the liberal arts in general, is that they do not prepare a person for a specific job or profession. They used to. The study of Latin in particular used to prepare a person for several possible careers. We can learn a great deal about the role the humanities used to play in Western society and what has happened to them by looking at the types of careers once available to students of the classics. In the early modern period, the study of classical antiquity not only shaped the modern individualistic self: it played a fundamental role in the evolution of the legal and political institutions of Western society.

Merchant Capitalism, the Absolutist State, and Roman Law

In his essay on "The Theory of Classical Education," Henry Sidgwick observed that while the classicists are the strongest supporters of a liberal as opposed to a professional education, they also argue that Latin and Greek are useful professionally. Sidgwick questions the validity of this argument and states that a knowledge of the classical languages is of direct professional use only in three instances: clergymen should know Greek in order to read the New Testament in the original; lawyers should be able to read Roman law, for the benefit of society, if not for their own careers; and scholars need to know Latin in order to study the early history of science and of any European nation (Farrar 1868, pp. 89–91).

What Sidgwick says about the direct usefulness of Greek and Latin for clergymen and scholars is still true today, even if few clergymen actually read the New Testament in its original Greek and fewer scholars than ever read Latin. But it is clear that by the late nineteenth century it was no longer necessary for one to have a firsthand knowledge of Roman law in order to be a lawyer. This again was a fairly recent change. From the Middle Ages up to modern times, the extensive use of Roman law provided an immediate and direct contact between daily life in Western Europe and the culture and civilization of classical antiquity; the study and adaptation of Roman jurisprudence to contemporary needs played a crucial role in the transition from feudalism to capitalism in Europe, and in the emergence in the sixteenth century of the centralized monarchies of France, England, and Spain.[1]

Already toward the end of the eleventh century the Italian jurist Irnerius (c. 1055–1130), founder of the school of law at Bologna which for centuries to come would attract students from all over Europe, including Petrarch, began a systematic study of the *Corpus iuris civilis,* the codification of Roman law carried out in the sixth century under the emperor Justinian. Over the next hundred years, Irnerius' school of Glossators methodically reconstituted and classified the legacy of the ancient Roman jurists.

The Church was the first to make use of this legacy in the shaping of its centralized administration, and it quickly saw the value of administrators trained in Roman law. But Roman legal concepts and procedures left their most lasting mark in secular society. Let us look first at Roman civil law, and its importance for urban merchants, bankers, and manufacturers.

In the feudal society of the Middle Ages, there was no legal concept of absolute and unconditional private property. Property rights were multiple and overlapping.[2] They were juridically defined by the concept of *conditional private property*. The distinction between *dominium directum* and *dominium utile* or *usufructus,* for example, was invented in the late twelfth century "to account," as Perry Anderson puts it, "for the existence of a vassal hierarchy and hence a multiplicity of rights over the same land" (Anderson 1979, p. 25). The notion of "seisin," which Marc Bloch defines as "possession made venerable by the lapse of time" (Bloch 1961, p. 115), offers another example of medieval thinking on ownership. It defined "an intermediate conception between Latin 'property' and 'possession,' which guaranteed a protected ownership against casual appropriations and conflicting claims, while retaining the feudal principle of multiple titles to the same object . . . " (Anderson 1979, p. 25).

This concept of conditional and multiple ownership was never wholly adequate to the economy of the towns which grew up during the medieval period, an economy based upon trade, banking, and manufacturing, that is, upon the production and exchange of privately owned commodities. The importance of Roman civil law, from an economic point of view, lay in its recognition of *absolute, unconditional private property,* and of the buying and selling of such property. The reemergence of Roman law in the Middle Ages led to legal efforts, inspired by classical precedents, to delimit notions of ownership. Anderson points to the reappearance of the concept of single and unconditional ownership of land, expressed by the maxim *superficies solo cedit* ("the surface becomes the property of a single person") (ibid., p. 26). Furthermore, in the cities, where for several centuries merchants had gradually evolved new forms of legal expression concerning trade but with no uniform framework of legal theory or procedure, the superiority of Roman law lay not only in the clarity of its notions of private property, but also in its procedures of equity and contracts that regulated the exchange of private property. The revival of Roman civil law, then, played an essential role in the juridical regulation and rationalization of early capitalism, and was a powerful cultural and intellectual weapon in the merchants' and manufacturers' struggle to free themselves from the restraints of feudal lords and feudal conceptions of property.[3]

Roman law was equally important, though for entirely different reasons, in the emergence of the absolute monarchies of France, England, and Spain during the course of the sixteenth century.

Classical Roman jurisprudence recognized two kinds of law: civil law (*jus*), which regulated economic transactions between private citizens, and public law (*lex*), which dealt with the relationship between the State and its subjects. Roman public law, especially those juridical concepts and procedures elaborated after the fall of the Republic and under the reign of the emperors, was by far the most powerful intellectual weapon available to the new monarchies for furthering their program of territorial integration and administrative centralization. Although in practice the monarchs did not always and everywhere achieve absolute power, the Roman jurist Ulpian's famous maxim, *Quod principi placuit, legis habet vigorem,* "what pleases the ruler has the force of law" (*Digesta* I, 4, 1), became the constitutional ideal of the new Renaissance monarchies.

Part of the reason for the rapid success of the new curriculum of the *studia humanitatis* throughout Western Europe was the fact that the original humanities came into being during an extensive and ongoing revival of Roman law. The "rebirth" of classical antiquity in the Renaissance, after all, was dictated by practical concerns: businessmen used the authority of ancient Rome to justify and regulate the buying and selling of private property, kings and princes used it to justify the consolidation of their power. Both the merchants' use of Roman civil law and the monarchs' adoption of Roman public law encouraged the study of the laws and political institutions of ancient Rome. Although they later ridiculed it, both Petrarch and Bruni studied law at the university before turning to classical literature, history, and moral philosophy. Bruni may have urged Niccolò Strozzi to devote himself to the *studia humanitatis* rather than civil law, but from another perspective it is easy to see that the *studia humanitatis* were in essence merely a broadening of the study of classical antiquity which had already begun with the revival of Roman law.

It is important to realize too, in explaining the initial success and the later decline of the humanities, that the curriculum of the *studia humanitatis* itself provided one with definite career opportunities. *Humanista* was the name given by fifteenth-century Italian university students to a teacher of the *studia humanitatis*. As people who could teach, write, and speak good classical Latin, the humanists were preceded by the earlier medieval profession of *dictatores* and notaries, people trained in writing and drawing up legal contracts and documents, and in carrying on diplomatic correspondence. With the economic and territorial growth of the cities of central and northern Italy, and as increasingly well-educated merchants began drawing up their own contracts, these *dictatores* and notaries gradually shifted their traditional literary activities from private business to public employment in the growing municipal bureaucracies. The society of central and northern Italy had always been much more urban, and much more closely tied to Roman political institutions and to the memory of Rome than the primarily agrarian, feudal society north of the Alps. Now, beginning in Florence in the late fourteenth century, the Italian Renaissance city-states consciously emulated the great cities of classical antiquity, especially Rome and Athens, as Leonardo Bruni's oration *In Praise of the City of Florence (Laudatio Florentinae Urbis)* so clearly shows. A knowledge of classical Latin thus enabled one to find employment as a teacher, a diplomat, or an official in the municipal chancery. The profession of the medieval *dictator* and notary thus evolved into that of the Renaissance humanist.[4] At the same time, a knowledge of ancient history was becoming increasingly useful for a career in politics. It is striking, in fact, how quickly the early humanists influenced the political language of their age. A recent study of material in the Florentine archives has revealed that as early as 1413–1414 Florentine politicians were using examples from Roman history in their debates in the town hall.[5]

The acquisition of a classical education as a road to professional advancement which began in Florence in the early Renaissance became common north of the Alps two centuries later, though with the significant difference that now it was the old feudal aristocracies, and not just the new merchant and banking classes, who encouraged their children to learn Latin and Greek. We can understand why the new *studia humanitatis* found favor among the feudal aristocracies by looking at the nature of the absolute monarchies, and the role they played in enabling the nobility to retain its power in early modern Europe.

In the sixteenth century, centralized monarchies in England, France, and Spain replaced the pyramidal, fragmented sovereignties of the medieval period, along with their estates and liege systems. The abolition of serfdom and the emergence of centralized monarchies did not, however, signal the decline of the feudal aristocracy, but rather its reconstitution. The peasant revolts of the fourteenth and fifteenth centuries threatened the power of the feudal lords, who saw the traditional basis of their power, juridical coercion and personal dependence, weakened. But these revolts did not destroy feudal relations in the countryside. Despite the fact that the new centralized state had the power to break or discipline individuals or groups within the nobility itself, the absolute monarchies actually ministered to the collective needs of the feudal aristocracy by using the new centralized and militarized royal power to maintain the nobility's domination of the peasants in the countryside.

The absolute monarchies introduced standing armies, national taxation, codified law, and a permanent bureaucracy administered by lay officials, in contrast to the clerical bureaucrats of the medieval period. They thus continued, on a much larger scale, the process of centralization and secularization of government that had already occurred in the Italian Renaissance communes, a process in which the emulation of the classical city-states played a fundamental ideological role, as the history of the art and culture of early Renaissance Florence so clearly shows. To an increasing extent, the absolute monarchies were administered by officials drawn from the feudal nobility. Indeed, it was primarily in the royal administrations that the feudal aristocracy reconstituted itself, passing from a rural and military elite to become a service elite, in part through the sale of offices and tax farms. And the best way to obtain a post in the royal administration was now to acquire a humanistic education. Let us look at the example of England.

It was during the reign (1485–1509) of Henry VII that the *studia humanitatis* were taken up seriously in England. The transition from clerical to predominantly lay administration at all levels of English society, a steady increase in schools (new colleges were founded at Oxford and Cambridge at this time), and a rapidly growing public for books, as evidenced by the number of new "gentlemen" who had private libraries, made England much more receptive than it was at the beginning of the century to a new educational program formed along Italian lines.[6]

During the reign (1509–47) of Henry VIII, the scions of the titled nobility began to flock to Oxford and Cambridge, and filled up the great grammar schools, "pushing the poor out of the scholarships."[7] Feudal aristocrats, who for centuries had been content to give their eldest sons a traditional courtly and military training, now began to send them to universities and secondary schools, domains of learning formerly reserved for men destined for some kind of clerical career. The education they acquired was the new classical, humanistic one, imported from Italy and modified by the writings of Northern humanists such as Erasmus. We have already pointed to the role which Roman public law played in the emergence of the new monarchies. Now, in the new conditions of a centralized and secularized administration, the *studia humanitatis* offered a curriculum which promised to train wise and loyal public servants who, through the study and emulation of Roman examples, would be inspired to serve their prince, and would acquire the practical wisdom to govern the commonwealth and the virtue to do so out of only the highest of motives.

Sir Thomas Elyot describes this new kind of education in *The Boke named the Governour*, published in 1531. Elyot himself is an example of the new governing class in England. His father Richard was a Wiltshire gentleman who served as Crown Receiver in his native county, was then made Sergeant-at-Law, and finally Judge of Assize. During Thomas's boyhood his father lived chiefly in London and frequented the humanists who gathered around Thomas More. Thomas Elyot was thus exposed to the new *studia humanitatis* as a young man. He even learned Greek from the scholar Linacre. In 1511 his father obtained the position of Clerk of Assize for his son, and Wolsey later appointed him Clerk to the Privy Council.

By "governors" Elyot means all lay officials: royal secretaries, judges in the King's Court, justices of the peace, sheriffs, clerks of the Exchequer or the Chancery.[8] His book prescribes for them a classical education in the belief that such training in the classics will provide the state with loyal and trusted servants.

Elyot's curriculum begins with poetry. "[P]oetry," Elyot writes, "was the first philosophy that ever was known: whereby men from their childhood were brought to the reason how to live well . . ." (Elyot 1962, p. 46). By the end of his thirteenth year, the boy destined to serve in the governance of the commonwealth will have read, in the original, parts of Aesop, Lucian, Aristophanes, Homer, Vergil, Ovid, and Horace. Elyot speaks of the power of poetry in words reminiscent of Petrarch's: ". . . the child's courage, inflamed by the frequent reading of noble poets, daily more and more desireth to have experience in those things that they so vehemently do commend in them that they write of" (ibid., p. 33).

At fourteen the boy turns to the study of classical prose, reading the orators and writers on rhetoric, then geographers and historians. At the end of his seventeenth year he passes on to the third stage of his education, the study of classical moral philosophy. Here we see how very much in line Elyot is with the earliest Italian humanists, such as Bruni and Petrarch, not only in the content of his curriculum, but also in its stated purpose. The goal of this entire program of study is not learning, but wisdom, "so excellent wisdom that throughout all the world should be found in no common weal more noble counsellors . . ." (ibid., p. 52). This is practical wisdom, "Prudentia" or "Sapience," a combination of knowledge and virtue applied to practical affairs (Woodward 1967, p. 292). It was what built Rome. And in it lies true nobility. "Let young gentlemen," Elyot writes,

> have oftentimes told to them, and (as it is vulgarly spoken) laid in their laps, how Numa Pompilius was taken from husbandry which he exercised, and was made king of Romans by election of the people. What caused it suppose you but his wisdom and virtue, which in him was very nobility, and that nobility brought him dignity? (Elyot 1962, p. 105)

Feudal governance knew no centralized State. It was based upon parcellized sovereignty, personal dependence, and, in the countryside, a direct relationship between lord and peasants. It was thus highly personal and individual. The value of the humanities for the landed nobility of the new absolute monarchies was that ancient Rome now provided them with an example of a State, and service to it. In France, a century before Elyot wrote *The Governour,* Ghillebert de Lannoy wrote an essay of advice to his son on education. He urged him to read "Valerius Maximus, Tully [Cicero], Lucan, Orosius, Sallust, Justin, and other historians," explaining that "you will wonder at the many virtuous examples of how our predecessors loved honor and the public weal and faced death for the good of the land" (quoted in Hexter 1961, p. 64).

Ideally, the *studia humanitatis* could train anyone for public service. But the nobility believed that they were especially suited for government office. In their treatises on the education of aristocrats, Humphrey Gilbert in England, Montaigne and François de la Noue in France, and Philippe de Marnix in the Netherlands, pointed out to their fellow nobles that the prince or commonwealth had a proper claim to their good service, and offered advice on why or how aristocrats should educate themselves to provide such service. The two main reasons they gave for educating those born into the nobility, as opposed to men from other social classes, emphasized the importance of authority, duty, and honor: subjects are naturally more obedient to men born to authority than to those who are not; and it will ultimately cost the commonwealth more to give offices to those seeking public office for money and careers than to those bound to the State and the prince by duty and honor.[9]

We see then that the new *studia humanitatis* provided an ideal educational curriculum for bourgeois merchants and feudal nobles alike, for both the Italian city-states and Northern European monarchies. This is why Leonardo Bruni, who did so much to identify Florence with the "liberty" of Republican Rome,[10] could at the same time address his treatise *On Studies and Letters* to Battista di Montefeltro, wife of the feudal lord Carlo Malatesta, to whom Bruni's predecessor as Chancellor of Florence, Coluccio Salutati, had written as well about the new *studia humanitatis*. In a letter written in the late 1420s or early 1430s to one of the first Englishmen to take an interest in the new humanities, Duke Humphrey of Gloucester, Bruni says that while literary studies adorn other men, they are especially necessary to princes or rulers (*principes*). Are not, Bruni asks, the knowledge of things and of right living necessary above all for princes, "in whose hands and will the governance of cities and peoples is placed?" (Bruni 1969, p. 139). Leaders and princes above all, he says, need eloquence, the power to persuade and dissuade, to excite and calm souls. Since a knowledge of morals and the ability to speak well can be attained only through "letters and studies" (*litterae et studia*, that is, the *studia humanitatis*), "those who find fault with literary studies in a prince, find fault with excellence and authority" (ibid.). A century later we find Thomas Elyot saying the same thing to his fellow nobles.

These are some of the specific reasons why anyone looking for a career in "governance" during the Renaissance would have found it helpful to study the new humanities. To put it in contemporary terms, learning classical Latin and acquiring a ready knowledge of Greek and Roman history and moral philosophy were skills one needed to have in order to find a job in government. Now one needs them no longer. Why?

From Renaissance Governor to Modern Manager

In looking at the external factors which once fostered the rise of the humanities but which are no longer operative today, it is easy to understand why Roman law no longer commands the attention it used to: its contributions to the legal conceptualization and regulation of commodity exchange have by now been fully absorbed into our legal system.[11] In the case of Roman public law, which defined the relationship between the State and its subjects, whatever was of use in the rise of the modern nation state has already been incorporated into the legal tradition of the West, and that which was limited to monarchs, such as Ulpian's dictum that "what pleases the ruler has the force of law," died with the absolute monarchies. Although the rule of law, and to a great extent Roman law, distinguishes the civilization of the West from all other world civilizations, learning to read Latin in order to study Roman law, as Sidgwick observed over a century ago, is no longer necessary.

But Roman law, as we have seen, was only one point of contact between classical antiquity and the economic and political institutions of early modern Europe. As Petrarch and the early humanists never tired of repeating, the goal of study is to become good, not more learned. Acquiring wisdom and virtue, especially Roman virtue, now personalized and interiorized, was the highest goal of the *studia humanitatis*. Why has this ideal vanished in our own times? After all, this high goal of education was always expressed in universal terms; as an *ideal* it was tied to no particular form of government and to no social class, although certain classes may have believed, or preferred to believe, that they could attain it more readily than others. But as an ideal, education in wisdom and virtue for the purpose of serving one's fellow citizens in public office is as valid today as it ever was. Why has it disappeared from our discussions of the goal and purpose of education? The answer to this question takes us to a much more contemporary reason for the demise of the humanistic educational tradition.

The humanities emerged, as we have seen, out of Petrarch's attempt to triumph over contingency by distancing himself from it in his inner life. Unable to find order and harmony in the world around him, Petrarch turned within. He tried to fill his mind with the biographies of ancient Roman heroes in order to strengthen his own soul by comparing his courage to theirs. That their battles were real physical ones while his were, for the most part, psychological, made no difference to Petrarch: he wanted to be able to withstand the blows of Fortune by emulating what he believed was the *inner* strength of his ancient heroes. The original *studia humanitatis,* as a program of primarily literary studies formulated by Petrarch's followers, contain this ideal of forming, shaping, molding one's inner self through the study of other human lives, especially the ancient Romans.

Although he was deeply concerned about contemporary political issues, Petrarch never held public office, nor was he interested in doing so. But some of his famous early followers did: Coluccio Salutati and Leonardo Bruni, for example, held the office of Chancellor of the Republic of Florence. In addition to being directly useful in preparing one to study the legal and political institutions of ancient Rome, in the fifteenth-century Italian city-state or the sixteenth-century absolute monarchy, nothing prepared a person better for leadership and public service than the molding and shaping of an autonomous inner self, which Petrarch, through his writings, first popularized.

The new classical curriculum of the *studia humanitatis* found favor among both feudal lords and princes, and also among wealthy merchants and bankers. The original humanities offered these people self-confidence in a quite literal sense: it held out for them the hope that through the deep and ongoing study of Greek and Roman moral philosophy and history they could acquire the strength of character to withstand the blows and the guiles of Fortune wherever they might meet her, and the wisdom and the virtue necessary to rule their own lives, and the lives of others. Let us look at a concrete example of the belief that the cultivation of an inner self was essential in governing other men.

Guarino Guarini of Verona (1374–1460) was one of the most successful of the early humanist teachers. His school in Ferrara attracted students from all over Europe. In 1422 he taught a course in Verona on Cicero's treatise on duties, the *De officiis.* In his introductory lecture he tells his pupils what his course has to offer them. The study of moral philosophy, Guarino says, will enable one to exercise dominion over his own passions, to set his household in order, and to govern his city or his state. Then he continues, speaking all the time of moral philosophy:

> Here are provided those arms which enable one not to fall when broken by bad fortune and not to swell up when elated by good fortune. Here are found weighty counsels for action and here impetuosity, the enemy of reason, is avoided. Here faith, constancy, fairness, and liberality towards friends and foreigners, and finally respect for mankind, is learned. Here the impulses of souls and the reins for desires are set in order, so that nothing is done effeminately, nothing is done weakly, nothing is done dishonourably. (Sabbadini 1964, pp. 182–83)

That Guarino believed that the study of works such as Cicero's *De officiis* led to practical results is attested by a letter he wrote several years earlier, in 1419, to his friend Gian Nicola Salerno, who was then the chief magistrate of the city of Bologna. Guarino writes:

> I have learned that when civil tumult and internal discord recently moved the people of Bologna to take up arms, you showed no less the courage and eloquence of a soldier than you had previously shown the justice of a magistrate. . . . You thus owe no small thanks to the Muses. Imbued with (*imbutus*) and formed (*institutus*) by them from boyhood on, from them you learned to govern, order, and manage, restore and maintain, yourself, your family, and the business of your city. You therefore demonstrate that the Muses rule not only strings and lyres, but also public affairs. (Guarino Guarini 1959, p. 263)

Who today would say that the Muses rule public affairs? The Muses have now been replaced by the so-called "science" of management. The ideal Renaissance leader, whether the ruler of a city or a state, the citizen of a free republic, or a military commander, was well-read in the Greek and Roman classics, firmly in control of his or her own passions, and able to make or justify military or political decisions on the basis of the lessons derived from the study of ancient history. The modern bureaucratic manager, whether working for a corporation, the government, or a labor union, is, ideally, a person who can weigh costs and benefits, and who strives to adjust means to ends in the most economical and efficient manner. The manager makes, or at least justifies, his or her decisions on the basis of quantitative data—market research, for example. The goals of leadership, and the justification for the exercise of power, have thus changed radically since the period in which the humanities were born.

Our curriculum reflects this change. From the Renaissance up through the last century, the humanities, with their claim that the study of the Greeks and the Romans formed character and taught wisdom and virtue, provided the basis for the education of leaders in Europe and in America. This kind of education has now been replaced by another. Behind the figure of the modern bureaucratic manager lies the claim of the so-called social sciences that it is possible to discover scientifically verifiable laws of human behavior which enable those in positions of power to predict and manipulate such behavior. Thus while the justification for the Renaissance leader's exercise of power lay in part in his or her moral character as shaped by literary training, the justification for the modern manager's exercise of power rests in his or her ability to appeal to a body of scientific, and above all social scientific, knowledge.

Alasdair MacIntyre has argued that Max Weber's theory of the modern bureaucratic organization describes the social context for the deterioration of moral thinking in our own time. Speaking of the connection between the "practical intelligence," the knowledge necessary to the exercise of judgment in a particular case, and the moral virtues in Aristotle's ethics, MacIntyre observes that

> those characters so essential to the dramatic scripts of modernity, the expert who matches means to ends in an evaluatively neutral way and the moral agent who is anyone and everyone not actually mentally defective, have no genuine counterpart in Aristotle's scheme or indeed within the classical tradition at all. It is indeed difficult to envisage the exaltation of bureaucratic expertise in any culture in which the connection between practical intelligence and the moral virtues is firmly established. (MacIntyre 1984, p. 155)

Weber distinguished between traditional, rational, and charismatic authority. In explaining the former, Robert A. Nisbet (1966) quotes from Weber's *The Theory of Social and Economic Organization:*

> The person or persons exercising authority are designated according to traditionally transmitted rules. The object of obedience is the personal authority of the individual which he enjoys by virtue of his traditional status. The organized group exercising authority is, in the simplest case, primarily based on relations of personal loyalty, cultivated through a common process of education.

Nisbet comments:

> Traditional authority thus draws its legitimacy not from reason or abstract rule but from its roots in the belief that it is ancient, that it has inherent and unassailable wisdom transcending any one man's reason. *Its social essence is the direct personal relation between those affected*: teacher to student, servant to master, disciple to religious leader, and so on. No clear differenti-

ation in such a system is made between "political" and "moral" authority. (p. 142. My emphasis)

Rational authority, on the other hand, "is characterized by bureaucracy, by rationalization of the personal relationships which are the substance of traditional society. . . . The emphasis is on the rules rather
than on persons or on mores. . . . Function, authority, hierarchy, and
obedience all exist here, as they do in the traditional order, but they
are conceived to flow strictly from the application of organizational reason" (Nisbet 1966, p. 143).

The Renaissance humanities, simply put, anointed one not only
with the authority of tradition, but with the most imposing tradition
of all, the classical tradition, with its morality of duty, obedience, self-
domination, and civic virtue. The attraction of a classical education
was thus bound to weaken as the authority of tradition was replaced
by the authority of bureaucratic rationality. Conversely, the tradition
of the humanities, with its classical and Renaissance conceptions of virtue, could certainly be revised and reappropriated as an alternative to organizational reason. If the rationalization of government, Nisbet observes in his discussion of Weber, "is prevented from evolving further
to a more complete, even totalitarian, mode of bureaucratic rationalization, it will be only because of the continued force of moral and es-
thetic values which men will somehow continue to see as limits on
pure rationality" (p. 145).

Perhaps nowhere in our society can we observe the passage from traditional moral authority to rational bureaucratic authority as clearly as
we can in our universities, where this transition is still going on. The
university president used to be a moral and intellectual leader; now he
or she is becoming a bureaucratic manager. "Administration has become a self-contained profession," Leon Botstein, president of Bard College, observed recently. "College presidents have become enamored
with bureaucracy. Rarely are they scholars of note who are integrally
connected with the functions of learning on campus" (quoted in the
Christian Science Monitor, 1 December 1986, p. 37).[12]

Much of what MacIntyre says about the contemporary demise of
the tradition of moral philosophy associated with the ancient Graeco-
Roman concept of "virtue" applies equally well to the demise of the humanities in the modern world. From the Renaissance on, the *studia
humanitatis* were the chief conduit in the West for major texts of classical moral thought. They internalized and individualized the classical
ideal of *virtus,* and thereby adapted a classical standard of moral behavior to the very unclassical world of early modern Europe, in which
the unity of individual, society, and cosmos had been shattered. But

the concern with "virtue" remained, as did part of the vocabulary of classical moral philosophy.

This individualization and interiorization of virtue played a key role in the formation of the Renaissance ruling classes. As during the Middle Ages, so too in early modern Europe, governing was still dependent upon individuals, although the direct personal dependency and parcellized sovereignty of the feudal Middle Ages had been replaced by urban oligarchies in Italy and centralized monarchies in the north. The military commander, the urban magistrate, the diplomat, even if they derived their office and power from others, acted for the most part individually; they were neither supported by nor constrained by large organizations. In one sense then, they enjoyed a degree of autonomy unknown to the modern bureaucratic manager or the modern military commander, who has become just another manager of a large and unwieldy organization. But in another sense, the Renaissance commander, magistrate, and diplomat had traditional "moral" constraints entirely unknown to the modern manager: he was tied to the individual, social group, or class in whose interest he held office by virtues such as duty, honor, and loyalty. It was the acquisition, or at least the perfection of these virtues, along with the virtues of courage, wisdom, and prudence, the exercise of wisdom in particular circumstances, that a classical education was intended to provide.[13]

The modern bureaucratic manager has a moral autonomy that his or her Renaissance predecessor did not have: the ideology of technical expertise, of the understanding and application of the principles of "scientific" management, has replaced the exercise of virtue as a justification for power and authority. This is not to say that modern managers need give no thought to virtue: their subordinates will probably still respect truthfulness, honesty, and fairness, and do the tasks assigned to them more willingly and with greater care because they recognize these qualities in their superior. But the manager's authority does not derive from moral character; it is based upon his or her ability, as MacIntyre put it, to match "means to ends in an evaluatively neutral way" (p. 155). Furthermore, it is no longer the practice of virtue, especially duty and loyalty, that binds the modern executive to the organization he or she manages, but rather the very organization itself, as the title of William H. Whyte's famous *The Organization Man* so vividly suggests.

The difference between the Renaissance ruler and the modern bureaucratic manager perhaps can be seen most clearly in the question of "personal" responsibility. The Renaissance ruler was directly responsible for his actions in a way the modern manager is not. Because of his power and autonomy, the success of his leadership often depended on himself alone, on his eloquence, and on his own personal courage and wisdom. He had no organization to hide behind, no faceless "system" to blame if he failed in his office. The modern manager, on the other hand, especially when it is a question of legal and ethical violations, is tempted, at least in the United States, to blame the organization, of which the manager is only a small part. When the old and respected First National Bank of Boston pleaded guilty in early 1985 to illegal cash transfers in what the Treasury Department said looked like a scheme to launder millions of dollars of drug money, its chairman, William L. Brown, absolved the bank's management of any wrongdoing by imputing the illegal cash transfers to a "systems failure"—a phrase untranslatable into Renaissance or classical Latin.

From the point of view of "governance," the Greek and Roman classics could be useful in the "Education of a Christian Prince," to use the title of Erasmus's treatise. But the primarily literary curriculum of the traditional humanities has little to offer any modern manager whose ideal world is one of quantification and predictability, and who therefore must play the role of seeming to make decisions on the basis of efficiency rather than virtue. But the tradition of the humanities will certainly remain of interest to those who, in business, government, and the academic community, have difficulty accepting the theory of bureaucratic rationality, who question not only the value but the very possibility of quantifying and predicting human behavior, and who are therefore searching for alternative ways of structuring and understanding human interaction.[14]

It is interesting to observe that the "science" of management came into being toward the end of the last century, pioneered by the American engineer Frederick Winslow Taylor.[15] Max Weber conducted his analyses of bureaucracies in the early part of this century, at the same time that the hegemony of Greek and Latin was broken in the schools. Educational systems change slowly, but we can now see that the rise of modern philosophies of management parallels the decline of the humanities as a curriculum for the ruling classes.

The ideal of bureaucratic efficiency, however, is part of an even larger cultural change which has contributed enormously to undercutting the relevance of the humanities today: the cult of the new and the death of the past.

The Death of the Past

The original *studia humanitatis* were a curriculum based exclusively on the classical languages and literatures. The early humanists believed that the culture and institutions of Greece and Rome were directly relevant to the present. "What else, then, is all history," Petrarch asked, "if not the praise of Rome?" (Petrarca 1965, p. 1187. Quoted in Mommsen 1959, p. 122). Bruni urged Battista di Montefeltro to read the Greek and Roman historians for lessons she could apply to the present. As we have seen, in the early 1400s Florentine politicians tried to draw lessons from the history of Greece and Rome in debating courses of action to follow in the present. During the Renaissance, decisions concerning the governance of the city or the State were made on the basis of, or at least justified by, reference to the past, especially to classical antiquity.[16] This practice continued all the way up into our own century. The founding fathers of our republic used the memory of the ancient Roman Republic to give the authority of history and tradition to the new nation that had just freed itself from the control of the English monarch. That ancient Roman emblem of authority, the fasces, a bundle of rods bound together around an ax with the blade projecting, is still stamped on every American dime, a silent reminder of the republican tradition out of which the United States came.

References to the actors and events in the histories of Greece and Rome could of course be used to support widely divergent points of view, as Frank M. Turner shows so well in his recent book *The Greek Heritage in Victorian Britain* (Turner 1981), and as Harold T. Parker, in his *The Cult of Antiquity and the French Revolutionaries: A Study in the Development of the Revolutionary Spirit,* showed earlier in the case of the French Revolution (Parker 1965). Already in the Renaissance, the history of Rome could be used to justify republics or tyrannies, depending upon the propagandist's point of view.[17] Nor should we forget that if the French Revolution began under the banners of Republican Rome, Napoleon conquered Europe under the banners of the Empire. Benito Mussolini, and after him Adolf Hitler, likewise brought back the ghosts of ancient Rome—though like Napoleon, Imperial, not Republican, Rome—in order to blot out the all too recent memory of class conflict with the myth, as Hitler stated it, of "one empire, one people" (*ein Reich, ein Volk*). The word *fascism,* after all—*fascismo* in Italian—comes from the Roman *fasces.*[18] The point is not that the intellectuals and propagandists of times previous to our own agreed upon the meaning of classical history, or the use to which it could be put in the present, but that they understood the present in terms of the past, especially the classical past. The past, for them, supplied standards of comparison for the present. What characterizes our own time is that we do not use the past at all.

Despite the continued relevance of the classical republican tradition to the preservation of democracy and representative government in the United States today, American politicians no longer look to the history of Greece and Rome for insight and inspiration in determining and debating public policy; like their counterparts in the business world, they often use numbers and statistics to argue for particular courses of action—even when the numbers are phony, as David A. Stockman, former budget director for the Reagan administration, reveals in his book *The Triumph of Politics: Why the Reagan Revolution Failed* (Stockman 1986).

Our lack of interest in the history of Greece and Rome is due in part to a reaction in the last century to the hegemony of Greek and Latin in the curriculum. Speaking of what he calls "the historical study of literature," Henry Sidgwick wrote:

> . . . the branch of this study which seems to have the greatest utility, if the space we can allot to it is limited, is surely that which explains to us (as far as is possible) the intellectual life of our own age; which teaches us the antecedents of the ideas and feelings among which, and in which, we shall live and move. Such a course, at this moment in history, would naturally contain a much larger modern than ancient element: it would be felt in framing it more imperatively necessary to represent French, German, and English thought of recent centuries, than to introduce us to any of the older influences that combined to determine our immediate intellectual antecedents. (Farrar 1868, p. 103)

But this reaction to the hegemony of Greek and Latin does not explain the lack of interest in the past—any past—that has now become such a characteristic part of our culture that the British historian J. H. Plumb could write a book in 1969 which he entitled *The Death of the Past*. Sidgwick was asking for a balance in the curriculum between the ancient and the modern. He would never have imagined that a century later not only had the Greeks and the Romans disappeared from the consciousness of most students, but also the "French, German, and English thought of recent centuries" that he championed.

We live now in a culture which, at both an individual and collective level, has at best only a tenuous relationship to its past. For the moment, in our rapidly changing world of cultural fads and fashions, this relationship is characterized by nostalgia, which becomes evermore superficial as it is mined as a source for new commodities of mass consumption. But for the most part we live only in the present. Even within the present, we have no sense of historical continuity but experience reality as a series of discontinuous fragments served up nightly on the evening news.[19]

Plumb argues that "the present weakness of the past" is due primarily to the nature of industrial society:

Industrial society, unlike the commercial, craft and agrarian societies which it replaces, does not need the past. Its intellectual and emotional orientation is towards change rather than conservation, towards exploitation and consumption. The new methods, new processes, new forms of living of scientific and industrial society have no sanction in the past and no roots in it. The past becomes, therefore, a matter of curiosity, of nostalgia, of sentimentality. (Plumb 1969, pp. 14–15)

We can get an even clearer picture of what has happened to our sense of the past by turning back to the nineteenth century. Today we are almost completely tyrannized by the present. We treat it the way we do the weather, as an inevitable part of nature, over which we have no control. But thinkers in the last century, since they were closer in time to a past and a way of life that was coming to an end, could sometimes see the changes more clearly than we can. This is certainly true of the essayists in F. W. Farrar's 1868 volume on liberal education: while they attacked the hegemony of classical education in the British schools, they also knew what this classical education was and why it was defended. In the same way, the clearest and most famous explanation for the death of the past is the one which Marx and Engels give in *The Communist Manifesto* of 1848:

> The bourgeoisie cannot exist without constantly revolutionizing the instruments of production, and thereby the relations of production, and with them the whole relations of society. Conservation of the old modes of production in unaltered form was, on the contrary, the first condition of existence for all earlier industrial classes. Constant revolutionizing of production, uninterrupted disturbance of all social conditions, everlasting uncertainty and agitation distinguish the bourgeois epoch from all earlier ones. All fixed, fast-frozen relations, with their train of ancient and venerable prejudices and opinions, are swept away, all new-formed ones become antiquated before they can ossify. All that is solid melts into air, all that is holy is profaned, and man is at last compelled to face with sober senses his real conditions of life, and his relations with his kind. (Marx and Engels 1968, p. 7)

"All that is solid melts into air." This is the experience of modernity, as Marshall Berman argues in his book (1982), for which he chose as his title this phrase from *The Communist Manifesto*. Marx and Engels experienced the Industrial Revolution in England, and the French Revolution was much closer to them in time than it is to us two centuries later. They could thus see clearly how the bourgeoisie was by far the most revolutionary ruling class in history, in part because they had a clearer sense of the feudal aristocratic culture which it tore down, especially in France. Marx's formula M–C–M', in which he describes the "process of continuous transformation of capital-as-money into capital-as-commodities, followed by a retransformation of capital-as-commodities into capital-as-more-money," as Robert L. Heilbroner puts it so succinctly in his book *The Nature and Logic of Capitalism* (1985, p. 36), explains well the experience of *constant change* that characterizes our society. Capital is not a thing but a process: one begins with money, invests it, and, if successful, comes out with more money, which he then reinvests. The drive to make money sends the capitalist looking for ever-new commodities to buy and then resell for more money. We experience this process in many ways in our daily life, of which perhaps the most visually striking is the constant transformation and retransformation of our urban landscape, as real estate speculators tear down old buildings and put up new ones.

But the business executive experiences this process in an even more specific way, a way which gives us clear insight into the relationship between a waning sense of the past and life in a capitalist society.

Between September 1974 and September 1975, the Conference Board, a national business organization, organized three-day meetings for groups of senior executives from across the country to exchange views on the past, present, and future social responsibilities of business. The Conference Board invited Leonard Silk, an economist and columnist for the *New York Times* and David Vogel, of the University of California, to join these meetings as observers and write a book on what they heard. Their observations on the chief executives' relationship to their past accomplishments tell us a good deal about our society today:

> For most executives, fame and immortality are beyond reach. In a business civilization there seems to be no place for permanent status: the only relevant standard for judgment is last quarter's earnings. A vibrant business system cannot be satisfied with the past performance of its leaders. In that sense, there is something a bit sad about *Fortune* magazine's recently established "Business Hall of Fame." In commenting on it, Max Ways notes that most businessmen, even when they achieve public recognition, are usually recognized for their nonbusiness achievements, i.e., "statesmen" (George Washington), "inventors" (Eli Whitney, Thomas Edison), or "philanthropists" (Peter Cooper). . . .
>
> Oddly enough, the pervasive business values—values that emphasize change and performance today and tomorrow—make the executive feel unappreciated for his past efforts. As one executive noted, we have fewer and fewer corporations that bear their managers' or founders' names. Executives nowadays have only a short spell at the top—five or six years, typically. What distinguishes the current generation of top executives from the previous two or three is their anonymity. . . . Today, the names of

the chief executive officers of corporations that have been most heavily in the public spotlight—one thinks of the executives of the major oil companies—are virtually unknown to the general public. Said one executive:

The oil companies have done a great job; they deserve a medal.

Regardless of the merits of this assessment, America, being a thoroughly bourgeois society, has no equivalent of the Queen's honor list; thanks to the success of our revolution, we have no aristocratic honors to bestow for distinguished pecuniary performance. The only "medal" we have to bestow is the applause of the financial community at the increase in earnings reported each quarter, and that recognition, as every executive knows, is rather ephemeral. (Silk and Vogel 1976, pp. 107–108)

The chief executives who participated in these conferences seemed to have been clearly aware that "[i]n a business civilization," as Silk and Vogel put it, ". . . the only relevant standard for judgment is the last quarter's earnings." M-C-M': the drive to amass capital, the constant metamorphosis of money into commodities and commodities into more money, not only creates a world of constant change and transformation; it knows no past.

Our economic system has a profound effect on people's values, even those who are not driven to make "big bucks." The movement of money underlies "the fast pace of modern life." The obsession with money even influences the way we think. It shapes our language, and thereby gives us some of the concepts we use to make sense of our lives and the world around us. "The bottom line" is one of the most widely used metaphors in our speech today. By it we mean "the end result" of something. It comes from the world of business: it is the last line on a financial statement, showing net income or loss. It is the last quarter's earnings. The past can have little or no meaning in a society ruled by the bottom line.

PART THREE

Looking Forward

INTRODUCTION TO PART THREE

Words not only articulate thought; they provide the categories in which thinking takes place. To use words with broad and vague meanings can become an excuse for not thinking, for it permits us to appear to understand more than we really do. Our current use of the phrase "the humanities" does just that: because it lacks any substantive denotation, it lets us talk about the humanities without really knowing what we are talking about. Consider how we now use the term. We employ it indiscriminately to designate the modern as well as the classical languages and literatures, and commonly extend the rubric "humanities" to include the languages and literatures of non-Western cultures.

Using the term so broadly provides a convenient administrative category for dividing up the liberal arts curriculum into the sciences, the social sciences, the arts, and the humanities: whatever subject or discipline fails to fit into the first three areas goes into the last. The broad and indefinite application of the phrase "the humanities" serves as well, when the need arises, to suggest that aspect of a liberal arts education concerned with what is truly human. But here we run into trouble: What do we mean by "human"? What in fact is the "humanistic" dimension of a liberal arts education? Since we cannot define the humanities, we are for the most part forced to answer these questions negatively, explaining what the humanities are by contrasting them with what they are not, usually the sciences.

The ongoing national debate about the quality of education in the United States invites us to do some serious thinking about the curriculum of our schools. The humanities can help us do this thinking—but only if we are willing to put aside the broad and increasingly indiscriminate use of the term and return to its original meaning as the study of the language and literature of ancient Greece and Rome.

But why insist on such a narrow definition of the humanities? What do we have to learn from an educational tradition which has so deteriorated in our own time as to be almost unrecognizable? This is a question we would easily ignore except for one unavoidable fact: classical education may be dead, *but we have found nothing to replace it.* Speaking of the vital spirit that went out of the teaching of Greek and Latin in the last century, Marcel Piérart writes:

> The miracle is that it [the teaching of Greek and Latin] survived so long. But I wonder if this is due in part to the fact that the adversaries of the ancient languages were unable to propose effective replacements for it: if one had been able to develop in our laboratories of pedagogy a formula which had a formative value as sure as Latin and Greek, the case would

doubtlessly have been decided a long time ago. (Piérart 1986, pp. 127–28; my translation)

Concerning the teaching of Greek and Latin today, Piérart goes on to observe that "[t]he best justification for the Graeco-Roman humanities is, in short, the incapacity of Western man up to present to think about himself outside of the ancient world" (ibid., p. 130).

We have no choice: if we want to think about education seriously today, we must engage in a dialogue with our classical and Renaissance pasts. That we do not explains the emptiness of our current discussions of the humanities. We are living in the vacuum created by the disappearance of the Greeks and the Romans. Since the hegemony of classical education was broken in the last century, our curriculum has slowly degenerated into a smorgasbord of courses with no focus, no unity, no integrating design. The result is that whenever we talk about improving our schools, we sidestep the question of the actual content of what we teach and focus instead on the technology and techniques of teaching.

This obsession with technique leads nowhere. Choosing the specific books and authors that students will read is vastly more important than deciding how they will read them, just as choosing the food we eat is more important to our health than deciding what utensils we will eat it with. Yet it seems well-nigh impossible today to talk about the actual content of our curriculum. This is because we are tyrannized by the present: having no sense of the past, we can think and talk about only what we presently experience. But our present experience is an intellectual vacuum as far as the content of a liberal arts curriculum is concerned. The only way to free ourselves from the tyranny of the present is by engaging in a dialogue with our past. Only such a dialogue can liberate us from the present incoherence of our curriculum, because acknowledgment of a tradition is incompatible with a cafeteria approach to education: a tradition is not a smorgasbord, but specific works and authors.

Entering into a dialogue with the tradition of the humanities is not, however, a conservative endeavor. It can lead only to something new: the very deterioration of this tradition forces us to correct and transcend it, not reenact it. This is why we must take the death of the Renaissance humanities seriously. We must not presume that they ceased to exist for superficial reasons, and can thus be brought back to life again by an act of will. In fact, one of my reasons for delineating the major internal and external causes for the demise of the humanities has been to dispel the belief (Bennett 1984, Bloom 1987, Kramer 1980) that the humanities have lost coherence and direction in our schools because of a "failure of nerve" by faculty and administrators during the protests of the sixties. The Greeks and the Romans had vanished from our classrooms long before the Civil Rights Movement and the war in Vietnam, for reasons that go much deeper than the question of authority in our schools. We need leadership and courage in our schools more than ever today. But what is even more important is that leadership and courage be informed by a sound understanding of the pedagogical traditions we inherit.

Where does this understanding lead? It leads us first of all to recognize that the tradition of the humanities as we inherit it is now composed of three major components: the Renaissance perception of classical antiquity, along with the Renaissance conception of an autonomous inner self, which determined its understanding and use of classical antiquity; classical antiquity itself, the study of which constituted the core of the humanities curriculum; and our present perspective on both the Renaissance and classical antiquity. I mention our present situation as the third major component of the tradition of the humanities not just because the present is where we happen to be, but because, from the perspective of the history of the humanities, our current situation constitutes a totally new phase: the death of the original humanities in our own time permits us, indeed forces us, to look at this tradition from the outside, and to become conscious and critical of it in a way no previous generation could. The very vacuum created in our curriculum by the disappearance of the Greeks and the Romans, in spite of the confusion and disorientation it has created, gives us the freedom to decide what aspects of our past we can use today. Indeed, we are now in an ideal position to revise and reappropriate the tradition of the humanities. A century ago it had become a dead weight, and people had to struggle to get out from under it. Today it is weightless. The use we make of this tradition depends primarily upon our understanding of it and of the specific problems facing us in the present. I have spoken at length of the Renaissance and classical ideals of education. Now we need to see which of them might be relevant today. Let us begin by looking at the first major component of the tradition of the humanities as we inherit it: the Renaissance's appropriation of classical antiquity.

CHAPTER 7

LESSONS FROM THE
RENAISSANCE

❧

MOST PEOPLE TODAY identify strongly with the Renaissance, primarily because the sense of self that came into being in the Renaissance is still to a large extent our own, despite our growing awareness of its limitations. For this reason, we have much to learn from Petrarch: we can see the advantages and the limitations of a personal sense of self better in him than in any other major figure in our tradition. But there are also other aspects of Renaissance culture which can help us now.

The Revolt against Technique

We have much to gain by adopting the humanists' attitude toward learning. Petrarch lived at a time of methodological fads. Medieval university culture was obsessed with the *techniques* of research and the display of intellectual brilliance. Abélard (1079–1142) paints a striking picture of this world in his short and moving biography *The Story of My Misfortunes*. After writing a tract for his students on the unity and trinity of God, he got into trouble with his colleagues. Here is how he explains what happened:

> Now, a great many people saw and read this tract, and it became exceedingly popular, its clearness appealing particularly to all who sought information on this subject. And *since the questions involved are generally considered the most difficult of all, their complexity is taken as the measure of the subtlety of him who succeeds in answering them.* As a result, my rivals became furiously angry, and summoned a council to take action against me. . . . (Abélard 1922, p. 36. My emphasis)

Our university culture today bears some striking similarities to this medieval world of higher learning. We are obsessed with techniques

146

and pass quickly from one methodological fad to another. We tend to judge scholarship by brilliance of insight, mental acuity, and the mastery of technique, regardless of content. In fact, it no longer matters much whether one writes about comic books or Shakespeare's sonnets, so long as what he or she says about them is new and clever. Like their medieval counterparts, too many scholars, and too many of their graduate students, are intent on proving what good minds they have.

Petrarch and his followers provided a critique of this approach to learning by arguing that the ultimate purpose of study was not to become learned, but to become good. Wisdom and virtue, they believed, are much more useful in one's daily life than erudition. But do not learning and study help one attain wisdom and virtue? Not necessarily. We can see why by looking at another aspect of the humanists' attitude toward learning which is relevant today: their recognition that some subjects were not worth studying.

We have already heard Leonardo Bruni tell Battista di Montefeltro to avoid reading contemporary theologians, and not to waste too much time with geometry and arithmetic. Lorenzo Valla was even more direct. Drawing an image from contemporary attempts to save the Ptolemaic conception of the universe, Valla described the latest methodological fads in theology as dazzling contemporary theologians "like the ninth sphere and the planetary epicycles" (Camporeale 1976, p. 37–38). But he himself was not to be taken in. "I am in no way dazzled (*admiror*) by these things," Valla wrote, "nor do I believe it matters very much whether you know them or not, and perhaps it is better not to know them as impediments to [knowing] better things" (Valla 1962, p. 350).

Valla is not only saying that some things are not worth knowing; he is saying that knowing some things may actually get in the way of knowing other, better things. For Valla this meant that the study of logic and metaphysics, which dominated theology in his time, was an impediment to knowing God. Applied to our own university culture, Valla's general principle helps us to see that most of the current methodological fads in our universities today, such as quantitative analysis in the social sciences and the latest literary theories in the so-called "humanities," are of such limited application that having these techniques in one's head can often be an impediment to serious thinking. Quantitative analysis and the construction of mathematical models in the social sciences, for example, or deconstructionism and "postdeconstructionism" in the literary disciplines, just as logic in the medieval universities and classical philology in the great German universities of the last century, tend to become ends in themselves. They may dazzle the initiated, or intimidate the unin-

itiated, but they also hamper serious thinking, for they limit and prede-
termine the kinds of questions one can ask of a society or of a literary
text. As the pollster Daniel Yankelovich once put it in describing the fallacies of quantitative thinking:

> The first step is to measure whatever can be easily measured. This is
> okay as far as it goes. The second step is to disregard that which can't be
> measured or give it an arbitrary quantitative value. This is artificial and mis-
> leading. The third step is to presume that what can't be measured easily
> isn't very important. This is blindness. The fourth step is to say that
> what can't be easily measured really doesn't exist. This is suicide.
> (Quoted in Smith 1972, p. 286)

Furthermore, the creation of mathematical models without the use
of empirical data in the social sciences, and deconstructionism in the literary disciplines, are examples of total intellectual permissiveness: anything goes, because there are no pragmatic criteria, as there are in the natural sciences, to test a particular theory or interpretation.[1]

Keeping abreast of the newest methodologies, moreover, takes time:
if scholars try to keep up with all the secondary literature in their
fields, they have little time or energy left for reading anything truly significant. If they want to understand the humanities, they need to find
the time to read and reread Cicero and Petrarch. Practicing the latest
techniques of literary criticism may help them to publish quickly, or
say something new or clever about Petrarch or Cicero, but it will
blind them to bigger and more important questions. Rather than helping them escape from the tyranny of the present so they can learn something new from the past, it will lock them into a relationship with a technique, and thereby imprison them in contemporary ways of thinking.

Beware of the illusion of techniques! Learn Greek and Latin and return to the sources! This is one of the more important lessons the Renaissance humanists can teach us. Of course some contemporary scholars,
in their obsession with technique, like to think, or need to think, that
only they have the training and insight to understand fully the cultural ar-
tifacts we inherit from the past. This attitude is not so different from
that of the scholastic theologians in Petrarch's and Valla's time, who believed that you could not know God unless you had mastered the logic
and metaphysics of scholastic Aristotelianism. That we have to fight
against a new kind of scholasticism is not surprising, given the similarities of our own university culture and that of the Middle Ages. As the
history of the humanities shows, the professionalization of learning and
its segregation in universities foster an obsession with technique. We
thus need to remind ourselves, especially those of us who teach in colleges and universities, that there is historical precedent for turning

away from obsessions with methodology and technique. We are certainly in good company in feeling compelled to do so. The constant reminder of the humanists' insistence on wisdom and virtue as the goal of learning can help us guard against this kind of academic degeneration.

The Uses of Inspiration

The authors of *Habits of the Heart* (Bellah et al., 1986) point to the classical republican tradition as one of America's secondary "languages" which could now help us articulate our desire for "commitment and community." But how can we learn to speak again this forgotten language? We shall have to return to its sources, and familiarize ourselves with the classical concept and practice of "virtue." That we may encounter some initial difficulty in doing this is not surprising. We live, as the title of Alasdair MacIntyre's book puts it, *After Virtue*. The tradition of the virtues, of which the Renaissance humanities constitute an important and significant part,[2] is now unrecognizable, so greatly has it deteriorated since the Enlightenment. MacIntyre addresses this problem first by trying to explain the decline of the concept of virtue in the modern period, and then by showing how Aristotle's theory of the virtues could be used to reconstruct a coherent moral theory practicable in our own times. One need not necessarily agree with the use MacIntyre makes of Aristotle in order to see the importance of the kind of historical understanding he is trying to attain.

The question we must ask ourselves, however, as we mull over the problem of how to teach moral values in our schools, is whether theoretical coherence is sufficient for encouraging the practice of virtue. The Renaissance humanists can help us think about this question. They remind us that the actual practice of virtue, at least in postclassical societies, needs more than an intellectually coherent theory of virtue. It needs examples of virtuous actions capable of inspiring other actions; and, if Petrarch is right, it needs as well a rhetorical presentation of these deeds powerful enough to move us to want to undertake them. Petrarch's observation that after studying Aristotle's ethics he realized that he was more learned, but not morally better (Petrarca 1906, p. 68, translated in Cassirer 1948, p. 103) is probably still true of anyone who studies Aristotle today. Petrarch read Aristotle not as a participant in the community of the ancient *polis*, but as an autonomous self. So too do we. Despite our recognition of the limitations of isolated individualism, we too continue to experience ourselves as isolated centers. Petrarch's humanism was an attempt to find a unity within to make up for the lost unity without. It was a reaction to the subject-object dichotomy, the new technical reason, which Anselm articulated for the first time in the West. Until this rift between the knower and the known, and the individual and the cosmos, is healed, it is probable that we shall need to do what Petrarch did: read authors whose descriptions of virtuous deeds, and whose uplifting style, can enkindle in us the love of wisdom and virtue.

There is an important difference, though, between the Renaissance humanists' ability to be inspired by the lives and writings of the ancients, and our own. The difference has to do with the Renaissance experience of community. Petrarch's perception of personal autonomy was based upon a bond of psychic community with other human beings, however distant in time. His awareness of individual autonomy was shaped and sustained by a consciousness which was both social and historical: he sought to discover who he was, and to mold and shape his own character, by comparing himself to the ancients. Few people today have this kind of historical consciousness. Indeed, it is precisely the absence of historical consciousness that distinguishes our own culture so sharply from that of the Renaissance. Their communion with the past gave inward-turning Renaissance men and women an experience of community for the most part lacking in modern cultures.

In truly communal societies, such as ancient Rome, there are individuals, but no isolated autonomous selves. One looks outward, not inward, for the meaning of his or her life, as Cicero did after the death of his daughter Tullia. The Renaissance, in a sense, marks a half-way point between the classical community and modern postcommunal society. No matter what its humanist propagandists, such as Leonardo Bruni, said in its favor, Renaissance Florence was not ancient Athens, nor was it ancient Rome. It lacked the community of the Athenian *polis*, or the Roman *civitas*. But Renaissance man, for all of his devotion to finding a center and final resting place within himself, still belonged to a community: the community of wise men. At the beginning of his widely read *De remediis utriusque fortunae*, "On Remedies for Good and Bad Fortune," Petrarch says that except for the exertions of a noble soul, and conversations with wise men, nothing helps one confront the anxieties of the human condition better than "the continual and night-long reading of the records (*monumenta*) of noble writers, provided that to their healthful counsels is not lacking the soul's consent, which I would not be afraid to assert is the one living fountain of sane counsel on the earth" (Petrarca 1965, vol. 1, p. 2). While the individual self has become central to Petrarch's thinking, as we see here from his emphasis on the soul's consent, this self is not completely alone: it takes advice and counsel from the wisdom of the ancients. This is even clearer in what follows. If we can be grateful to plebeian writers, Petrarch says, for opening up the way to others,

> how much more gratitude, I ask you, is owed to renowned and esteemed writers, who, having passed their time on the earth many centuries before us, through their divine geniuses and most sacred teachings, with us live, dwell, and converse? (Ibid.)

He goes on to speak of these ancient writers as guides:

> In the midst of souls' perpetual billows, like so many bright stars affixed to the firmament of truth, like so many pleasant and happy breezes, so many industrious and skillful sailors, they show us the port of peace, and move there the slow sails of our will, and guide the rudder of the wavering soul, until, tossed about by such storms, it at last steadies and tempers its deliberations. (Ibid.)

Petrarch did not like the century in which he was born. "Among many other subjects, I attached myself especially to a knowledge of antiquity," he writes in his famous *Letter to Posterity*, "since I always disliked this age; so that, were it not that love for those who are dear to me pulled me in a different direction, I would always have rather been born in any other age; and I have tried to forget this age, always putting myself in spirit in other ages. I thus delighted in history . . ." (Petrarca 1955, p. 6). The crucial difference between Petrarch and Freud, certainly one of the most influential representatives of modern culture, is that Petrarch blamed his ills on his own times, whereas Freud accused civilization in general. The lesson Freud taught is that civilization involves the repression and sublimation of one's basic impulses. Petrarch and his followers, on the other hand, looked to culture, to civilization, albeit an earlier one, for salvation from the present world. The humanistic cultivation of the self, then, while it marked a retreat from the ancient plenitude of community, constituted nevertheless a community: a community of men and women, who, though distant in time, shared a common search for wisdom and virtue. The Renaissance self thus existed in a kind of dynamic tension in which it was held back from total narcissism by its very program of self-cultivation: it had to measure itself against the illustrious men and women of classical antiquity. Once the particular relationship which the Renaissance established with the classical past fell apart, the self was freed from the claims of civilization, and could now sink down completely into its own analysis.

Classical civilization was a civilization based upon authority, especially the authority of the past. It was a community, based upon a culture of commitment. The new view of the human condition that receives its first, and in some ways still most complete, expression in the writings of Petrarch, while it prepared the ground for modern psychoanalysis, was still a culture based in part, at least, on the authority of the past, and on a commitment to a psychic community of present and past. But after Freud, as Philip Rieff puts it,

> [i]n sociological terms, psychoanalysis became what we shall call the symbolic mode of a "negative community." It is held together by the analytic attitude, as most moderns are who think too much about themselves. Psychoanalysis is yet another method of learning how to endure the loneliness produced by culture. Psychoanalysis is its representative therapy—in contrast to classical therapies of commitment. It is characteristic of our culture that there is no longer an effective sense of communion, driving the individual out of himself, rendering the inner life serviceable to the outer. (Rieff 1966, p. 32)

The Romans, as we saw so clearly from Polybius' description of a Roman funeral, experienced this communion to the fullest. The Renaissance humanists could still have a partial experience of it through reading the ancients, and through the still strong sense of community which had survived through the Middle Ages. This communion is gone today, and in its place is the "negative community" of the modern intellectual, who, priding himself on his independence of mind and conduct, as Rieff observes, is attracted to psychoanalysis precisely because of its adversarial stance vis-à-vis the demands of society and civilization. From Rieff's point of view, both the analyst and the modern intellectual, as "charter members of the negative community," in which members have few obligations and "the corporate effort is devoted mainly to objecting to the rule," are condemned to feel the futility of their vocation. But there seems to be little they can do about it. Rieff argues that

> despite growing regret among its critics, the civilization of authority continues to fade into history; more accurately it has become dysfunctional. Freud was acutely aware of this. Seen from the vantage point of membership in the negative community, all positive ones appear either fraudulent or stupid. . . . (Rieff 1966, p. 33)

The result is tragic. "Since a less negative sense of vocation can be instilled only in a community blessed with both a rank order of vocations and some objective means of assigning vocations, as in a civilization of authority," Rieff observes, "*the patient, when he is sent out 'cured,' can only make himself his own vocation*" (Ibid. My emphasis).

The risk in Petrarch's life, and in the life of any post-Renaissance man seeking to find the meaning of his earthly existence through the study and emulation of the ancients, is that he make himself his own vocation. This risk was avoided precisely because the act of self-fashioning, self-perfecting, could be achieved only by looking outside the self to other selves, or, as Arnold puts it so often in *Culture and Anarchy*, in using the ancients to pass from one's ordinary to one's "better self."

The extent to which anyone living in the modern world can transcend his or her intensive self and feel the ancient unity of the individual with the whole world of being is an open question. It may be that we can arrive at some kind of experiential understanding of the ancient extensive self only in stages. If this is the case, then the first stage in this process lies in rediscovering the Renaissance's sense of a community across time. We need to bring ourselves into the company of the ancients and establish a psychic community with them. This is what Petrarch and the humanists did, and we can do it too. Furthermore, this kind of community with the ancients, if we use it to go beyond the Petrarchan intensive self, may very well prepare us psychically and morally for the social community that *Habits of the Heart* believes Americans deeply, though unconsciously, yearn for. In short, in trying to learn to speak again the language of "commitment and community" of the classical republican tradition, we need to be inspired to love virtue. But for this inspiration to have any lasting effect upon us, we must break out of our cultural isolation and narcissistic autonomy by engaging in a dialogue with our past. Nothing will help us better to do this than the historical consciousness we inherit from the Renaissance. So let us look more closely now at what this consciousness is.

The Discovery of History

Classical antiquity and the Middle Ages were aware of and used the past. They made it actual. Polybius describes how at the funeral of a noble Roman his heir recounted the man's deeds while surrounded on the rostrum by men wearing the wax masks of the deceased's ancestors (see above, chap. 2). Dante chose Vergil, the poet of the Roman Empire, to guide him through Hell, and up to Beatrice in Purgatory. For the Christian Middle Ages, history is the story of God's intervention in time. During the *pax romana* of the reign of Augustus, Rome brought the world to justice, and thus prepared it for the coming of Christ. The allegorical significance of Dante's journey with Vergil in the *Divine Comedy* is based upon the belief that this same pattern is repeated in the life of each individual Christian in whom the natural light of reason (Vergil) prepares the soul for the reception of supernatural grace (Beatrice).[3] Classical antiquity and the Middle Ages thus saw a continuum between present and past. The Renaissance saw a break. And it was in its recognition of a disjunction between the present and the past that the Renaissance discovered history.

Petrarch played a key role in this discovery because it was he who first spoke of a darkness which fell over the West with the end of the Roman Empire, thereby pointing to a break in the continuity of Western culture between his own time and classical antiquity.[4] He recognized, moreover, the difficulties in overcoming this cultural disjuncture. Thomas M. Greene points to a certain pathos in Petrarch's letters to the ancients, as in his final words to Homer, "I realize how far from me you are" (*Fam.* XXIX, 12, 42. Quoted in Greene 1982, p. 29). Greene concludes:

> Petrarch precipitated his own personal creative crisis because he made a series of simultaneous discoveries that had been made only fragmentarily before him. It was he who first understood how radically classical antiquity differed from the Christian era; he also saw more clearly than his predecessors how the individual traits of a given society at a given moment form a distinctive constellation; he understood more clearly the philological meaning of anachronism. (Greene 1982, pp. 29–30)

Renaissance humanism, as we have seen, represented a major reorientation of thought in the West: in their attempt to recover the culture of the ancients, scholars were struck by the differences between their own times and classical antiquity, and this recognition of the disparity between the present and the past led to the discovery of historical change and cultural relativity (see chap. 1, note 7).

These discoveries probably constitute the Renaissance humanities' most enduring heritage. I have spoken of the death of the humanities in the modern period. But some of the academic disciplines and ways of thinking which came into being with the Renaissance *studia humanitatis* still live on today. The disciplines of history, philology, archeology, and cultural anthropology, for example, continue to use the Renaissance humanists' discovery of historical change and cultural difference. The members of the American Council of Learned Societies who helped Congress define the humanities when it drafted the law creating the National Endowment for the Humanities[5] were thus certainly correct, from a historical point of view, in attempting to single out specific academic disciplines for inclusion under the rubric "humanities." Not only were the Renaissance *studia humanitatis* themselves identified as a specific group of disciplines; the disciplines which made up the Renaissance humanities were informed by a clear consciousness of historical change and cultural relativity, as most of the disciplines which the NEH defines as "humanities" still are today (though these disciplines, in order to preserve what is fresh and vital about them, need to beware of the danger of elevating technique over substance). This book itself, in its attempt to tell the history of the humanities, and describe profound differences between the ancient and the Renaissance understanding of the human, can surely be seen as a product of the historical consciousness we inherit from the Renaissance.

It has been my intention, however, to provide a definition and an understanding of the humanities which is even more historical than that given by the NEH, which limits its definition of the humanities to a list of disciplines. We have seen what happens to the tradition of the humanities when academic disciplines become ends in themselves. What we need today is a definition of the humanities which invites us to think about more than just the areas of our curriculum and the divisions of scholarly research. The humanities are nothing without their history, and this history includes not only the old disciplines that the Renaissance *studia humanitatis* transformed (grammar, rhetoric, poetry, moral philosophy, and jurisprudence), and the new disciplines which they brought into being (history, philology, and archeology), but the original object of these disciplines' investigations: the culture and civilization of classical antiquity.

I have tried, moreover, to use the historical consciousness and sense of cultural relativity we inherit from the Renaissance to go beyond the Renaissance in our understanding of what it means to be a human being. Petrarch was keenly aware of differences between ancient culture and his own. Yet he treated the Romans as if they had personal selves similar to his. It is only now, as we struggle to free ourselves from the tragic narcissism of our own times, that we can see the limitations of the modern intensive self, and recognize, as Petrarch could not, how much we have to gain from pondering the ancient unity of the individual, society, and the universe. In the final analysis, what we owe most to the Renaissance humanists is thus that they lead us back to the ancients. If the questions we ask now of the Greeks and the Romans are different from the ones the humanists asked, we must be grateful to the humanists for giving us the historical consciousness both to ask, and, let us hope, to answer them.

CHAPTER 8

THE RELEVANCE
OF THE ANCIENTS

❧

THE MOST COMMON argument advanced today for making the study of the Western tradition, beginning with the Greeks and the Romans, central again in our schools is that it is, after all, our tradition, and that we cannot understand ourselves and our institutions without a deep understanding of our own past. I agree with this argument. And I believe that the Greeks and the Romans in particular can help us think about our past, for they stand at its very beginning. But here I want to add another reason for studying the Greeks and the Romans: they can help us think about our future too.

"One of the great fallacies of American thinking," Alfred North Whitehead once remarked,

> is that human worth is constituted by a particular set of aptitudes which lead to economic advancement. This is not true at all. Two thirds of the people who can make money are mediocre; and at least one half of them are morally at a low level. As a whole, they are vastly inferior to other types who are not animated by the economic motives; I mean artists, and teachers, and professional people who do work which they love for its own sake and earn about enough to get along on. (Whitehead 1954, pp. 251–52)

Renaissance individualism, which was to a certain extent mitigated by the Renaissance's dialogue with classical antiquity, has now degenerated into a pathological narcissism which is manifested in many ways.[1] One that particularly afflicts our students, as they plan their careers, is a concern for money, for private gain as opposed to public service. In order to live according to what is highest in them, our students need ideals which point to more in life than making money, ideals which show them a fuller humanity than is possible when purely economic motives predominate. The ancient concept of the human, now shorn of

156

the Renaissance idea of an inward-turning self, can help them find a higher meaning for their lives. Its power to do so lies in the ancient vision of human life as participation in a larger whole. This vision can help us counteract the tendencies toward narcissism in our society by offering perspectives on three relationships which have become deeply problematic in the modern world: our relationship to nature, to society, and to the mystery of our own existence.

The Unity of Mind and Nature

Our relationship to nature is determined to a great extent by our attitude toward science. Modern science mesmerizes people in two ways: through its promise to unlock eventually all the mysteries of the universe; and through its demonstrated power to transform the natural world. Now we find ourselves forced to reexamine both its promise and its power.

The nineteenth century was a great age of Faith, not in God, but in Science.[2] Toward the end of the century many believed that within a short time science would unlock the mysteries of the universe: all the theories seemed to be in place, only a few details remained to be worked out. Then came quantum mechanics and the theory of relativity. The whole picture of the universe suddenly changed. One explanatory paradigm of reality was replaced by another, radically different one, and science's understanding of the material universe was utterly transformed. Alfred North Whitehead lived through these dramatic years. Here is how he recalled them:

> We supposed that nearly everything of importance about physics was known. Yes, there were a few obscure spots, strange anomalies having to do with the phenomena of radiation which physicists expected to be cleared up by 1900. They were. But in so being, the whole science blew up, and the Newtonian physics, which had been supposed to be fixed as the Everlasting Seat, were gone. Oh, they were and still are useful as a way of looking at things, but regarded as a final description of reality, no longer valid. Certitude was gone. (Whitehead 1954, pp. 6–7)

We now know that it is precisely total conceptual changes of this sort that characterize pivotal moments in the history of science, as Thomas S. Kuhn showed in his influential study, *The Structure of Scientific Revolutions* (Kuhn 1970).

This understanding of the actual history of science is important precisely because the mesmerizing power that the word *science* exercises over people is due to a greater extent than most of us realize, not to what modern science actually reveals about the structure of the universe, but to what it *promises* to reveal: modern science always seems to be on the verge of unlocking the riddles of the universe. But it has not, and, if our understanding of the history of science is at least partially correct, there is no reason to believe that it ever will. Discoveries of new "facts" always raise new questions, some of which serve primarily to throw current theories into doubt. The future of science thus promises to be a repeat of its past: an alternation of periods of "crisis" in which new discoveries throw into doubt the prevailing theories, followed by conceptual revolutions in which totally new paradigms replace the old ones, followed in their turn by new crises which throw into doubt the now consolidated paradigms.

We may be living through just such a period of crisis now. The discovery of phenomena such as quasars, pulsars, black holes, anti-matter, etc. has raised more questions concerning our understanding of the nature and origin of the universe than scientists can answer. Sooner or later what is now called the "new physics" will be replaced by an even newer physics, and with it a radically different understanding of the nature of physical reality, perhaps so different that no one could possibly imagine it today.

It is important to remember, furthermore, that theories are theories, not reality, and that while theories are logically constrained by facts, they are *underdetermined* by them. As Mary Hesse puts it, "while, to be acceptable, theories should be more or less plausibly coherent with facts, they can be neither conclusively refuted nor uniquely derived from statements of fact alone, and hence no theory in a given domain is uniquely acceptable" (Hesse 1980, p. 187). Theories, of course, can be tested by pragmatic criteria in the natural sciences, but even here it is impossible to say that the ability to make successful predictions supports just one particular theory. "The spaceship still goes," Hesse observes, "whether described in a basically Newtonian or relativistic framework" (ibid., p. 192). In other words, our ability to send a space probe to Venus and beyond demonstrates that natural science since the seventeenth century has indeed been successful in utilizing the "laws" of nature; it does not prove that modern science will ever understand these laws completely. In short, there is really no basis for believing that modern reason, enshrined in the subject-object, mind-nature dichotomy of modern science, will ever understand the nature of reality, and this may be because reality itself knows no such dichotomies.

But what of the spaceship, and all the other incredible technological applications of modern science? Do these not demonstrate the preeminent power of modern science over the natural world, even if we grant, for the sake of argument, that science will never explain reality fully? This is the second reason science mesmerizes people: it seems so powerful in bending nature to its will. But now we know it does not. Nature reacts. The Greeks were right: the tree nymph punishes the woodsman who fails to ask her permission before cutting down one of her trees. Since the United States dropped the atom bomb on Hiroshima and Nagasaki, and Rachel Carson published *Silent Spring* in the 1950s, our attitude toward the technological applications of modern science has become increasingly ambivalent. People all over the world are beginning to be troubled by modernity's relationship to nature. They fear an ecological catastrophe. Seveso, Love Canal, Three Mile Island, Bhopal, and now Chernobyl; acid rain, the "greenhouse effect," and the conversion of the Amazon rain forests into pasture land, with the resulting alteration of the ecosystem on a large scale, constitute a series of increasingly urgent warnings that unless we stop turning nature into an object which we ruthlessly exploit, all organic life, including our own, may someday become impossible on the earth.

Changing our relationship to nature means changing, in no small degree, our understanding of this relationship. The sciences and the humanities both posit a radical dichotomy between mind and nature, between the knowing subject and the natural world. Modern science highlights this dichotomy; the humanities try to help us live with it by promising an interior unity and integration to make up for the lost exterior one. But narcissism on the one hand, and the deterioration of our natural environment on the other, now make it urgent that we overcome the modern objectification and desacralization of the natural world, and recapture the ancient vision of the unity of all being.

Some of the conceptual changes necessary to do so come from within the scientific community itself. Aspects of the "new physics," especially quantum mechanics and Heisenberg's principle of indeterminacy, have begun to blur the traditional dichotomy between mind and nature, at least as far as the investigation of sub-atomic particles is concerned.[3] Stephen Toulmin's most recent book has the indicative title *The Return to Cosmology: Postmodern Science and the Theology of Nature* (1982). He argues that a "postmodern" science is now on the horizon which attempts to unify formerly separate disciplines and transcend the mind-nature, subject-object dichotomy upon which modern science has been based. Speaking of the work of Gregory Bateson, the titles of whose books, *Steps to an Ecology of Mind* (1972) and *Mind and Nature: A Necessary Unity* (1979), may serve as signposts to the future, Toulmin writes:

We can no longer view the world as Descartes and Laplace would have us do, as "rational onlookers," from outside. Our place is within the same world that we are studying, and whatever scientific understanding we achieve must be a kind of understanding that is available to participants within the processes of nature, i.e., from inside. (Toulmin 1982, pp. 209–10)

Toulmin goes on to observe that once we begin to look for a science which "accommodates human beings—including scientists—along with all the other inhabitants of the natural world," the distinction between mind and matter, material and mental processes, "ceases to be terribly useful or fundamental for science" (ibid.).

That a growing number of people today, and not just theoretical physicists, are receptive to these kinds of conceptual changes can be seen from popular attitudes toward illness and disease. Many Americans now look at illness and disease from an ecological perspective: they are quite willing to attribute their bodily ills to poisons in their environment. At the same time, as a result of the immense influence of Freud, many people believe that the mind affects the body; illness and disease may arise out of prolonged anxieties and deep inner conflicts, of which, perhaps, they are not even aware. It is probably not clear in the minds of most people, what, if any, relationship exists between ecological and psychosomatic theories of disease. But the popularity of these theories shows that people today are starting to look for wholes, not dichotomies. They see their bodies as part of their environment, and as mirrors of their minds.[4]

Once we begin to make these conceptual changes, we open ourselves up to the possibility of recovering the lost wisdom of the ancients. Works such as Cicero's *Tusculan Disputations* and *On the Nature of the Gods* become surprisingly relevant to our own attempts to understand the relationship between the body, the mind, and the universe. In talking about the fear of death, the endurance of pain, the alleviation of mental distress, and other ills of the soul, Cicero, in the *Tusculan Disputations*, offers insights into the nature and power of mind which may ultimately prove more useful, and certainly more edifying, than Freud's, since for Cicero the alleviation of whatever ills plague the mind, and therefore the body, lies not in resolving hidden inner conflicts, but in rising in contemplation above the human, and in becoming one with the reason and the harmony of the universe.

But just as musicians like to point out that Bach is never the same after we have listened to Beethoven, so too whatever the shape of postmodern science may be, the unities it achieves between mind and nature, between man and the universe, between the knower and the known, can never be quite the same as they were in classical antiquity, because Western categories of thought from 1100 A.D. on are marked by a dichotomy which, since it has been so much a part of Western thought for so many centuries, will doubtlessly leave its own peculiar mark on our efforts to transcend it. We cannot repeat the ancient experience of the unity of all being because we are not the ancients; we are ourselves. But we can emulate them in striving to experience this unity anew. We can recognize that the ancient problem of the One and the Many has come back to haunt us, and we can study the particular solutions to this problem worked out in classical antiquity as a step toward arriving at our own. We can, finally, do what Cranz has tried to do: through reading and rereading the ancient texts, we can try to experience something of the ancient knowledge of the "immediacy" and "ultimacy" of the ground of all being, and let this experience guide us in our own search for the unity of mind and nature.

If postmodern science, as the title of Toulmin's book suggests, will be characterized by a return to cosmology and a theology of nature, it will entail profound changes in our values. We can see this clearly in the ecological movement, which has already deeply affected our attitude toward the natural world. Here again we find the ancients standing in our future, not in our past. A theology of nature will lead to the rediscovery of the sacred. A sense of the sacred will help us balance our ability to transform the natural world with a recognition of the peace, joy, and personal transcendence to be gained from contemplating its beauties.

This brings us to the question of contemplation in general. At the end of the *Nicomachaean Ethics*, Aristotle states that the highest and the happiest life for man is the theoretic life, the life of contemplation. Such a perspective has all but been forgotten in the modern world. "Modern industrial society," E. F. Schumacher has written, "is immensely complicated, immensely involved, making immense claims on man's time and attention." And he observes:

> Paradoxical as it may seem, modern industrial society, in spite of an incredible proliferation of labor-saving devices, has not given people more time to devote to their all-important spiritual tasks; it has made it exceedingly difficult for anyone, except the most determined, to find any time whatever for these tasks. In fact, I think I should not go far wrong if I asserted that the amount of genuine leisure available in a society is generally in inverse proportion to the amount of labor-saving machinery it employs.

"Proper physical work," Schumacher believes, "even if strenuous, does not absorb a great deal of the power of attention, but mental work does; so that there is no attention left over for the spiritual things that really matter." He concludes that "it is a great evil—perhaps the greatest evil—of modern industrial society that, through its immensely involved nature, it imposes an undue nervous strain and absorbs an undue proportion of man's attention" (Schumacher 1979, p. 25).

We often equate modernity with "progress." But there is no reason to believe that there is more real joy, happiness, and contentment in the twentieth century than in former ages. There is probably much less. We would all lead happier, more peaceful, and certainly more dignified, lives if we could find a way of balancing the work ethic and the culture of consumption with the classical ideal of *otium*, leisure devoted to study.[5] Kerenyi (1962) has called our attention to the festal nature of Greek and Roman religion. Here, in these lines from the Greek playwright Menander, we find a vision of nature, and an ideal of happiness, which remind us of a fuller humanity:

> I'll tell you, Parmenon,
> Who seems to me to have the happiest life: the man
> Who takes a steady look at the majestic sights
> Our world offers—the common sun, stars, water, clouds,
> Fire; and having seen them, and lived free from pain, at
>   once
> Goes back to where he came from. These same sights
>   will be,
> If you live to a hundred, always there, always the same;
> And equally if you die young; but you will never
> See more majestic sights than these. Think of this time
> I speak of, as a people's festival, or as
> A visit to some city, where you stand and watch
> The crowds, the streets, the thieves, the gamblers, and
>   the way
> People amuse themselves. (Fragment 481, in Menander
> 1967, pp. 235–36)

The Community of Self and Society

Growing dissatisfaction with the autonomous self is another sign that people today are searching for a new and more satisfying understanding of meaning and purpose of human life.[6] We have already seen how Petrarch's autonomous self becomes elusive and evasive once it has lost the community with the ancients which the humanities provided, and is forced to stand alone, the sole object of its inquiry. A study of the mores of middle-class Americans in the 1980s suggests that much of the pervasive emptiness and dissatisfaction that plagues the lives of materially comfortable and often economically successful people in this country derives from the American cult of individualism, which encourages people to center their lives completely upon themselves.

Habits of the Heart (Bellah et al. 1986) shows that people in America become self-centered because they literally have no other way of thinking about the meaning and purpose of their lives. The primary language of America is individualism. It provides the concepts and categories by which most Americans think and talk about moral, social, and political matters. Even when, in their interviews across the country, they came upon men and women whose lives served larger, more communal purposes, the authors found that these same people were unable to talk about their broader commitments in anything but the language of individualism. This is an extremely important insight, for it shows that our pathological narcissism is not simply a product of the social and economic institutions of capitalism, of the particular ways in which people are forced to live and work in order to survive materially; it is due as well to the way people *think*, to the concepts and ideals they use in making sense of their world, in choosing their careers, and in deciding what kind of society they want to live in.

Those who use the language of individualism, especially phrases like "dog-eat-dog" and "survival of the fittest," to describe human nature as they believe it always was and always will be, suffer from the terrible cultural amnesia that is the hallmark of modern civilization. The first step toward attaining a fuller humanity lies in overcoming this amnesia.

Awakening from the amnesia of modern industrial society may be easier than it seems. Material wealth and physical comforts have not brought greater happiness. Most people in advanced industrialized countries are tense and nervous. The quiet desperation Thoreau observed in the lives of modern men isn't so quiet anymore: it has become frenetic. The myth of progress is fading. And as it fades, people will begin to search for higher and happier visions of the meaning and purpose of human life than those provided by narcissism and greed.

Our own past provides such visions. As the authors of *Habits of the Heart* so rightly observe, the language of individualism, although it is the primary language of most Americans, is not their only language. Americans have inherited two secondary languages which, although overshadowed by the primary one, still provide part of their moral thinking and discourse, and in so doing keep individualism from becoming completely dominant. These are the languages of the Bible, and of the classical republican tradition. We learn about the latter primarily through the humanities, for the humanities lead us into a dialogue with our classical and Renaissance pasts.

But while the biblical and republican traditions continue to provide us with some modicum of meaning and coherence in our lives, the authors of *Habits of the Heart* ask if we do not now face "the danger that the erosion of these traditions may eventually deprive us of that meaning altogether?" (Bellah et al. 1986, p. 282). They speak of "the profound yearning for the idealized small town" they found among most of the people they talked to, a yearning for meaning and coherence which the culture of individualism denies. And they state that

> it is worth considering whether the biblical and republican traditions that small town once embodied can be reappropriated in ways that respond to our present need. Indeed, we would argue that if we are ever to enter the new world that so far has been powerless to be born, it will be through reversing modernity's tendency to obliterate all previous culture. We need to learn again from the cultural riches of the human species and to reappropriate and revitalize those riches so that they can speak to our condition today. (Ibid., p. 283)

The Greeks and Romans have much to teach us about community. They have not only given us our basic political institutions; the ideal of community embodied in the classical city-state has never been surpassed. It is, moreover, a fundamental part of our culture: only in the West can we find man defined, as Aristotle defined him, as *politikon zoon*, a "political animal," that is, a living being specifically characterized by his participation in the life of a *polis*. Our word *politics*, in fact, comes from the Greek *polites*, citizen, from *polis*, city. Our word *citizen* derives ultimately from the Latin *civitas*, city or state, from *civis*, citizen. For the ancients, one's status as a human being was originally dependent upon membership in a civic community; exile from one's city was equivalent to death. In the *Apology*, for example, Plato has Socrates explicitly refuse banishment as an alternative to the penalty of death. The strength of the ancient bond of community can be seen in the fact that while suicide, for Thomas Aquinas, is a sin or injustice (*iniuria*) against God, and for Dante a sin against one's own self, for Aristotle it is a sin against the *polis*.[7] In developing their ontologies, it was in the concept of citizenship that the ancients solved the problem of the relationship of the part to the whole. From a Greek and Roman point of view, the malaise of the modern liberal state, composed as it is of individuals each seeking their own private gain, lies in its inability to solve this problem. The words of Hans Jonas are worth repeating here:

According to classical doctrine, the whole is prior to the parts, is better than the parts, and therefore that for the sake of which the parts are and wherein they have not only the cause but also the meaning of their existence. The living example of such a whole had been the classical *polis*, the city-state, whose citizens had a share of the whole and could affirm its superior status in the knowledge that they the parts, however passing and exchangeable, not only were *dependent* on the whole *for* their being but also *maintained* that whole *with* their being: just as the condition of the whole made a difference to the being and possible perfection of the parts, so their conduct made a difference to the being and perfection of the whole. Thus this whole, making possible first the very life and then the good life of the individual, was at the same time entrusted to the individual's care, and in surpassing and outlasting him was also his supreme achievement. (Jonas 1963, p. 248)

One reason for the almost pathological fear of aging and death that seems to afflict so many Americans can be found in their lack of any experience of participation in a whole which will surpass and outlast them.

In talking about the relevance of the ancients today in our own search for community, it is important to be clear about what held the ancient community together. If man is, as Hobbes saw him, a selfishly individualistic animal at constant war with other men, then there can be no real community; the State serves merely as a policeman to keep individuals from seriously harming one another. The ancient conception of the human was completely different. In his discussion of Aristotle's account of the virtues, Alasdair MacIntyre makes some useful observations concerning the ancient community. The citizens of the *polis* all shared the same goal: as a community, they strove to realize not just this or that good, but the human good in general, which, to a certain extent, is synonymous with citizenship itself. The particular kind of bond between citizens which, according to Aristotle, constitutes a *polis*, springs from their broad agreement on the nature of goods and virtues. Of these, the virtue of friendship is one of the most important. MacIntyre comments:

> The type of friendship which Aristotle has in mind is that which embodies a shared recognition of and pursuit of a good. It is this sharing which is essential and primary to the constitution of any form of community, whether that of a household or that of a city. . . .
>
> This notion of the political community as a common project is alien to the modern liberal individualist world. This is how we sometimes at least think of schools, hospitals or philanthropic organizations; but we have no conception of such a form of community concerned, as Aristotle says the *polis* is concerned, with the whole of life, not with this or that good, but with man's good as such. It is no wonder that friendship has

been relegated to private life and thereby weakened in comparison to what it once was. (MacIntyre 1984, pp. 155–56)

The passages I have quoted from Polybius' account of a Roman funeral, from the *Aeneid*, and especially from Cicero's letters to Atticus (see above, pp. 57–58, 75, and chap. 3 respectively), give specific examples of the experience of community in the ancient world. In every case we see how a person, in crucial moments of his life, is seen as part of a larger whole: young Lausus becomes an example of *pietas*, the son of the deceased becomes the bearer of his family's history, which is also the history of Rome. Cicero fled to Astura after Tullia died not because he wanted to be alone with his grief, but because his grief threatened to break the bonds of community, and thus keep him from fulfilling his duties and obligations as a Roman. And his friends Atticus and Brutus, as Cicero himself did two years later for Brutus, fulfilled some of the *duties* of ancient communal friendship by helping Cicero remember that he was a part of a whole, a citizen of Rome. The ancients, in sum, conceptualized and experienced their humanity not as separation, but as *participation* in the whole order of being. Their experience and their ideals can help us now as we begin to grope for new communal ideals and a language in which to express them.

It is this search that makes a book such as Cicero's *On Duties (De officiis)* important reading today. At a time when deep cynicism pervades so much of our public life, and so many young people use the amount of money they hope to earn as the standard for choosing their future careers, Cicero's treatise presents the ancient ideal of public service and civic virtue as one of the higher goals of a human life.

A New Perspective on the Mystery of Human Existence

I have tried to show how the ancients can help us achieve a new understanding of the unity of mind and nature, and of the individual and community, by inviting us to ponder their experience of the harmony and symmetry between these realms of being. But they can do even more. They can give us a new perspective on the mystery of our own existence.

Many people today seem to be searching for a new vision of man and his place in the universe. In many instances they are seeking a dimension of reality which both transcends and gives meaning to their lives. This search is often expressed as a call to turn our attention to "religious" questions, the ultimate questions one can ask concerning the nature of the universe and man: Is there something higher than man? Is there spirit as well as matter?[8]

Science itself, or better, the limits of science, invite us to ask these questions. This is true not only of the physical sciences. The theme that runs through the works of Ernest Becker, a cultural anthropologist and a popular writer whose final book, *The Denial of Death*, won the Pulitzer Prize for General Nonfiction in 1974, is that the insights and discoveries of anthropology, sociology, psychology, and psychiatry, taken as a whole, lead to a conception of man as a creature in search of something greater than himself. "If I were asked for the single most striking insight into the human condition," Becker once wrote, "it would be this: that no person is strong enough to support the meaning of his life unaided by something outside him" (Becker 1969, p. 130). For Becker, this "something," the highest level of power and meaning to which a human being can turn, is the sacred (Becker 1971, p. 186). Questions concerning the "problem of man" raised by the social sciences, he argues, can thus be answered only by religion and theology.

This increased attention to "religious" questions, coming as it does from scientific quarters, may be a sign of a significant change in our consciousness of ourselves and the meaning of our lives. Charles Trinkaus has spoken of "the gradual development of a 'deification' of man, or a displacement of the consciousness of God as the prime directive force in the universe by a notion of human powers and of natural forces, which . . . begins in the Italian Renaissance" (Trinkaus 1976, p. 688). Now, five centuries later, with the Renaissance, the Scientific Revolution, and the Industrial Revolution all behind us, we are beginning to wonder again if there is something in the universe beyond human powers and natural forces.

It is one thing, however, to ask religious questions, and another thing to pursue them. We won't find much help from the academic community. While the social sciences, as Becker argues, may point beyond themselves to religion and theology, the academic study and teaching of religion has moved away from theology and metaphysics, and has adopted instead the disciplines of anthropology, sociology, and psychology to describe and explain the experience of the sacred. Since their methodological perspectives require that they explain whatever phenomenon they may be studying as a human construct, these disciplines are incapable of considering the existence of anything which transcends the human. When they meet the belief in the divine, they reduce it to the product of social, cultural, or psychological factors. As Arthur Green, president of the Reconstructionist Rabbinical College, put it recently, "There is no place for religion as a divine rather than a human creation in the general academic community" (Green 1986, p. 86).

The modern mind, insofar as it tries to find a "scientific" explanation of reality, is uncomfortable with mystery, complexity, and paradox. It is always tempted to explain whatever phenomenon it seeks to understand by reducing it to a lower order of being. It explains the human in terms of the animal, and life and consciousness in terms of atoms and molecules.[9]

The Greeks and the Romans did not think this way. The fundamental characteristic of classical thought is its attempt to understand the human condition in terms of its relationship to that which transcends the human. "[T]he Greeks of the early and classical periods," Bruno Snell has written, "used the term, 'human' in contradistinction to the notion of divinity: the human being is a mortal (*brotos, thnetos*) thing, whereas god is immortal (*athanatos*). Man is a frail and feeble being, the shadow of a dream" (Snell 1960, p. 246). Speaking of modern misconceptions concerning the Greeks, Snell writes:

> It is sometimes averred that the Greeks in their art did not portray any one man with his accidental traits, but that they represented *man* himself, the idea of man, to use a Platonic expression which is not infrequently used to support the argument. The truth is that such a statement is neither Platonic nor even Greek in spirit. No Greek ever seriously spoke of the idea of man. . . . If we want to describe the statues of the fifth century in the words of their age, we should say that they represent beautiful or perfect men, or, to use a phrase employed in early lyrics for purposes of eulogy: "god-like" men. Even for Plato the norm of judgment still rests with the gods, and not with men. (Snell 1960, pp. 246–47)

For Cicero, a person becomes truly human only by rising above the human through the contemplation of the eternal and the divine. This is one of the meanings Cicero gives to the word *humanitas*. In a passage we looked at earlier, he writes:

> But what dominion, what magistracy, what kingdom can be more excellent than for one, looking down upon everything human and considering it inferior to wisdom, never to revolve anything in his mind except that which is eternal and divine? Such a one is persuaded that while others may be called human (*homines*), only those are who are polished by the proper arts of humanity (*humanitatis artes*). . . . (*De re publica* I, 17, 28)

The ancients lived with the awareness of a dimension of reality which both transcends and gives ultimate meaning to human life. Furthermore, as Cranz has shown (see above, chapter 4), the subject-object dichotomy of modern reason was absent from their epistemology, so that in thinking about the eternal and the divine, the Greeks and the Romans could become one with it.

The Greeks and the Romans, then, offer us a rich source of concepts and insights upon which we can draw in exploring the mystery of our lives. Furthermore, if ancient epistemology is based upon a unity between the knower and the known, then the actual *experience* of the sacred found in classical antiquity may serve as an ideal against which we can measure our own attempts to find support for the full meaning of our lives in something outside of us.

The question of the meaning of human existence is one that no person can avoid. It is thus a vital question for us to raise in our schools. Students will decide for themselves whether they want to believe there is something which transcends the human. But their education will be limited and one-sided unless they are given a chance to consider this possibility. Studying the Greek and Roman experience of the divine is an excellent way of raising religious questions in a pluralist society. This is because the Greeks and the Romans can lead us to ponder "religion" in its original sense. As Carl Kerenyi puts it in the introduction to his study *The Religion of the Greeks and the Romans*:

> I have here used the word 'absolute' as a description, as non-commital as possible, for everything before which a man stands *religiously*, as before the divine. We have here the original sense of the word 'religious', not referring to a particular religion, but to an attitude of respect, or beyond that, of worship, or more still, a feeling of giddiness on the edge of the abyss, of the Nihil, or 'nothingness.' This attitude may refer either to a god, who will be addressed as 'thou,' or to the festal reality of the world—a godly world or a world full of gods—or even to the Nihil in a completely godless world, a *kosmos atheos*. . . . (Kerenyi 1962, p. 14)

Utterly noncommittal as far as any of the world's contemporary religions are concerned, the ancients can provide us with a sense of life lived in the awareness of an absolute, with an ideal of humanity, as Cicero says, which looks upward to the eternal and the divine.

In studying the ancients we are reminded that there have been in the past, and therefore certainly can be in the future, other ways of understanding and experiencing the mystery of existence. The ancients cannot solve this mystery for us. We have to face it on our own, the way every generation does. But they can help us face it. They have stood, as Kerenyi puts it, at the edge of the abyss. They can give us the courage to stand there too. They can challenge us to question some of our modern beliefs, such as our faith in technological reason, and our retreat into narcissism. They can inspire us to contemplate the wonders of nature, and to love civic virtue. And they can hold out for us the possibility of grounding our lives in something greater than ourselves.

CHAPTER 9

A CURRICULUM FOR TODAY

❧

The Humanities in College

THIS IS A BOOK about the humanities. Many people reading it, however, will want to know how an understanding of the tradition of the humanities can contribute to undergraduate education in general. Can the humanities help us formulate a coherent curriculum? Can they help us agree upon some body of common learning which every liberal arts student should be expected to master? People raise these questions because they are unhappy with the amorphous, fragmented, and to a great extent haphazard, character of liberal arts education today. They want our colleges to offer more intellectual guidance. They want them to answer, more clearly than they now do, the question: What should a college graduate know?

College faculties and administrations recognize the importance of these questions, but they have trouble answering them: they can never reach agreement among themselves on what an ideal liberal arts curriculum should be. Whenever they do come up with some core curriculum which every student should be expected to complete, it is more often than not the result of political compromises between various factions of the faculty, rather than an internally logical and coherent program of studies.

As far as the role of the humanities in addressing these questions is concerned, let me state the obvious: the humanities cannot specify a complete liberal arts curriculum because they themselves are only part of the liberal arts. They can, however, offer some perspectives on what a liberal arts education should *include*. For if my description of the tradition of the humanities is at least partially correct, this tradition itself can suggest some important issues which all liberal arts students should face today. The reader will judge how successful I have been in drawing these issues and perspectives logically out the tradition of the humanities, but turning to a dialogue with this tradition

170

seems to me one way of solving the problem of lack of agreement among faculties and administrations concerning what our students should study and why.

In chapter 1, I discussed Bruni's letter to Battista di Montefeltro. I pointed out that of the specific subjects Bruni wants Battista to study, moral philosophy was the most important. Bruni wants Battista to see what "the greatest minds of the philosophers have handed down" concerning "the good life" (*bene vivendum*). In his attack on scholastic Aristotelianism, Petrarch raised the question of the relationship between learning and goodness. For Petrarch, the only learning that really matters is that which helps us to know "man's nature, the purpose for which we are born, and whence and whereto we travel." From the point of view of the tradition of the humanities, the primary purpose of education is moral: it is to help us acquire the learning we need in order to think about the meaning and purpose of our lives. Furthermore, insofar as this thinking raises questions of moral philosophy, that is, to use Bruni's terms, questions concerning the good life (*bene vivendum*), happiness (*beata vita*), and virtue, the tradition of the humanities invites us, as Bruni did Battista, to ponder the answers which the ancients gave to these questions. This, then, is the first contribution the humanities can make to liberal education today. They can remind us that the most important instruction we can give our students is that which will help them seek wisdom and virtue. Let us look at this goal more closely.

For Petrarch, there is an implied distinction between the liberal arts as they were practiced by the scholastics and those studies which would come to be known as the humanities. This distinction is useful to keep in mind as we think about the goal or goals of a liberal arts education today. In the 1350s, Petrarch wrote a letter, which we looked at earlier in the context of "mental discipline," about a man who was still teaching logic in his old age, and presenting it as the most important of all the disciplines. Petrarch is careful to point out that he is not against logic, or dialectic, in itself:

I know how much the Stoics, that strong and masculine sect of philosophers our Cicero mentions so often, especially in his book *De finibus*, attribute to it. I know it is one of the liberal arts, and a stepping-stone for those who are pressing upwards to higher things. It is not useless armor for those who walk through philosophers' thickets. It arouses the intellect, marks off the path to truth, and shows how to avoid fallacies. Finally, if nothing else, it makes people quick and witty.

Notice how similar Petrarch's description of the uses of logic is to what college presidents say about a "liberal arts" education today: they argue that it prepares young people for good jobs after graduation by teaching them how to think clearly, judge critically . . . and even express themselves with urbanity and wit.

From Petrarch's point of view, however, the acquisition of reasoning skills and a quick wit cannot be the goal of a person's life. He goes on to say:

> But where we passed through with honor, we do not remain with praise. On the contrary, the traveller who, because the road is pleasant, forgets the goal he has set for himself, is of unsound mind. Praise for the traveller lies in having passed quickly through many things, and never having stopped short of the end of the journey. And who among us is not a traveller? We all, for a brief and hostile time, as during a rainy day in winter, make a long and difficult journey. Dialectic can be a part of this journey, but surely not the goal. And it can be the part of this journey we make in the morning, not in the evening. (*Fam.* I, 7, 13–14)

Petrarch closes his letter with this advice:

> So stir up the pupils of that old man with my words. Don't deter them, but encourage them, not that they hasten towards dialectic, but through it on to better things. Tell the old man, then, that I do not condemn the liberal arts, but childish old people. (*Fam.* I, 7, 18)

As we have seen, the humanities emerged, in part, as a reaction against this attempt to reduce learning to the acquisition of intellectual skills and research techniques. The *studia humanitatis* did not do away with the liberal arts. But the humanities changed the so-called "liberal arts tradition" by merging into it and by adding another goal to secondary and university education: the subjugation of all concern with methodology and preprofessional training to a search for the meaning of human life, and the shaping and molding of moral character. I realize, of course, that the distinction between the humanities and the liberal arts is a modern one; it did not exist in classical antiquity, as I showed in chapter 1. The ancient unity of all the disciplines and areas of learning remains a powerful ideal to strive for, and a standard against which to measure and judge our own increasingly fragmented and incoherent curriculum. But that unity does not exist today. Our situation is strikingly similar to Petrarch's. So his response must be ours, at least until we can find a new unity of all the areas of learning. The distinction Petrarch makes between technical and preprofessional training, and learning which can accompany us through life, reflects what he perceived as the inability of the university education of his time to address moral questions. There is thus a tension built into the very pedagogical tradition we inherit between the humanities and preprofessional training, between a concern for the acquisition of "marketable skills," to use a present-day term, and a longing for the wisdom and the virtue which will guide us on our life's journey, to use Petrarch's analogy. The major contribution the tradition of the humanities can make to the liberal arts curriculum today is to help us choose the latter as the primary goal of liberal learning.

Where can we learn about wisdom and virtue today? The tradition of the humanities tells us to study the ancients. But this tradition has deteriorated in our own times, for internal as well as external reasons. The whole point of studying the history of the humanities is to arrive at an understanding of this deterioration which will permit us to see why we can no longer read and teach the ancients the way our ancestors did. So what are we to do? We must avoid looking back with nostalgia to the Renaissance, or even to the nineteenth century, and recognize instead that the classical education which nourished the culture of Europe and later America from the fifteenth through the nineteenth century has died. And yet, as I have argued, we still need a dialogue with the Greeks and the Romans. The challenge facing us now, therefore, is to find a new and fresh way of studying our classical and Renaissance pasts. It is precisely in taking up this challenge that we discover a solution to the fundamental problem of liberal arts education today: its lack of direction and coherence. Recognition of the deterioration of the tradition of the humanities brings with it the possibility that the very project, the very activity of trying to understand, revise, and reappropriate this tradition could, in itself, give continuity and coherence to the liberal arts curriculum, and moral consciousness to our students. This is the second major contribution the humanities can make to liberal arts education today. They not only give us a goal for liberal education; they can help us achieve it. Let us see how.

Our understanding of the meaning and purpose of our lives is closely bound up with our understanding of what it means to be a person, that is, with our concept of the self. I have argued that it is time for us to reexamine this concept. This is what the humanities can help us do, for it is within the tradition of the humanities that the concept of a unique, autonomous, inward-turning self received its fullest cultural expression. If we want to understand our ideals of radical autonomy and individual self-perfection, and why these ideals have degenerated into the pathological narcissism that afflicts our society today, we need to study the history of the humanities. Furthermore, it is this kind of study that can draw us out of our narcissism. By looking carefully at how the Renaissance humanists read a modern self back into the ancients, we discover another kind of self, the ancient extensive self, with its ideal not of autonomy and radical freedom, but of harmony and unity with the whole world of being. The humanities thus not only give us a history of the modern self; they remind us that our own culture, our own past, contains experiences and ideals which can help us transcend this self and find other ways of experiencing our humanity.

By inviting us to study the Renaissance's transformation of the Greek and Roman concept of the human, the tradition of the humanities offers a way of understanding both Renaissance and classical culture. But it does not stop there. It offers a unique perspective on modern culture as well. One way of understanding the development of modern science, philosophy, and later the social sciences, is to see it as a series of attempts to come to terms philosophically and morally with the autonomous, inward-turning self Petrarch first described in his writings, and with the relationship of this autonomous subjectivity both to nature and to society, especially society as we know it after the French and Industrial Revolutions. If the condition of modern man is one of intellectual fragmentation and moral disorientation, *one* of the reasons is that these attempts have failed, and this despite the brilliance of those who undertook them.

Furthermore, in leading us into a dialogue with classical antiquity, the project of revising and reappropriating the tradition of the humanities frees us from two imprisoning conditions of modern culture. First of all, in part because of the failures mentioned above, modern society has lost wisdom and virtue as ideals. If Alasdair MacIntyre's analysis of the history of moral philosophy from the Enlightenment up to the present is correct, it is impossible to be modern and moral, for the fully autonomous self knows no morality other than the expression of its own desires and principles.[1] This is a crucial issue which every student attending a liberal arts college should be expected to confront, because in deciding how to resolve it, one is in effect answering the question of the meaning and purpose of his or her life. Secondly, I have argued that one of the factors which has contributed to the deterioration of the humanities in our own time is the death of the past. This is another issue every student should be expected to face. The great collective amnesia which now hangs over us has given rise to one of the most alarming aspects of modern society: the fact that so many people can be deeply disturbed by modern life but nonetheless resigned to it. This happens because of the nature of thought itself. Thinking takes place through comparison and contrast; if people have nothing to compare the present to, they have no way of thinking about it, and no way of imagining anything different. Modernity has thus not only destroyed the possibility of moral discourse; by destroying the past, modern industrial society has also destroyed the basis for critical thought.

The attempt to regain moral consciousness thus becomes an attempt to regain historical consciousness as well. It is only by studying the ideals of previous ages that we can understand and evaluate our own. The attempt to understand and use the tradition of the humanities is thus a way of acquiring historical and moral consciousness. The Renaissance humanists can give us the courage and the inspiration to do as they did: turn back to classical antiquity in an effort to understand and evaluate the moral and intellectual life of the present. The Greeks and the Romans can give us examples of wisdom and virtue, and can show us that the two great dichotomies of modern culture which so deeply influence our understanding of the human condition, the division between mind and nature, and between the individual and society, are by no means part of the natural order of things, but are products of a certain conception of the human which we are now challenged to transcend.

The humanities can thus help to give continuity and coherence to our increasingly fragmented liberal arts curriculum in three general ways. They can help us choose a goal for liberal education which addresses our highest needs; they can offer a perspective on Western history; and they can show us how to use this perspective to understand and evaluate our own times. How can we translate all of this into a specific curriculum? The humanities do it for us. Their history raises a series of questions concerning our past, present, and future which every graduate of a liberal arts college should be able to answer:

1. What is the Greek and Roman concept of the human? How did the Greeks and the Romans understand the relationship of the individual human being to nature, society, and to that which transcends the human?

2. How and why did the Renaissance humanists transform the classical concept of the human?

3. What are the humanities? Why did they begin in the Renaissance? Why has the tradition of the humanities deteriorated in our own time?

4. What understanding of the self, of nature, and of society underlay the scientific revolution of the seventeenth century and the Enlightenment of the eighteenth century?

5. What problems concerning the Renaissance/modern understanding of the self and nature did Kant and Hegel attempt to solve? What have been the consequences of their attempts for modern thought?

6. When and how did the social sciences come into being? As moral theories, what do the social sciences say about the nature of the self, and the meaning and purpose of human existence?

7. What are the differences between ancient and modern moral philosophy? How can one attain wisdom and virtue today?

There are several ways of preparing our students to answer these questions. The Oxford/Cambridge system of tutorials, university lectures, and students reading for comprehensive exams would be the best: it encourages students to read and think on their own, gives them the confidence that they can educate themselves, and helps them acquire habits of self-disciplined learning which will serve them in good stead throughout their lives.

In the United States it is more likely that teachers will prefer to discuss these issues through a series of courses. In this case it would still be useful to give incoming freshmen these or similar questions, with the understanding that they will be expected to answer them, either in written or oral examinations, at the end of their senior year. This would be a good way of giving our students something coherent and continuous to think about during their four years at college, and it could raise considerably the intellectual tone of their lives.

What might such a series of courses look like? This is something individual faculties will have to decide. There are many ways of discussing in the classroom the issues which the tradition of the humanities raises today, and we should encourage diversity of approach in order to keep these questions from becoming stale and rote. Purely by way of example, then, let me suggest a series of four courses, each of which could be one or two semesters in length:

FRESHMAN YEAR   Classical Antiquity and Its Transformation in the Renaissance: The Birth of the Autonomous Self.

SOPHOMORE YEAR   Science and Philosophy in Early Modern Europe: The Autonomous Self and the Objectification of Nature.

JUNIOR YEAR   The Social Sciences as Moral Theory: Individual Autonomy and the Origins of Modern Society.

SENIOR YEAR   Moral Philosophy: The Search for Wisdom and Virtue.

FRESHMAN YEAR: CLASSICAL ANTIQUITY AND ITS TRANSFORMATION IN THE RENAISSANCE

This is the most important course of the humanities curriculum, for it is the foundation of everything that is to come. Its goal is to enable the students to understand the radical difference between ancient and modern categories of thought, and experiences of the human. Students should begin by studying the texts I cite in chapter 4. When they have some sense of the differences between ancient conjunctive vision and the modern subject-object dichotomy, they will be ready to study the differences between the ancient and the modern self. The best way of perceiving these differences is to see how Petrarch and the early humanists turned the ancient extensive self into the modern intensive self, and how the humanities came into being as a curriculum for the new self. For this study I have chosen the following seven texts: Cicero's philosophical and moral works *The Tusculan Disputations* (*Disputationes Tusculanae*) and *On the Nature of the Gods* (*De Natura Deorum*), and his short *Speech on Behalf of Archias the Poet* (*Pro Archia*); St. Augustine's treatise *On True Religion* (*De vera religione*); Petrarch's *Secret* (*Secretum*) and his treatise *On His Own Ignorance and That of Many Others* (*De sui ipsius et multorum ignorantia*); and finally Leonardo Bruni's treatise *On Studies and Letters* (*De studiis et litteris*).

A full and sustained dialogue with our classical and Renaissance pasts would certainly include other authors. Homer, Sophocles, and Vergil, Plato and Aristotle, Erasmus, More, Machiavelli, and Montaigne, among others, come readily to mind. I have chosen to begin with these particular texts by Cicero, Augustine, Petrarch, and Bruni because not only can they help us to understand the ancient and Renaissance/modern conceptions of what it means to be human; when read as a unit they will help us see the differences between the two. They are the texts which I have found most useful in describing the origins of the humanities, and in explaining the humanities to students and other audiences.

Students should begin their study of the Renaissance's transformation of classical antiquity by reading Cicero. Although the approach to the humanities I am proposing calls for a radical revision of the understanding of classical antiquity which we inherit from the Renaissance humanists, the author they made the basis of their curriculum, Cicero, serves our present needs admirably well. Cicero is a concise and eloquent writer who strove to make Greek philosophical speculation available to his Latin compatriots. A careful reading of his works offers us a vicarious experience of ancient Rome, and a useful introduction to Greek thought. Cicero's letters, orations, and philosophical writings, by their very number and breadth of topics, constitute an exceptionally full picture of ancient life and thought. Furthermore, Cicero wrote in Latin rather than Greek; since English derives in part from Latin, and since Latin is much more widely studied than ancient Greek, there is a greater chance that those who begin to read Cicero in

English, or in bilingual editions, will become sufficiently interested in what he has to say to learn enough Latin to read his works in the original.

I have chosen Cicero's *Tusculan Disputations* because this work treats, from the point of view of the ancient unity of the individual, society, and the cosmos, problems which the Renaissance attempted to solve through the creation of an inward-turning autonomous self, and which we all still struggle with today: the fear of death, physical pain and suffering, mental anguish and depression, emotional turmoil, and the search for happiness.

On the Nature of the Gods may seem strangely discordant in our own age, but its portrayal of the individual as part of the cosmos is of great relevance to recent developments in modern science, developments which have led, as we saw in the previous chapter, to a renewed interest in cosmology and natural theology. One of the challenges facing us today, moreover, as we see from the ecological movement, is to recapture a sense of the sacred and the divine, especially as far as the natural world is concerned, in a nondenominational language acceptable to everyone regardless of religion or creed. Cicero's treatise on the gods provides a good introduction to the ancient experience of the cosmos as a sacred and ordered whole.

Finally, Cicero's short and famous speech *Pro Archia* contains his use of the phrase *studia humanitatis*. It helps to know what Cicero means by this term in order to see how the Renaissance humanists gave it a new meaning.

In his work the *Secret,* consisting of three short dialogues between himself and St. Augustine, Petrarch tells Augustine that he has recently read his treatise *On True Religion (De vera religione)*. I have included this work of Augustine's in my program of studies not only because it will let students see how Petrarch transforms the ancient program of "seeing with the mind," but also because *On True Religion,* which dates from an earlier period in Augustine's life in which he was deeply influenced by Plato's philosophy, contains passages that show the ancient preoccupation with the relationship of the Many to the One, and its solution through the participation of the human in an order of being beyond the individual self. For these themes it would be sufficient to read sections XXIX, 52 - LII, 101.

Having read Cicero and Augustine will enable the students to read Petrarch and the early humanists with historical insight. Petrarch wrote the *Secret* in midlife, and his treatise *On His Own Ignorance and That of Many Others* shortly before he died. These two works record his attempt to solve the problem of change and multiplicity by creating for himself an immutable unity within, just the opposite of what Augustine did. In reading the *Secret* and *On His Own Ignorance and That of Many Others,* the students will meet texts by Cicero and Augustine they already know, and will thus be able to see how Petrarch transforms them. Furthermore, the *Secret* in particular shows the limitations of the inward-turning self: Petrarch cannot, through will power alone, change his character.

Finally, Bruni's treatise *On Studies and Letters* will let students learn firsthand what the original humanities were. I have found, moreover, that asking students to imitate Bruni's treatise by writing a letter to a younger brother, sister, or friend about to begin college is an excellent way of getting them to think about education.

Discussing and comparing these texts over the course of one or two semesters gives us an opportunity not just to learn about the tradition of the humanities, but also to revise it. On the one hand, the texts by Cicero and Augustine are ones which the Renaissance humanists studied and taught. On the other hand, the questions which we, standing at a farther point in time, can now put to these texts are radically different from the ones which the early humanists, or even nineteenth-century humanists such as Nietzsche or Matthew Arnold, asked. It is crucial that we point out this difference to our students. Unless the student can actually see how the Renaissance humanists transformed the classical experience of the human by reading a personal self into it, he or she may end up doing exactly the same thing today, and thus miss the new perspectives on the mystery of human existence which come from discovering the ancient ideal of the unity of the individual with something greater than himself.

In preparing the courses for the sophomore and junior years, those who now teach courses in the history of science and technology, the history of modern philosophy, and the social sciences, should work together to address the question of how the twin concepts of an autonomous individuality and an objectified nature, including human nature, became so firmly rooted in Western consciousness during the seventeenth, eighteenth, and nineteenth centuries. As general goals, these two courses should help students to see that not only the social sciences, but also natural science and technology, are based upon a particular conception of the human. The objectification and the domination of nature, for example, presupposes that human beings are autonomous selves who stand over and against the natural world as subjects to objects.[2] Let us now look at these two courses:

SOPHOMORE YEAR: SCIENCE AND PHILOSOPHY IN
EARLY MODERN EUROPE

This course combines the History of Science and the History of Modern Philosophy courses now offered in most colleges and universities.

I would cover the standard authors now taught in these courses, but in introducing the students to Galileo and Descartes, and the scientific and epistemological revolution of the seventeenth century, it would be useful to have them study carefully the "Cranz Thesis" and the texts I have cited in chapter 4: we really cannot understand modern reason until we can contrast it with ancient reason.

Students should read only original texts. Those teaching this course will find that the first and last chapters of Charles Taylor's *Hegel* (Taylor 1975) give an overview of the moral and philosophical problems such a course could explore. The first chapter is an extremely lucid account of the attempt to define "the nature of human subjectivity and its relation to the world" (p. 3) from the scientific and epistemological revolution of the seventeenth and eighteenth century up to Hegel. Taylor sees the modern subject-object dichotomy as coming into being with Descartes. Cranz has found it much earlier in Anselm, and I have emphasized the key role Petrarch plays in defining the modern intensive self. But none of this detracts from the usefulness of what Taylor has to say about this central problem of modern philosophy. In his last chapter, "Hegel Today," Taylor offers some interesting observations on modern society, and on the way in which periodic revolts against modernity, such as the student movement of the sixties, return to themes first elaborated by the German Romantics and Hegel, and later by Marx.

One of the great challenges facing our high schools and colleges today is to revise radically the way we teach science. From the Enlightenment on, science has been modernity's chief superstition: despite the changing perceptions of modern science I discussed in the previous chapter, too many people still think of science as a kind of magic which will someday solve all of the world's problems. Scientists such as Lewis Thomas and Stanley L. Jaki have argued that the exaggerated claims made for science, and the popular misconceptions of science such claims have spawned, are the fault of scientists themselves, who either do not understand or do not discuss publicly the very limited, tentative, and provisional nature of so-called scientific "discoveries." Thomas believes that in introductory courses in science we should emphasize what science does not know (Thomas 1984, p. 151). Jaki stresses the importance of teaching the *history of science*. He takes issue with the assertion made by C. P. Snow in his book *The Two Cultures and the Scientific Revolution* (1959) that the split between the humanities and the sciences in the modern world is due to ignorance of science on the part of nonscientists, and that it can be repaired by adding more science courses in our schools. According to Jaki, the problem today is that not only nonscientists, but scientists themselves have a triumphalistic, superhuman, and basically distorted image of science, and this because they are ignorant of the *history* of science. "What is really needed," Jaki writes,

> is the determination to restore the truly human features in the portrait of science, and this means that both the successes and the failures of the scientific quest should be given proper emphasis. For, as the historical record shows, failures, limitations, and persistent frustration are not an irrelevant side aspect of the march of science. As the triumphs of physics unfold in connection with solving basic problems of the life sciences, so with each advance of physics are new aspects of the immense complexity of living matter revealed. In the same manner, man's conquest of one layer of matter reveals at the same time the outlines of a hitherto unsuspected one. Man's penetration into the realm of stars and galaxies shows the same characteristics, those of an apparently never-ending process. Again, all claims to the contrary, *physical science has relatively little to say about such crucial aspects of human endeavor as those manifested in ethics, social organization, religion, and the arts. Obviously, the metric tools of science are not the instruments for probing the depths of the non-metric dimension of human existence.* . . . Far from being the complete truth based on uncontrovertible facts, science even in its own field is not wholly objective or infinitely precise or unconditionally permanent or philosophically inescapable as regards its findings and laws. (Jaki 1966, pp. 505–506. My emphasis)

Jaki observes that the effects of science can be both beneficial and harmful, and that "the latter usually stem from a misunderstanding and misuse of science." He goes on to point out the need for a historical, as opposed to a technical, knowledge of science:

> The misunderstanding, however, can be based as much on worshiping science as on ignoring it. This is one of those truths about science that should be assimilated as widely as possible if we are to merge the two cultures again and prepare individuals and society alike to meet in a balanced manner the challenge of the second scientific revolution. *Such assimilation does not so much require technical information about science as it does a better insight into its history. It can be done without knowing calculus or matrix mechanics. But it cannot and will not be done if physicists remain as unaware of the varied history of their field as they are today.* (p. 513. My emphasis)

The tradition of the humanities, as I have described it, can make an important contribution to our comprehension of the history of science by helping us to understand how, and under what circumstances, the objectification of nature occurred in the West, and why modern science has nothing to say about wisdom and virtue.

Finally, this course would be the place to examine the differences between the ancient and the modern self vis-à-vis their relationship to the cosmos, that is, to the totality of being. Students will have read

Cicero's *On the Nature of the Gods* the year before, so they will know something about ancient cosmology and ancient views of the universe. Now they might want to discuss what relevance these views have for their lives today. For those teaching this course, Stephen Toulmin's book, *The Return to Cosmology: Postmodern Science and the Theology of Nature* (1982), especially part three, "The Future of Cosmology: Postmodern Science and Natural Religion," will be interesting reading, since Toulmin discusses some of the similarities and differences between ancient and modern views of the cosmos, and suggests what a modern cosmology might be like.

JUNIOR YEAR: THE SOCIAL SCIENCES
AS MORAL THEORY

"Major ideas in the social sciences invariably have roots in moral aspiration," Robert A. Nisbet has written. "However abstract the ideas may eventually become, however neutral they may come to seem to scientists and theorists, they do not ever really divest themselves of their moral origins" (Nisbet 1966, p. 18).

The social sciences influence our thinking today in two ways: they give us many of the words and concepts we use in thinking and talking about modernity, and they give us some of the words and concepts we use in defining our moral aspirations. Students need to be aware of both in examining their own thinking about the world they live in, and in contrasting what the ancients have to say about the meaning and purpose of human existence with modern answers to this question. It is important, then, that they have some understanding of the historical origins of the social sciences, and what the social sciences say, or imply, about human life and the nature of the self. Since the social sciences began, in part, as an attempt to apply the methodology of the natural sciences to the study of human psychology and society, this course should provide as well an opportunity to discuss the relationship between the social sciences and natural science.

The books which have influenced my own thinking about the social sciences as moral theories, and which might be of some use to those teaching this course, include C. B. Macpherson's study of the seventeenth-century roots of liberal-democratic political theory, *The Political Theory of Possessive Individualism: Hobbes to Locke* (1962); Robert A. Nisbet, *The Sociological Tradition* (1966); and Philip Rieff, *The Triumph of the Therapeutic: Uses of Faith After Freud* (1966). (Note the title of Rieff's previous book: *Freud: The Mind of the Moralist.*) The second chapter of Nisbet's book presents a useful overview of the effects the French Revolution and the Industrial Revolution have had on modern values and thought. The titles of two recent books are indicative of a growing body of literature on the moral underpinnings, often hidden under scientific rhetoric, of the social sciences: Barry Schwartz, *The Battle for Human Nature: Science, Morality, and Modern Life* (1986), and Donald N. McCloskey, *The Rhetoric of Economics* (1985).

I see a course of this kind as an opportunity to begin a fruitful dialogue between the social sciences and the tradition of the humanities. In some ways they share similar goals. Anthony Giddens, in his short book *Sociology: A Brief but Critical Introduction* (1987), writes:

> An understanding of the social world initiated by the contemporary industrialised societies—present-day society as first formed in the West—can only be achieved by virtue of a threefold exercise of the imagination. These forms of the sociological imagination involve an *historical*, an *anthropological*, and a *critical* sensitivity. (p. 13)

In describing the first, Giddens says that

> [t]he first effort of sociological imagination that has to be exercised by the analyst of the industrialised societies today is that of recovering our own immediate past—the 'world we have lost'. Only by such an effort of the imagination, which of course involves an awareness of history, can we grasp just how differently those in industrialised societies live today from the way people lived in the relatively recent past. (p. 14)

The truth of what Giddens says can be seen from the history of sociology itself. Why did the golden age of sociological thought occur in the last century, and not in our own times? Because the great thinkers of the nineteenth century had a historical imagination. The founders of modern sociology, men such as Comte, Durkheim, Le Play, Marx, Simmel, Tocqueville, and Weber, were much closer in time to the French Revolution than we are, and all of them experienced the Industrial Revolution firsthand. They were aware of, and were struggling to understand, the enormous changes then taking place in Western society and values. They contrasted industrial with preindustrial society, Christian-feudal values with the secular rationalism and democratic ideals of the Enlightenment and the French Revolution. In this sense both the social sciences, especially sociology, which has always been the most self-consciously moral of the social sciences, and the tradition of the humanities foster historical and moral consciousness: they both judge present-day society by contrasting it to the past.

But there are also fundamental differences between these two traditions. Three are particularly important here, and we need to keep them in mind in order for a dialogue between the social sciences and the humanities to prove fruitful. Historically, the social sciences have always looked to a more recent past against which to understand and judge the present: the preindustrial, precapitalist society of Christian-feudal Europe. Nisbet speaks of the "rediscovery of medievalism" as "one of the significant events in the intellectual history of the nineteenth century" (Nisbet 1966, p. 14). We have already seen the immense importance of classical antiquity in nineteenth-century thought and political debate. But Nisbet is right to remind us that when nineteenth-century sociologists sought to contrast their own age to a previous one, it was usually to the Middle Ages that they looked. However, as far as our fundamental *categories of thought* are concerned, "modern" consciousness begins, if Cranz is correct, not with Descartes, but already around 1100 A.D. The medieval mind, in its theological speculations, was already using modern reason. If we want to understand the dichotomy between knower and known, mind and nature, which characterizes the modern world, we need to contrast it with the conjunctive vision of the ancient world. While the contrast between feudal and capitalist society does indeed provide important insights into the nature of modernity (as anyone who has taught the *Divine Comedy* knows), the only way fully to understand modernity is to contrast it with classical antiquity. From this point of view, the tradition of the humanities, insofar as it provides a key to understanding the ancient self and ancient categories of thought, can considerably enhance the social scientist's understanding of modern culture.

The second fundamental difference between the tradition of the humanities and the social sciences lies in the social sciences' attempt to be "scientific" by uncovering universal "laws" which apply to all societies, not just our own. As Louis Dumont points out at the beginning of *Homo Hierarchicus,* his study of the caste system in India, "sociology is the product of modern society, or rather an integral part of it. It can escape this limitation only partially, and by a deliberate effort" (Dumont 1980, p. 4). What Dumont says about sociology is true of all the other social sciences as well: they are modernity's attempt to understand modernity; they are the modern mind's attempt to understand modern society, especially modern industrial capitalism. And thus they are limited. Whenever they attempt to understand premodern societies on the basis of concepts which they have worked out for analyzing modern society, they risk turning the past into a mirror of the present. For example, the most powerful explanatory model of the "laws of motion" of modern capitalist society is Marx's. In an age obsessed with methodologies, many people have found it convenient to adopt as universal laws of history, applicable to all societies, past as well as present, the concepts of "forces of production" and "relations of production," and of "base" and "superstructure," and the relationship between them that Marx sketches in the brief preface to his *Critique of Political Economy* (1859). In a careful analysis of what Marx and Engels actually wrote about this subject, Paul M. Sweezy shows that they never intended the schema set out by Marx in the preface to apply to any society other than capitalist society. As Sweezy observes, it does make a good deal of sense to separate the social and economic "base" of capitalist society from its cultural "superstructure," and to talk about the influence of the former on the latter (Sweezy 1981, pp. 11–25). But this model blinds us to understanding pre-, or even postcapitalist societies in which moral or religious obligations and duties may shape the tenor of life. We all, whether teachers of literature, economists, nuclear physicists, philologists, or modern philosophers, must thus make a deliberate effort to put aside modern categories of thought if we ever hope to learn something from the ancients. It is not as modern fragmented specialists that we must approach them, but as human beings in search of the meaning and purpose of our lives. As Pascal said, "People should not be able to say of anyone that he is a mathematician, or a preacher, or an eloquent man, but that he is a man. Only this universal quality pleases me . . . for this universality is the finest thing" (quoted in Jaki 1966, p. 533).

The third difference between the social sciences and the humanities lies in their attitudes toward tradition. In a recent article on "The Return to Values," Alan Wolfe, a sociologist by profession, examines E. M. Forster's novel *Howard's End*. Wolfe points out that this kind of "moral fiction" is no longer written today. Given what he sees as the decline of religion and tradition in the face of modernity, where, he asks, can modern people find moral values? Wolfe believes that part of the answer may lie in the social sciences' rediscovering their moral origins:

> The major question facing a revival of moral sociology is whether it is possible to posit ties that can hold people together without subjecting them to historical traditions or political decisions over which they have no control. . . . Realizing that modernity was inescapable, Durkheim tried to find a source of secular morality, an alternative to either the market or the state. He was not successful. It is not clear that contemporary sociologists will be either, but *attempting to reconcile modernity with morality is certainly the major task facing the more humanistic social sciences in the next years.* (Wolfe 1986, p. 63. My emphasis)

Wolfe's remarks show a convergence of interest now between what he calls the more "humanistic" social sciences, and the tradition of the humanities as I have described it: they are both concerned with moral values, with making some sort of statement about the meaning and purpose of human existence. But his remarks also show another fundamental difference between the social sciences and the humanities: if the social sciences reject tradition, *where* are they to find moral values? Once the students have looked into the origins of the social sciences, and have examined the moral philosophies underlying various economic, political, and social theories, this is the question they should try to answer: Where can a person find moral values today? In struggling to answer this question, they will prepare themselves for the course in Moral Philosophy they will take the coming year.

The two courses which I have just described, *Science and Philosophy in Early Modern Europe* and *The Social Sciences as Moral Theory*, could perhaps be put together out of existing courses now taught at most colleges and universities. My concern here has been to state some of the issues which I think such courses should address. Those who teach them will decide what original texts they want their students to read. It is important, though, that the students have read enough of Hobbes, Locke, and especially Hume, Kant, and Mill during their sophomore or junior years to be able to contrast the kind of "modern" moral philosophy that comes out the Scientific Revolution and the Enlightenment with the ancient moral philosophy they will meet in their senior year.

SENIOR YEAR: MORAL PHILOSOPHY

Many people now are talking about the need to teach moral values in our schools. But there is no agreement on how to do this, or even on what "moral values" are. The reason is summed up in the title of Christina Hoff Sommers's article, "Ethics without Virtue: Moral Education in America" (Sommers 1984). We are unable to teach moral values because modern society has lost the meaning of virtue. We no longer know what virtue is. This loss explains, in part at least, the success of the two most popular forms of "moral education" in our schools today: "values clarification" and "cognitive moral development," movements which Sommers describes and criticizes in her article. Both approaches to moral education are silent about wisdom and virtue.

If we can no longer tell our students what virtue is, who can? The Greeks and the Romans. This senior year course on moral philosophy will give the students a new perspective on the moral dilemmas of the modern age by inviting them to think about virtue the way the Greeks and the Romans did. The course thus serves as the culmination of the entire core curriculum. It uses the learning of the previous three years to address the moral predicament of modern society: to the ex-

tent that it strives to realize its ideals of complete freedom and autonomy, the modern self knows no morality other than the expression of
its own personal "values." If there is no way to justify morality today
beyond personal preference, how is one to be moral? Without a knowledge of the ancients, a person might conclude that this dilemma simply cannot be resolved. Ancient moral philosophy shows that it is a dilemma only for the modern world.

This course has two basic texts: Cicero's *De officiis,* and Aristotle's
Nicomachean Ethics.

A human being is not perfect, but "some little part of the perfect"
(*quaedam particula perfecti*), Cicero says (see above, chap. 1). As far as
human society is concerned, this means that it is participation in the
life of the civic community that gives meaning and purpose to an individual's existence. For the ancients, "ethics" and "politics," in the original meaning of these words, are thus inseparable. We no longer think
this way. According to the seventeenth-century theory of possessive individualism, which still to a large extent determines the ideals of the liberal democratic state, what makes us human is "freedom from dependence on the wills of others" (Macpherson 1962, p. 263). Ancient
moral philosophy sees the human condition in another light. It is not
by chance that Cicero entitled his treatise on moral philosophy *De
officiis,* "On Duties." To be a member of the ancient city-state is to
have specific moral obligations and duties. Cicero describes them in
his treatise, along with the virtues, especially prudence, justice, fortitude, and temperance, from which these duties spring, and the deeds
which exemplified these virtues in specific incidents in the history of
Greece and Rome. With its wealth of examples, the *De officiis* paints a
vivid and moving picture of ancient virtue.

Petrarch liked the Latin writers, especially Cicero, Seneca, and Horace, because he believed their words had the power to enkindle in one
the love of virtue. Aristotle, he felt, could bring one to know virtue,
but not necessarily to will it. The best approach to teaching ancient
moral philosophy today is to give our students both Cicero and Aristotle: after they have peopled their minds with the vivid examples of virtuous deeds they find in Cicero's treatise *On Duties,* the students will
be ready to read Aristotle's *Nicomachean Ethics* for a systematic account
of ancient virtue.

Studying Aristotle's ethics will show students how, in the modern
world, moral consciousness can be achieved only through historical consciousness. As Alasdair MacIntyre observes, ". . . Aristotelianism is
philosophically the most powerful of pre-modern modes of moral
thought. If a premodern view of morals and politics is to be vindi-
cated against modernity, it will be in *something like* Aristotelian terms

or not at all" (MacIntyre 1984, p. 118). The goal of having all liberal arts students read the *Nicomachean Ethics* is not to turn them into Aristotelians; it is to teach them to think coherently about virtue, and to give them a standard against which to measure the depth, seriousness, and coherence of contemporary moral discourse.

Once the students are able to contrast ancient with modern moral education, it will be important for them to understand and discuss how the study of classical virtue came to be replaced by contemporary forms of moral instruction. Those who teach this course will have to decide how they want to approach this topic. I have found Alasdair MacIntyre's *After Virtue* helpful and stimulating. In addition to its discussion of Aristotle's theory of the virtues, the book offers a critical perspective on contemporary moral thought, and a historical explanation for the deterioration of moral discourse in modern society.

In thinking about the place of the humanities in a liberal arts curriculum, it is important to keep in mind two distinctive features of the humanities. First of all, the humanities are the only area of our curriculum explicitly concerned with wisdom and virtue. They thus provide a goal for liberal education as a whole, and a vantage point from which all the other parts of the curriculum can be judged. But they can maintain this vantage point only by keeping in sharp focus what they are: a specific tradition of learning devoted to studying our Renaissance and classical pasts. We must be careful not to blur this focus. It is only insofar as they let us hear the voices of the ancients and their Renaissance interpreters that the humanities can make their special contribution to education today. We must not confuse the humanities with other areas of study which are often included under the rubric "humanities," but which actually lie outside of it.

A curriculum derived from the tradition of the humanities does not specifically address the problems of women and minorities, for example. This is because the contemporary relevance of this tradition concerns issues which transcend gender and race, such as the nature of civic virtue, the uses of historical consciousness, the relationship of mind and nature, and the mystery of human existence. Nor do the humanities, understood historically, include non-Western cultures. The humanities, as the etymology of the term shows, were synonymous with the study and teaching of the languages and culture of ancient Greece and Rome. The Renaissance humanists, in their recognition of cultural differences between their own age and classical antiquity, did indeed lay the basis for the study of non-Western cultures. Moreover, insofar as the humanities help us to understand better the culture of the West, they help us to see more clearly differences and similarities between ourselves and other peoples. But to speak of the "Asian humanities" or the "African humanities" makes no sense; it just adds to the current confusion over what the humanities are or what they could be.

The humanities, finally, when we define them historically, do not include the Judeo-Christian tradition. It is of course impossible to understand fully the history of the West and our own contemporary values, however confused they may appear to be, without coming to terms with the Judeo-Christian tradition. Most humanists, moreover—Petrarch is a prime example—identified with this tradition. Petrarch especially was aware of a tension in his life between his love of the ancients and his Christian faith. But while most humanists engaged in a dialogue with both the classical and the Judeo-Christian traditions, the latter is not definitive of the humanities, even though in many cases Christianity was the matrix within which classical culture was recovered in the West.

It is important to keep in mind, though, that the contrast between ancient and modern categories of thought and experience which we discover in the tradition of the humanities can help us understand certain aspects of the Judeo-Christian tradition. Cranz has argued in a paper on "St. Paul and Ancient Modes of Thought" (Cranz, pp. 47-75), that the ancient extensive self explains much better St. Paul's theme of "Christians *in* Christ" and "Christ *in* Christians" than does the modern intensive self. For example, the King James Version of the Bible translates Galatians 1: 15–16 correctly: "But when it pleased God . . . To reveal his Son *in* me. . . ." Why then did the translators of the Revised Standard Version decide to change "in me" to "to me"? The Greek text, as they point out in a footnote, is "in me." If Cranz is correct, it is because the modern intensive self, which experiences its relationship to everything, including the divine, as a subject juxtaposed to an object, has trouble understanding how God could reveal Christ *in* Paul. But Galatians 1:16 becomes quite clear when we free ourselves from the modern intensive self, and read it in terms of the ancient extensive self, in which the mind becomes one with, or takes in, that which it cogitates. Cranz argues that Paul's experience of the divine was much closer to the kind of union between knower and known that we find in the main Aristotelian and Platonic traditions than it is to the modern subject-object dichotomy that begins with Anselm around 1100 A.D.

To define the humanities historically is to equate them with the tradition of the study of classical antiquity that begins in the Renaissance. In speaking about the relevance of the ancients today, one sometimes hears the objection that classical education died because it was a curriculum for the ruling classes and could not survive the democratization of education in the twentieth century. This argument puts the cart before the horse. The problem is not that the ruling classes studied the classics (although, as we have seen, they often studied them poorly), but that the subaltern classes did not. The study of the virtues necessary for active participation in public life which Cicero offers in his treatise *On Duties* (*De officiis*), for example, is still today an excellent preparation for public service in a democratic republic. It is the kind of preparation sorely lacking in our schools, as the spectacles of Watergate and Irangate sadly show. And why should public service be limited only to the rich and the powerful? The histories of Greece and Rome both show that democracies and republics do not last forever; they eventually succumb to some form of tyranny. One way of avoiding this fate is to have more, rather than less, democracy. To accomplish this goal we must give everyone, not just the sons and daughters of the rich and powerful, a culture of leadership, and the confidence, expectations, and high sense of civic obligation that go with it. The classics can provide this as well now as they ever did in the past.

As I think is obvious, the curriculum I am proposing, as well as the conception of the humanities that underlies it, is quite different from recent proposals for a humanities or a liberal arts curriculum. Let us look at some of these differences.

The latest attempt to define a curriculum in the humanities is William Bennett's " 'To Reclaim a Legacy': Text of Report on the Humanities in Education" (Bennett 1984), to which I have already referred. I am in full agreement with what I consider Bennett's main goal: to shift the debate about the deficiencies of the liberal arts curriculum from a concern with technique and methodology to an interest in content: "A curriculum is rarely much stronger than the syllabi of its courses. . . . The syllabi should reflect the college's best judgment concerning specific texts with which an educated person should be familiar and should include texts within the competence and interest of its faculty" (p. 18). Bennett argues that there is actually much more agreement in the country than one would expect concerning great books that all students should read, and he lists what he believes are the most significant works in the humanities. His authors range from Homer and Sophocles to T. S. Eliot and Faulkner.

In focusing his attention on specific books and authors, Bennett is responding, in part, to the lack of focus, integration, and continuity in the undergraduate curriculum. I agree with him that nothing would be healthier for faculties today than to debate the works that all students should be required to read during their four years of college. If we want to improve our curriculum in a way which will not only improve our students' learning, but will also enrich our own intellectual lives and give us a greater sense of community, we should indeed center our discussions and debates around choosing specific books and authors all of our students should read. And the fewer titles the better. Albert William Levi begins his book *Philosophy and the Modern World* (1959) by describing the "personal fragmentation" characteristic of modern society. Speaking of the cultural unity of the Middle Ages, Levi writes:

> It is of the essence of intellectual integration that the number of books from which an age draws its inspiration shall be limited. This is one of the presuppositions which guarantees that any tradition shall be authoritative. And it is partly in these terms that we are to understand the intellectual crisis of the modern consciousness. For ours is the problem of a bewildering multiplicity. How many books may a man read and take seriously without losing his central orientation? This is the intellectual problem of the modern world stated in the language of a textual tradition. (Levi 1959, p. 7)

My criticism of Bennett is not that he proposes a list of books which everyone should read, and suggests that faculties across the country do likewise. My criticism of Bennett is that he and the people who helped him write his report do not define the humanities historically. After listing the disciplines which the federal legislation establishing the National Endowment for the Humanities defined as humanities in 1965, Bennett adds:

> Expanding on a phrase from Matthew Arnold, I would describe the humanities as the best that has been said, thought, written, and otherwise expressed about the human experience. The humanities tell us how men and women of our own and other civilizations have grappled with life's enduring, fundamental questions: What is justice? What should be loved? What deserves to be defended? What is courage? What is noble? What is base? Why do civilizations flourish? Why do they decline?
>
> Kant defined the essence of the humanities in four questions: What can I know? What should I do? What may I hope for? What is man? (p. 17)

These are good questions. But they are not a definition of the humanities. The humanities are nothing without their history. To revise and reappropriate the tradition of the humanities today is to enter into a new dialogue with classical antiquity, one which goes beyond the limitations which the Renaissance/modern concept of the self imposes on our understanding of the ancients. To describe the humanities as Bennett does just adds to all the confusion that surrounds them today. It is yet another example of the great amnesia that afflicts our intellectual and cultural life, even at its highest levels.

If "To Reclaim a Legacy" is not talking about the humanities, then what is it talking about? Exactly what it says it is: "the best that has been said, thought, written, and otherwise expressed about the human experience." Bennett is proposing another rendition of the Great Books program, with the addition of art history and music. What is wrong with this proposal? Nothing, as far as it goes. We might quibble with some omissions on Bennett's reading list, but I think as a whole "To Reclaim a Legacy" constitutes an important reminder that we need to encourage our students not only to read, but to read good books, the very best books. Every college and university in America should have a list of books that it believes every educated person should have read. Even if it did nothing more than make such a list available to students, this gesture alone would be a way of getting across the message that reading is important, and that some books are more worthwhile than others.

Such a reading list, however, will not in itself address the fundamental challenge confronting us today: how to understand and evaluate modernity. The Great Books approach to education is based upon an incorrect understanding of Western history. It fails to see the deeply problematic nature of our cultural and intellectual inheritance. We cannot understand Plato or Aristotle or even Dante without calling into question our contemporary beliefs concerning human subjectivity and the meaning and purpose of human existence. Like much academic scholarship, the Great Books approach to education sees continuities in our cultural and intellectual tradition where in fact there are profound breaks and transformations. It encourages students to think that they can read Homer with the same frame of mind that they read Tolstoy or Shakespeare because all great writers and thinkers, no matter when they lived and wrote, were struggling with the same basic questions. They weren't. As I pointed out in chapter 3, Polonius' injunction to Laertes, "To thine own self be true," would have made no sense to a Roman. Moreover, if we are not careful, the Great Books approach to education can end up being a justification for the present. Bennett writes: "Most of our college graduates remain shortchanged in the humanities—history, literature, philosophy, and the ideals and practices of the past *that have shaped the society they enter*" (p. 16, my emphasis). The relationship of the past to the present is not so simple. The acceptance of greed and self-interest as necessary and desirable character traits in a capitalist economy entailed the transformation of classical and medieval concepts of virtue.[3] As the authors of *Habits of the Heart* point out, there is a sharp conflict in American culture between the dominant language of individualism and the secondary languages based upon the republican and Biblical traditions. The real challenge facing us today is thus not to "reclaim" a legacy, but to *understand*, revise, and reappropriate it.

For this reason I have insisted throughout this book on giving the humanities an exclusively *historical* definition, a definition which is much narrower, and much more precise and focused, than most definitions of the humanities one finds today. To see the humanities as the *tradition* of classical education which began in the Renaissance and died in the twentieth century directs our attention more toward historical disjunctures than continuities, and thus forces us to think critically about our cultural inheritance, and the use we want to make of it. It means that if we want to belong to the *tradition* of the humanities, we have to study the Greeks and the Romans, just as Jews and Christians, if they want to participate in their respective traditions, have to study the Bible. This is not to say that we have nothing to learn from reading Dante or Shakespeare or Tolstoy. They are among my favorite authors. I even have the good fortune of being able to teach the *Divine Comedy* every year. But we create only confusion, and make it difficult to understand and use our cultural inheritance, when we include these writers under the rubric "humanities." They belong to other traditions.

The most recent proposal concerning the shape of the American undergraduate curriculum as a whole is a report of the Carnegie Foundation for the Advancement of Teaching, *College: The Undergraduate Experience in America,* written by Ernest L. Boyer (1987). This is a thoughtful analysis of American undergraduate education. I share fully the report's call that we balance the American tradition of individualism with a stronger commitment to community:

> We suggest, then, that within the traditions of individuality and community, educational and social purposes for the undergraduate experience can be defined. The individual preferences of each student must be served. But beyond diversity, the college has an obligation to give students a sense of passage toward a more coherent view of knowledge and a more integrated life. (p. 68)

The report then goes on to propose an integrated core of learning:

> What are common themes that cut across the disciplines? As one approach, we suggest seven areas of inquiry that, we believe, can relate the curriculum to experiences common to all people. Specifically, the following academic framework for general education is proposed:

• Language:	The Crucial Connection
• Art:	The Esthetic Experience
• Heritage:	The Living Past
• Institutions:	The Social Web
• Nature:	Ecology of the Planet
• Work:	The Value of Vocation
• Identity:	The Search for Meaning

It seems clear to us that an exploration of these universal experiences would be useful for helping students better understand themselves, their society, and the world of which they are a part. (p. 92)

This integrated core curriculum is not much different from the one proposed by the Association of American Colleges in its *Integrity in the College Curriculum: A Report to the Academic Community* (1985). The report proposes the following minimum required curriculum: (1) inquiry, abstract logical thinking, critical analysis; (2) literacy: writing, reading, speaking, listening; (3) understanding numerical data; (4) historical consciousness; (5) science; (6) values; (7) art; (8) international and multicultural experiences; (9) study in depth.

Note carefully that neither of these proposals is *internally coherent* the way the ancient liberal arts or the Renaissance humanities were. All of the areas of ancient learning led one beyond the human toward the contemplation of the eternal and the divine. All of the disciplines that made up the Renaissance *studia humanitatis* led one back to the ancients as models for perfecting an autonomous self. But there is no discernible relationship between the topics or themes these reports propose for integrating the curriculum, nor do the reports suggest any such relationship. The reason, I think, is clear. These and similar attempts to integrate the curriculum on the basis of themes, area studies, different disciplinary perspectives, and so forth, are struggling to come to terms with one of the distinguishing characteristics of modern society: intellectual fragmentation. Two centuries ago Hume wrote:

> . . . I may venture to affirm of the rest of mankind, that they are nothing but a bundle or collection of different perceptions, which succeed each other with an inconceivable rapidity, and we are in a perpetual flux and movement. Our eyes cannot turn in their sockets without varying our perceptions. Our thought is still more variable than our sight; and all our other senses and faculties contribute to this change; nor is there any single power of the soul, which remains unalterably the same, perhaps for one moment. The mind is a kind of theatre, where several perceptions successively make their appearance; pass, re-pass, glide away, and mingle in an infinite variety of postures and situations. There is properly no *simplicity* in it at one time, nor *identity* in different; whatever natural propension we may have to imagine that simplicity and identity. (Hume 1928, pp. 252–53)

"In finding human consciousness to consist in separate mental states detached from one another and from any discernible agency binding them together," Levi comments, "Hume expressed once and for all the crisis of contemporary intellectual life—the fragmentation of the thinking subject" (Levi 1959, p. 9).

What the Carnegie report calls "universal experiences" are actually what its authors perceive to be the common experiences of people today. But these experiences are incoherent. So any attempt to build a core curriculum around them will be likewise incoherent. It will take some or all of the fragments that make up the modern experience and require all students to study them. While this approach does overcome departmental narrowness, it does not create a coherent, meaningful curriculum. It just makes sure that all students are exposed to more fragments than the ones they meet in their major fields of study.

A core curriculum organized on questions raised by the tradition of the humanities, rather than around the categories of modernity, addresses this problem of integration in two ways. First of all, by introducing students to the ancient mind and to the unity of all the areas of the ancient curriculum, it gives them a direct experience of intellectual harmony, unity, and integration, and thus offers them a standard against which to measure the intellectual fragmentation they themselves may have taken for granted as part of the human condition. Secondly, by showing them the origins of modern reason and the modern self, it helps them *understand* why it is impossible for the vast majority of people in modern society to think in anything but fragments.

The best education will be one which challenges students to think about the questions raised by the tradition of the humanities. Such an education will lead them to see that wisdom and virtue are not only the highest, but also the most useful goals of learning. As Bruni said to Niccolò Strozzi, "the humanities as a whole aim at creating a good man, than which nothing more useful can be imagined . . ." (see above, chap. 1). Successful completion, through individual study and examinations, or specific coursework, or both, of a core curriculum in the humanities should be required of all students working toward a liberal arts degree. Sometimes, however, faculties are reluctant to vote in required general education courses. This is not just because they have trouble agreeing among themselves on what all students should be required to learn. Many teachers and administrators believe that college should be an experience in the exercise of choice: students should be treated as mature shoppers who can pick and choose what they want to study, and who can learn from occasional failures and disappointments.

There are several shortcomings to this approach to education. First of all, it is time that we recognize this obsession with choice for what it really is: an attempt to conceal ignorance. A surprising number of teachers and administrators in our schools today simply do not know what to say when a student asks them, "What should I study in order to get a good education?" They themselves have no coherent philosophy of education. They have few, if any, intellectual interests outside of their own academic speciality. They accept uncritically the fragmentation of the college and high school curriculum as somehow reflecting the nature of knowledge itself. They have neither the desire to think deeply and seriously about the nature and purpose of education, nor the historical consciousness such thinking demands. They suffer, in short, from the same intellectual fragmentation and cultural amnesia that afflicts our students. Such teachers and administrators are embarrassed by student demands for serious intellectual guidance, because they are unable to give it. So they pass the buck—to the students and their parents.

But most students today do not know how to give themselves a good education. They need, and, in my experience, want guidance. To preach choice and experimentation, to tell them to "shop around" for the right courses, actually demeans them because it does not *challenge* them to do any serious thinking and moral reflection during their four years of college. Furthermore, to replace wisdom as the traditional goal of learning with the exercise of choice means that a liberal arts education becomes, for most students, a completely haphazard, incoherent, and therefore ultimately meaningless experience. Finally, it means that most students will miss the last opportunity they will have in life to acquire historical consciousness, and with it to realize the extent to which contemporary culture actually *limits* their thinking and their ideals.

Herein lies the irony of erecting a Taj Mahal to choice: for all the myriad courses students may now choose from, they actually have little or no real choice at all. Most of the courses which make up the college and high school curriculum today are concerned only with the modern world: they either say nothing about the past, or turn the past into a mirror for the present by looking at it through the lens of one of the modern disciplines. But it is impossible to understand and evaluate modernity in terms of modernity. Anyone who uses modern intellectual standards to understand the modern world is using fragments to make sense of fragments. Sadly, most young people in America today know nothing but fragments. They are intellectually confused and morally disoriented. Those of us who are teachers thus abdicate our traditional role of providing moral and intellectual guidance to younger people if we do not show them how to use the past to see the present in a new way. Students are free to accept or reject this perspective. But let us at least get them to see that the real choice is not whether to take Biology at 8:30 or Italian at 11:30 A.M. (for some students do in fact choose their courses according to how late they want to sleep in the morning) or whether to major in English or History. The real choice concerns intellectual and moral ideals, the use of one's mind and will. From this point of view, one of the fundamental choices facing our students concerns their attitude toward material wealth: do they want to accept greed and selfishness as the controlling values of their lives, or do they look for other values to live by? There is no way students can make this kind of choice concerning the ultimate good unless they are aware of intellectual and moral perspectives different from the ones they have grown up with. The humanities can help students make this choice by letting them hear what the ancients have to say about the meaning of life. It is precisely for this reason that no student should graduate from college without knowing something about the classical conception of the human, and the Renaissance's transformation of it.

The Humanities in High School

Much of what students accomplish in college is determined by the habits of thought and mind they bring with them from their previous years of schooling. Any attempt to improve liberal education at the college level must thus begin in high school, during the formative years of a person's intellectual and moral life. College and high school faculties and administrations are in fact part of one common enterprise, and should work together more closely in setting goals for their students, and in discussing the means of achieving them.

There are three ways in which students can be introduced to the humanities in high school. First of all, students should begin to acquire a working knowledge of Greek and Latin. Why learn Greek and Latin? Because it will enable the ancients, and their Renaissance interpreters, to speak to our students directly. It is of course better to study the humanities in translation than never to study them at all. But a translation is *always* an interpretation. All too often the translators of the Greek and Roman classics do what Petrarch himself did, and what we are all tempted to do: they read our modern experience of the human back into the ancients. Students can easily learn enough Greek and Latin to be able to work with bilingual texts, and to check the translation against the original in those crucial passages in which they meet that which is most foreign to them: the ancient categories of thought, and the ancient experience of an extensive self.

I am perfectly aware, as I show in chapter 5, of how the institutionalization of classical learning in the schools turned the Romans—and the Greeks—into the "implacable enemies," as Dickens put it, of generations of schoolchildren. This is a danger we will have to guard against. We can do so by inspiring our students to love the ancients, and to turn to them for guidance. Richard A. Hawley, the Director of University School in Chagrin Falls, Ohio, points the way in his fine little book *The Purpose of Pleasure: A Reflection on Youth and Drugs* (Hawley 1983), in which he shows how classical moral ideals, especially the classical view of pleasure, can be used to address the problem of drugs in our schools. And it is not just the problem of drugs that haunts our high schools today; what are we to do about the increasing number of teenage suicides? High school students desperately need the kind of serious instruction in moral philosophy which the humanities can provide. Learning Greek and Latin is the first step in acquiring it.

In addition to teaching the classical languages, there are two other ways in which high schools can share in the project of studying and revising the tradition of the humanities. First of all, the faculty and administration of every school should discuss among themselves the issues raised by the tradition of the humanities, and find ways of addressing these issues across the curriculum, in as many different courses as possible. One could easily, for example, talk about the modern self in teaching *Hamlet,* refer the students back to Petrarch's *Secret* for the first full expression of this concept of the self, and then use Cicero's *Tusculan Disputations* to acquaint the students with the ancient soul, and the ancient concept of the self (see chapter 3). Even in science courses, in teaching the history of science instructors could touch upon some of the issues raised by the tradition of the humanities, and at the same time deepen their students' understanding of modern science.

Secondly, high schools could offer courses specifically on the tradition of the humanities. The course on *Classical Antiquity and Its Transformation in the Renaissance,* which I proposed for the freshman year of college, could easily be adapted to the senior year of high school. Or high schools could offer their seniors a course in moral philosophy based upon readings drawn from the freshman and senior year college courses I have described. Cicero's *On Duties* and his *Tusculan Disputations,* at least Book V, which takes up the question of happiness, would be excellent texts for such a course.

Who Should Teach the Humanities?

Who should teach the humanities? *Everyone.* The curriculum of our schools is fragmented and incoherent. So too is the collective mind of the faculty. Many men and women teaching today never acquired a good general education; their learning is narrow and specialized. How can we expect our students to become liberally educated if their teachers are not? We who teach can thus greatly improve the education we offer students by improving the education we give ourselves. Studying and teaching the history of the humanities is an excellent way for all teachers, regardless of their academic specialization, to acquire a liberal education.

It was common in American colleges slightly over a century ago for the college president to teach a course on moral philosophy to all seniors. Sometimes Cicero's *De officiis* was one of the texts used. This would be a useful tradition to bring back. But I would revise it, given the size of our student bodies and the intellectual specialization of our faculties, by suggesting that everyone, including members of the administrative staff whenever possible, teach the freshman and senior courses I have described, or a similar course during the senior year of high school. If everyone were to teach such a course on a rotating basis, each member of the faculty and administration would probably teach a humanities course every two or three years, depending on the size of the school. That should be easy to arrange. As we all begin to acquire the kind of culture which such a dialogue with our classical and Renaissance pasts provides, we will give ourselves the common learning we need in order to turn our colleges and high schools into true intellectual communities. This should be the ideal that guides us. In striving to achieve it, the tradition of the humanities will come alive again, for as people with different disciplinary backgrounds and different values teach the humanities, the tradition will automatically be reappropriated and revised, while those who enter into a dialogue with this tradition will find their own lives transformed as they begin to search for what Cicero called *humanitas,* that is, wisdom and virtue.

EPILOGUE

$\sim$

How would we recognize *humanitas* today? What would the soul of a person who sought wisdom and virtue in our own time be like? It would be remarkably similar to the soul of the wise man Cicero described some two thousand years ago. Here again are Cicero's words:

> Therefore the man, whoever he is, who through moderation and constancy is at rest in his soul and at peace with himself, so that he is neither wasted away by troubles, nor broken by fear, nor burns thirsting with desire for something he longs for, nor is he dissipated by exalting in futile joy—he is the wise man whom we seek, he is the blessed man, to whom nothing that happens to humans can seem unbearable to the point of casting down his soul, or so excessively joyful as to carry it away in elation. For what can seem of consequence in human affairs to a man who is acquainted with all eternity and the vastness of the universe. (*Tusc.* IV, 17, 37)

And here is Lucien Price's description of Alfred North Whitehead in the 1940s:

> He was now in his eighties. There was not the least evidence that his intellectual powers were waning. In fact, the current was being stepped up. During those final years at their apartment in the Hotel Ambassador, when our sessions might begin as early as seven-thirty in the evening and last until after midnight, he would finish fresher than he began. . . .
>
> The retention of his power he owed to moderation in all things. His abstemiousness was marked. He ate sparingly. Table wine was admissible. No smoking. He seemed never to have craved stimulants. The sight of this ruddy octogenarian, clear-eyed, clear-skinned, without a mark of the customary male indulgences, was, as time went on, not the least of his impressiveness. Another and greater impression was the spectacle of his living, in a four-room apartment, a larger life, more free, more spacious of spirit and intellect than most others could have lived in affluence. One grows accustomed in filial piety to indulging the aged in crotchets and caprices. In him there was nothing to excuse. His calm, his magnanimity, the vastness of his concepts reduced the trivialities of daily living to their true dimensions, yet at the same time abstract principles were raised into issues which must be stood up for stoutly. He was not above the battle, but the battle was on higher ground. This gave him a peculiar quality. He had met and solved more problems than most of us are aware of as existing at all. One felt that here was a man who was not afraid—not afraid

of those common enemies of mankind: illness, poverty, old age, misfortune, death; and then he was not afraid of the vast enigmas of human destiny or the immensities of the universe. In those awesome spaces he was at home and at his ease. This is what it means to be a philosopher, to have made friends with the enemy and to have domesticated the infinite in one's own soul. (Whitehead 1954, pp. 19–20)

APPENDIX
The Humanities and International Studies

My experiences over the past ten years both as a teacher of literature and as an administrator at a liberal arts college have convinced me that the most effective way of persuading others of the value of a humanistic education is to exemplify it in our own lives. In addition, we must find better ways of presenting the humanities in the curriculum, especially for students and their parents, who often see education primarily as a ticket to a job. When I wrote Chapter 9 I believed that students could best be introduced to the tradition of the humanities through individual courses, or through general education core curricula such as the one I suggested. I now believe that the tradition of the humanities can and should be used much more broadly. It can be taught across the entire curriculum. It can raise any discipline, including the natural sciences, to a higher level of engagement with contemporary reality. And most important of all, it can be a catalyst and a guide in the creation of new courses and interdisciplinary programs that address the material and spiritual challenges of modernity.

I speak from experience. Shortly after this book was published, and in part because of it, I was asked to create an international studies program that would exemplify the liberal arts tradition. It was a chance to test my understanding of the tradition of the humanities by using it to meet a specific educational challenge: prepare students to live and work in international settings. The ideas and inspiration we took from the tradition of the humanities helped to make the program a success; it now has a national reputation and attracts many good students to the college. These ideas, and the way in which we implemented them, can easily be applied to other new interdisciplinary programs and majors, such as conservation biology and environmental studies, which need the wisdom of the past in addressing contemporary problems.

In Part Three of this book I delineated some characteristics of the tradition of the humanities that can, in Nietzsche's words, have an effect on our own age to the benefit of a future age. Of all these, the best starting point for planning new courses and programs is to emulate the Renaissance humanists' discovery of history. All of our curricular innovations, even the most radical, are shaped by the specific educational traditions we inherit. Every institution of higher education in America, every professor's teaching and scholarship, and every new interdisciplinary program, center, institute, and curriculum is a unique blend of three different and often competing educational traditions: the tradition of the liberal arts college, the tradition of the state college and university, and the tradition of the research university. Rather than be passively influenced by these traditions, we should examine them and decide how we want to use them.

The most recent tradition, that of the German research university, began in the United States with the establishment of The Johns Hopkins University in 1876. Hopkins brought the German Ph.D. degree and graduate education to America. It was the first institution here that had as its primary goal the training of scientists and scholars. The model was so successful that it was quickly taken up by some of the older schools. According to this tradition, the goal of education is "the advancement of knowledge" through research and scholarship. This model can be seen in graduate and undergraduate international and area-studies programs that have as their primary aim the creation of "experts" in their fields, who identify themselves by the particular methodologies, primarily in the social sciences, they use in their research.

The second tradition dates from the Morrill Act of 1862, which gave the states federal lands for the establishment of colleges that would offer programs in agriculture, engineering, and home economics, along with the traditional liberal arts subjects. The Morrill Act stressed practical education, education that prepared students in the skills, trades, and professions that the country needed to industrialize. This tradition is utilitarian: it says that the goal of education is to get a job in an industrialized society. The growing popularity of international studies within a business or preprofessional context is an example of this tradition. The utilitarian tradition is particularly strong now because more and more businesses require undergraduate or graduate degrees as a condition of employment, and undergraduates and their families demand preparation either for specific jobs or for professional training at the graduate level (see Adam Yarmolinsky, "Constraints and Opportunities," in *Rethinking Liberal Education*, ed. Nicholas H. Farnham and Adam Yarmolinsky [New York and Oxford: Oxford University Press, 1966], p. 126).

Our oldest educational tradition is that of the liberal arts. The Pilgrims brought the English collegiate system with them to America. The English colleges can trace their lineage back, in part, to the new humanist pre-university schools of the Italian Renaissance, and farther back in time to the *artes liberales* of ancient Rome. At its point of origin in classical antiquity, the liberal arts tradition sees reality as an ordered whole, and all the disciplines as complementary ways of understanding this whole. It sees the individual as part of the whole, whether this be the cosmos or the city state. The highest goals of the liberal arts tradition are moral and political, the joy and tranquility of soul that come from general and lifelong learning, and the civic virtue that comes from using this learning for the common good (see above, pp. 14–20). In classical Rome as well as in colonial America, the liberal arts tradition prepared men of the ruling classes to become statesmen, legislators, and good citizens.

I have argued that the Renaissance humanists profoundly transformed this tradition by rejecting the study of nature as a means for understanding the human condition. We continue to live with the dichotomy they created between the humanities and the sciences and mathematics, even though our ecological problems are now forcing us to overcome this dichotomy. The highest manifestation of the liberal arts tradition today will thus be an alliance between the Renaissance humanists' goal of achieving moral and historical consciousness and the ancient liberal arts vision of the complementarity of all disciplines, including the sciences. I hope that we can one day achieve a lived moral consciousness that will include nature. But I suspect that in our experience of self we are still much closer to Petrarch than to Cicero, so that the alliance I speak of will continue to be epistemologically problematic. It does work, however, at a pedagogical level, and provides a better philosophy of education than anything else we have today. This philosophy, grounded in the liberal arts, can direct and give higher purpose to the research and utilitarian traditions.

In 1989 at Connecticut College we inaugurated a Center for International Studies and the Liberal Arts (CISLA, now endowed as the Toor Cummings Center for International Studies and the Liberal Arts), the heart of which is the undergraduate International Studies Certificate Program. One of its guiding presuppositions is that students in the program must work toward the goals of each of the three educational traditions we have inherited. Their professors expect them to do research in the major; their parents want them to get jobs or go on to graduate school; and many of their professors and parents hope that they will get a broad liberal arts education as well. The program is thus not a major but an opportunity for students to internationalize whatever subject they choose to major in. It recognizes that the tension between globalization and localization is a fact of modern life, and that all students preparing for positions of leadership and responsibility have an international destiny.

Following the traditional liberal arts, concern for the development of moral character, we structured our International Studies Certificate Program so as to attract and support young people who will take increasing personal responsibility for their studies and their work. Students of all majors apply for admission in October of the sophomore year. To be admitted they must reach an approved level in an oral proficiency interview conducted in a foreign language (we use the ACTFL [American Council of the Teachers of Foreign Languages] methods and guidelines) and write an application essay in their best English prose. This essay proposes a work/study internship, a research topic for a senior project, and a core of related courses outside of the major. The students must also have and maintain at least a 3.0 cumulative grade point average.

Students in the program take a core of five courses outside the major; go on a two-month work/study internship abroad during the summer between their junior and senior year, for which each student receives a stipend of $3,000; take a research seminar in the fall of their senior year; and do a special senior research project in which they integrate their major, internship, foreign language, and knowledge of the modern world as a whole. In addition, in order to receive the certificate when they graduate, students must demonstrate increased oral proficiency in the foreign language during an interview given their senior year by an outside tester.

The senior integrative project, which the students must conceptualize, at least in general terms, by October of the sophomore year when they apply to the program, brings the students into contact with the *research tradition*. Once admitted to the program, each student is paired with a librarian who will teach the student how to use all the research resources of the library for the next two and a half years. The library mentors also help the sophomores prepare an annotated bibliography on their research topic. In April of the junior year, students submit a revised research proposal, along with a letter of approval from a faculty advisor in their major area. Students do the actual senior integrative projects as either an honors thesis or an individual study in the field of their major. The research seminar that they take in the fall of the senior year forces them to begin writing their research projects sooner than many of them would otherwise do.

Students don't need to be introduced to the *utilitarian tradition*: getting a job is already on their minds. The experience of working in a foreign country, and the advantage of making contacts there, the high level of ACTFL-certified oral proficiency in a foreign language, and the general and incalculable maturing that occurs as a result of the program's specific challenges, give the students skills, experiences, and poise that make them stand out in job interviews. Most of our students find very good jobs, or go on to graduate school, or both.

Satisfying the requirements of the research and utilitarian traditions is not, however, the highest goal of our IS Certificate Program. In fact, the considerable successes we have had in these areas are due in large measure to a seriousness of moral purpose and climate of intellectual striving provided by the traditions of the humanities and of the liberal arts. I agreed to become Founding Director of CISLA in part because I feared that our IS Certificate Program could easily become just a foreign language, or a research-oriented social science program, with exclusively preprofessional goals. Such an international studies program would be too narrow. It wouldn't correspond to all of our students' human needs. And it would give them a false sense of the world. Students have much to gain from learning how to do careful research. But they also need to be aware of the limitations of highly specialized research. How is it possible, for example, that the break-up of the Soviet Union took the experts in Soviet and East European area studies completely by surprise? (See George Weigel, *The Final Revolution: The Resistance Church and the Collapse of Communism* [New York: Oxford University Press, 1992] for a critique of academic social science.)

As far as undergraduate education as training for a skill or a profession is concerned, once again we have to be careful not to give our students over-specialized training, regardless of what they and their parents might believe about its value. Some sociologists and economists are now predicting that most people will hold four or five different kinds of job during their lives. Our aim should be to give students skills and experiences that will not only help them find jobs when they graduate, but will prepare them to find another job, perhaps even another profession, when they lose or leave the first one! Even from a purely economic point of view, they will need to be lifelong learners.

Although the liberal arts tradition is constantly under attack, honored with clichés but rarely practiced, it will prove to be the most enduring and the most useful of the three traditions, because it is the only one that addresses *all* of our human needs, including the practical need of finding work throughout one's life. Furthermore, the liberal arts tradition warns us of the dangers of being too narrowly educated and of missing opportunities to enlarge our minds and expand our thinking. In lines reminiscent of Cicero's own definition of the liberal arts (see above pp. 14–16), John Henry Cardinal Newman writes, "That only is true enlargement of mind which is the power of viewing many things at once as one whole, of referring them severally to their true place in the universal system, of understanding their respective values, and determining their mutual dependence." He goes on to observe that "[m]en, whose minds are possessed with some one object, take exaggerated views of its importance, are feverish in the pursuit of it, make it the measure of things which are utterly foreign to it, and are startled and despond if it happens to fail them" (*The Idea of a University*, Discourse 6.6, ed. Frank M. Turner [New Haven: Yale University Press, 1996], pp. 99–100). In order not to take an exaggerated view of the importance and explanatory power of any single discipline, we and our students need to be able to view specialized research and training in the context of all the disciplines.

Finding a pedagogical structure that would stimulate this "enlargement of mind" was one of the greatest challenges of our program. The solution we found was to create a broader context for research in the major by challenging our students to struggle for two and a half years with three overarching questions that are simply too broad to be addressed by any single discipline:

> *What are the origins and dynamics of modern global society?*
> *What we can gain from a dialogue with the past?*
> *What are some of the material and spiritual challenges of modernity?*

These questions are meant to open students up to something larger than themselves, to invite them to ponder the modern world as a whole by stepping outside it and looking at it from the perspective of the past. They challenge the students to expand their horizons by taking in the viewpoints of other people and other cultures, including those of past ages. And they encourage students to think about the civic responsibilities of their education. We want students to realize that every single discipline can contribute a partial answer to these questions; no single discipline alone can provide a satisfactory one.

Students ponder these questions in three ways: in a special sophomore course; in courses they agree to take as part of their core curriculum for the IS Certificate Program; and in their senior integrative projects. In order to count toward the IS Certificate, the senior project normally puts research done for the major into the broader context of the three questions. In some cases the research topic, such as new religious movements in the former Soviet Union, fits easily into this broader context. In other cases, such as the zoology major who studied a specific microorganism in the Bay of Naples and in the Atlantic Ocean as an honors thesis in zoology, addressing the three questions requires a separate paper.

During the first two years of the IS Certificate Program, we had a group of faculty teach a special senior integrative seminar to help students think about these three questions. It didn't work; the students complained that they were unprepared to think about such broad questions their last semester in college. They urged us to turn the senior seminar into a sophomore course for students just admitted to the IS Certificate Program. We followed their advice, creating a new sophomore course, "Perspectives on Modern Global Society." We also require our students to send us, from wherever they may be in the world, a five-page paper at the end of every core course taken through the junior year, in which they explain how the course addressed at least one, and preferably all, of the three questions. The goal is to keep them thinking about these questions, even if the course does not address them specifically.

Getting the students to generalize, to think about the big picture, to ponder the social responsibilities of their privileged education, remains by far the biggest challenge for those who direct the program. This kind of moral and theoretical thinking goes against the grain of the specialized research and the intellectual fragmentation of the modern university. I have colleagues who tell me that there is no big picture. Others dismiss the questions as too broad to be of any interest. The students, on the other hand, experience the joy of learning when they see connections between disciplines and, more important, between their lives and something bigger.

The liberal arts tradition complements and raises to a higher level the research and utilitarian traditions in another and equally important way. The Renaissance humanists believed strongly in the power of inspiration to nourish and sustain the actual practice of virtue (see above, pp. 149–53). The International Studies Certificate that students receive at a special ceremony on the day before graduation is designed not only to acknowledge what they have achieved, but to inspire them to follow the ideals of the humanities and the liberal arts throughout their lives. The certificate comprises three large words arranged vertically on the page: *Sapientia, Virtus, Eloquentia*—"Wisdom," "Virtue," "Eloquence." To the left is a translation of a passage from Book Five of Cicero's *Tusculan Disputations* in which he describes these three virtues and addresses the importance of using them for the common good (24.69–25.72). Superimposed on the Latin words is a brief statement of what the recipient of the certificate has accomplished: an understanding of the origins and dynamics of modern global society; a high level of oral proficiency in a foreign language; a work/study internship abroad; and a senior integrative research project. Before the students receive the certificate, the director talks about its meaning, especially the passage from Cicero, as a *vade mecum* for life. I would sometimes remind them that as the years go by and their eyesight changes many of them will be able to read only the words that really matter: *Sapientia, Virtus, Eloquentia*.

Here, in sum, are three lessons that our International Studies Certificate Program has taught me about using the tradition of the humanities to foster curricular innovation:

1. *Have a clear philosophy of education to guide your program.* Clarity of purpose helps to guide and sell it. If you don't think through your phi-

losophy of education at the outset, you'll end up passively following other educational traditions. Like the pilot I describe in the Preface, you'll be lost, but making good time!

2. *Make sure your program satisfies the goals of all three traditions.* Some faculty will not participate in a program unless it involves research and scholarship. Students and their families expect their studies to help them find a job, or at least prepare them to pursue higher degrees. And unless you involve all the disciplines and strive to give the students the "big picture," your program will not be studying reality.

3. *Fight hard to have the liberal arts tradition—of which the humanities constitute an important part—guide the other two.* The liberal arts tradition is the only educational tradition we inherit that addresses all of our human needs. It is also the one most often under attack today, because it goes against the grain of modern capitalist society. The utilitarian tradition, and even aspects of the research tradition, can probably be carried on by capitalist corporations. The liberal arts tradition cannot, because it aims to produce a person *capax universi*, capable of taking in the whole of existence. Furthermore, it is grounded in a recognition of the importance of leisure and contemplation that dates from premodern societies, and which is inimical to the totalitarian claims of work, as Josef Pieper argues so well in his classic *Leisure: The Basis of Culture* (New York: New American Library, 1963). It now requires constant vigilance to keep the liberal arts tradition alive. Yet it is the only tradition capable of creating courses and programs that address the material and spiritual challenges of modernity in a deep and lasting way. *The formula we discovered for using the liberal arts requires giving the research and utilitarian traditions their due, but then transcending their limitations.*

Here we come full circle, back to the tradition of the humanities. Emulating the humanists' love of history teaches us to acknowledge the traditions we have inherited. Emulating their revolt against technique, and their use of inspiration, helps us give our students the education they deserve.

NOTES

Introduction

1. Garin 1976, Grafton and Jardine 1986, Oberman 1975, Percival 1976, and Woodward 1963, 1967, give accounts of the new humanist pedagogy and its spread from Italy to the rest of Europe.

2. On this obsession with technique, "[t]his 'fetishization' of large, complex issues, by singling out a narrow, simplistic approach to them," see Becker 1969, pp. 166–68.

3. For a further discussion of the "circle of the moon," see Singleton 1967, pp. 127–30.

1. The Humanist Transformation of Classical Antiquity

1. In addition to his writings on education, Bruni contributed to the development of the humanistic disciplines of history, moral philosophy, and rhetoric. His *History of the Florentine People* (*Historia Florentini populi*) set new standards of accuracy and elegance in the writing of history; his translation of Aristotle's *Nichomachean Ethics* and his own introduction to ethics, the *Isagogicon moralis disciplinae*, mark an important stage in the beginning of humanist moral thought; and his speeches, letters, and dialogues concerning the city of Florence show the humanist use of rhetoric in a civic context. For Bruni's historiography, see Wilcox 1969. Kristeller 1965 offers a good overview of humanist moral thought. The classic study of Bruni's "civic humanism" is Baron 1966.

2. See Baron 1966, p. 246, and Bracciolini 1966 [1741], pp. 665–66.

3. I use Hans Baron's text of *De studiis et litteris* (Bruni 1969) as corrected by Ludwig Bertalot (Bertalot 1975).

4. See Greene 1982 and Quint 1985.

5. See D'Amico 1984.

6. On the history of the word *humanist* see Avesani 1970, Campana 1946, and Kristeller 1979.

7. Greene 1982, chap. 3, Kelley 1970, and Panofsky 1972 provide a good introduction to the humanist discovery of history. Donald R. Kelley writes:

> The point is that Renaissance humanism represented not merely new knowledge of and new appreciation for classical antiquity—that is an old story—but a major reorientation in thought. What happened, in brief, was that the mere problem of gaining access to the past began to supersede the problem of how to make use of it. Increasingly, scholars were struck by the distance and the disparity between themselves and men of former ages. . . . Even those humanists who, beguiled by nostalgia or national sentiment, tended to idealize antiquity could not avoid the fact of historical change, so conspicuously reflected in the vicissitudes of literary style, social customs, and religious practices. . . . Wrestling with this anthropological dilemma (still one of the fundamental problems of historical thought) led them toward what was, in effect, a principle of cultural relativity. (Kelley 1970, pp. 23–24)

Concerning the humanist recognition of cultural relativity, Charles Trinkaus (1983, pp. 364–403) has argued that the scholarly origins of the modern discipline of cultural anthropology, "the comparative study of the vast varieties of human cultures encountered in the new and old worlds since 1492" (p. 364), can be traced back to the writings of some of the humanists of the late Renaissance.

8. *Instituere* is a difficult word to translate. It comes from *in* + *statuo* = to put or place into, set up. Its literal meanings include to construct, build, organize, arrange. Its figurative meanings include to train and to teach. But even when used figuratively, its literal meanings remain as part of its connotation. These literal meanings are lost in the English word *teach*.

9. The Renaissance humanists knew that *humanista* was not classical Latin, and they tended to avoid the term whenever they were concerned with writing good Latin. The Italian *umanista* was much more commonly used, even in literary works in Italian. See Avesani 1970, and Campana 1946.

10. I thank Benjamin G. Kohl of Vassar College for sharing with me, from his unpublished paper "The Changing Concept of the *Studia humanitatis* in the Renaissance" (1986), this information on the first use of the phrase *studia humanitatis* in the Renaissance. For Salutati's first use of the phrase see Salutati 1891–1911, vol. 1, p. 106, line 31.

11. Schadewaldt 1973 discusses the meaning of *humanitas* in Cicero's time. See also Giustiniani 1985, pp. 183–86.

12. See the discussion of Cicero's use of the word *litterae*, "letters," on p. 20.

13. See Wagner 1983, p. 1.

14. Insofar as they denote all the areas of ancient learning, what Cicero calls the *studia humanitatis* are thus not only synonymous with the *artes liberales*; they are the Roman equivalent of the Greek *enkyklios paideia*, "general education." But it is misleading to state, as Alan Bullock does, speaking of *paideia* in his recent book *The Humanist Tradition in the West*, that "the Latin word *humanitas* . . . was itself a Roman version of an older Greek idea" (Bullock 1985, p. 11). This seems to be a common misconception, born perhaps of a desire to believe in an unbroken tradition of humanistic learning in the West which begins with the Greeks and extends all the way up to our own time. In arguing that the Roman *humanitas* is the Greek *paideia*, many modern scholars, such as Werner Jaeger in his well-known book *Paedeia: The Ideals of Greek Culture* (1945, p. xxiii, and p. 415, note 7), refer to this sentence from the *Noctes Atticae* of the Latin grammarian Aulus Gellius (c. A.D. 165): ". . . but they called 'humanitas' that which the Greeks in a like manner call *paideia*; we say 'eruditio institutioque in bonas artes'" (XIII, 17). But we have to be careful how we interpret Gellius. Commenting on Heidegger's view that every "historical" humanism, such as Italian Renaissance humanism and German eighteenth-century *Neuhumanismus*, constitutes a revival of Greek *paideia*, Vito R. Giustiniani writes:

> . . . Heidegger is misled by the Latin translation of *paideia* with *humanitas*, a term which easily suggests a connection with humanism. To be sure, this translation is endorsed by a famous passage of Gellius, who equates *humanitas* with *paideia*. But beyond this equation, Gellius more properly translates *paideia* with 'eruditio institutioque in bonas artes.' The whole passage must be correctly assessed by the modern reader: since *humanus* means *also* 'learned', *humanitas* means *also* 'learning', but it includes other values (character, *virtus* etc.), while *paideia* focuses mainly on culture. These values are much more important than Heidegger seems to admit.

Humanitas does not have any corresponding term in Greek. (Giustiniani 1985, pp. 184–85).

Schadewaldt 1973 shows why *humanitas* has no corresponding term in Greek. Although influenced by Greek ideas, the concept of *humanitas* is a product of the particularities of the Roman character and history. It is worth summarizing Schadewaldt's observations here, for they enrich our understanding of the history of the humanities.

The word *humanitas* is pure Latin in origin, formed by adding *-itas* to *humanus*. *Humanitas* came into being in opposition to, and as a complement of, the older Roman virtues of *gravitas, dignitas,* and *severitas.* It builds on another set of preexisting virtues suggested by the old Roman words *clementia, fides, aequitas,* and, in another sense, by *comitas, hilaritas, iucunditas,* and *lepos.* The ancient Romans were a stern people, organizing their public and private lives around the scrupulous observance (*religio*) of ritual, ceremony, and a strict moral code. *Humanitas* brings that which is *suave, mite, dulce*—"human," in short—into this stern world.

Schadewaldt argues that the concept of *humanitas* enters the Roman world in the middle of the second century B.C. through the circle of Scipio the Younger (c. 185–129 B.C.). He points both to Scipio's own sayings and to what Cicero says about him in his dialogues, and he argues that Scipio's *humanitas* was not just an awareness of the frailty of the human condition and a love of learning, but had a political motivation as well: by virtue of the old Roman *severitas, disciplina,* and *virtus,* the Romans, after the battle at Pydna (168), the destruction of Carthage (146), and the conquest of Corinth (146), had gained control of the whole known world. They realized that in order to maintain their military and political hegemony, they had to win cultural hegemony as well. This realization led them to enlarge their concept of *virtus,* which they did by broadening the old Roman *virtus* through *humanitas.* The Greeks helped them carry out this ideological change.

Scipio had a Greek education. He carried a copy of Xenophon's *Cyropaedia* around with him. He was close to two Greeks, Polybius (c. 202–120 B.C.) and Panaetius (c. 180–c. 110 B.C.), who understood and admired the Roman character. Schadewaldt believes that it was through Panaetius, who had such an influence on Cicero's own work, that the Greek ethical tradition, beginning with Plato and Aristotle, and transformed by the Stoics into a specific idea of human comportment, met the old Roman *continentia, aequitas,* and *clementia maiorum nostrum* and broadened them into a comprehensive *humanitas.* This *humanitas* then became an educational program for the new Roman statesmen and governors (as can be seen in Cicero's letter to his brother Quintus I [I.1], 18–23, 27, where he talks about the virtues of a statesman, and in his treatise *De officiis*). Cicero, moreover, broadened the meaning of *humanitas* by extending it into the areas of law (*humanitas* joins *aequitas*), moral philosophy ("quid sit humaniter vivere"), and culture, education, and polite discourse (*studia humanitatis*).

Schadewaldt's explanation of the origin of the word *humanitas* gives us an important insight into the original meaning of the phrase *studia humanitatis.* If the *studia humanitatis* are equivalent to all the liberal arts, all the areas of ancient learning, why does Cicero use (or invent) the term *studia humanitatis*? What does it tell us that the more common terms *artes liberales, ingenuae artes,* and *bonae artes* do not? The answer is found in the passage from the *Pro Archia* quoted above, where Cicero speaks of Archias's leaving behind his boyhood and "those arts by which the age of boyhood is wont to be *shaped towards humanity* ("ab eis artibus quibus aetas puerilis *ad humanitatem informari* solet") (3, 4. My emphasis). The phrases *artes liberales* and *ingenuae artes* denote the socio-economic and juridical status of those "free" men who in their *otium*, or studious leisure, devote themselves to the "free arts"; the phrase *studia humanitatis* denotes the goal or result of such study: being shaped or educated toward *humanitas*. From this point of view, *humanitas*, as Giustiniani observes, does not mean learning so much as it means *the particular virtue or virtues that result from learning*. Cicero uses this meaning of *humanitas* effectively throughout the *Pro Archia*, especially in his final remarks to the jury, where he beseeches them to protect Archias, "so that he is seen to be raised up by your humanity (*humanitas*) rather than violated by your harshness (*acerbitas*)" (12, 31). The full meaning of *humanitas* as the virtue or state of mind to which learning leads becomes even clearer when we realize that true virtue, for Cicero, lies above man, in the heavens; the humanities (*artes humanitatis*), at their highest level, enable one to become truly human *by rising above the human* through the contemplation of the eternal and the divine.

15. I follow F. E. Cranz, whose explanation of the change from ancient to modern categories of thought I discuss in chapter 4, in using the words "extensive" and "intensive" to contrast the ancient and the modern self.

2. Petrarch and the Origins of the Humanities

1. For the opinion of Renaissance writers that it was Petrarch who initiated the revival of learning, see Weisinger 1940.

2. Witt 1982 offers a useful discussion of Renaissance humanism as a profession and good references to previous literature on this topic.

3. Camporeale 1972 and especially 1976 gives a clear and intelligible account of this aspect of scholastic theology, and the humanist critique of it.

4. On Ockham and scholasticism, see Leff 1975, esp. p. 139.

5. Trinkaus 1983, p. 8, points to similarities between nominalism and the humanists.

6. Peter Abélard (1079–1142) offers a striking contemporary account of this vicious competition in his autobiography *Historia calamitatum* (Abélard 1922).

7. On nominalism, scholasticism, and humanism, see Courtenay 1982, Gilbert 1976, Leff 1975, O'Malley 1974, and especially Perreiah 1982.

8. Petrarch's obsession with the constant change and transformation beneath the circle of the moon may have helped to prepare the way, at least at a cultural and psychological level, for the recognition of change that underlies modern science. Before setting out to measure change, as Galileo did, one must believe that the changeable, as opposed to the immutable, is worth thinking about. Petrarch made it culturally acceptable to think and write about change. Without the immense cultural changes Petrarch and the earliest humanists set in motion, it is possible that Galileo could not have written the following. It is a celebration of the alterable and the mutable which he has one of the interlocutors of his 1629 *Dialogue Concerning the Two Chief World Systems* deliver in defense of the modern view that the kind of change that takes place beneath the circle of the moon occurs throughout the universe:

I cannot without great astonishment—I might say without great insult
to my intelligence—hear it attributed as a prime perfection and nobility

of the natural and integral bodies of the universe that they are invariant, immutable, inalterable, etc., while on the other hand it is called a great imperfection to be alterable, generable, mutable, etc. For my part I consider the earth very noble and admirable precisely because of the diverse alterations, changes, generations, etc. that occur in it incessantly. (Galileo 1967, p. 58)

This is another example of the common origin of the humanities and modern science. While modern science turns outward and the humanities turn inward, they both, from the point of view of the ancients, confine their gaze to the world beneath the circle of the moon.

9. On "Prosper" and "Aesop" and other medieval Latin textbooks, see Garin 1958, pp. 91, 96–97.

10. Rico 1974 argues that Petrarch wrote the *Secret* in 1347, and revised it in 1349, and then again in 1353. Baron 1985, in the most recent discussion of the making of the *Secret*, accepts Rico's dating.

11. Mann 1980 discusses the popularity of the *De remediis* in the Renaissance. See also the useful introduction by Benjamin G. Kohl to Thomas Twyne's 1579 English translation of the *De remediis* (Petrarca 1980).

12. On the humanists' interest in the will, see Trinkaus 1970, p. xx.

13. Perreiah 1982, pp. 13 and 16.

14. Camporeale 1972 and 1976 gives useful accounts of Valla's theology.

15. The phrase, I believe, is Eugenio Garin's.

16. It is important to keep in mind that insofar as Petrarch deepened his sense of autonomy by studying and comparing himself to the ancients, his new consciousness of autonomy was at the same time a *social* consciousness and a *historical* consciousness. Unlike the lonely individuality many people experience today, Petrarch's sense of autonomous individuality was thus still very much tied to an experience of a psychic community with other human beings, however distant in time.

17. *Auctoritas* is a difficult word to translate into English. Of its many meanings, "prestige" and "dignity" are certainly present here. For a discussion of *auctoritas* see Balsdon 1960.

18. See Ramage 1960 and 1963.

19. In Book VIII, chapter 9 of his *History of Rome* Livy describes the Roman ceremony of devotion and gives the words the state priest (*pontifex*) told Decius to say to the gods in vowing to sacrifice his life in battle for the safety of his legions and the people of Rome.

3. Cicero in Grief

1. I have used D. R. Shackleton Bailey's edition (Cicero 1966, 1977, 1980) for texts of Cicero's letters. In citing a letter, I follow the editor's practice of including the standard reference to the letter as it appeared in editions previous to his.

2. On Dante's purpose in writing the *Vita Nuova*, see Singleton 1958.

3. See the figure of Ajax "hiding his emotion in his cloak" in Williams 1980, p. 139.

4. Since Cicero's identity as a Roman was constituted by what his peers thought of him, his struggle, in essence, was between his exterior and his interior, between the grief that gripped his soul and the external social constitution of his identity.

5. See Shackleton Bailey's note on *Att.* 251: 3, 5 (Cicero 1966).
6. See Shackleton Bailey's note on *Att.* 278: 1, 4 (Cicero 1966).
7. See Bailey 1971, p. 277.
8. In pointing to sharp differences between the Greek and the Roman experience of the person, and our own, I do not mean to imply that the Greeks and the Romans had no "inner self." They obviously did. Cicero's *Tusculan Disputations* describes it. But it was an "extensive," not an "intensive" self. When thinking about the individual self, the ancients turned outward, not inward, and strove to become one with the reason and harmony of the universe. Explaining the meaning of the famous saying "Know thyself," Cicero says that to the soul examining and pondering the heavens, "there comes that knowledge enjoined by the god at Delphi, that the mind know its own self and feel itself united with the divine mind . . ." (*Tusc.* V, 25, 70).
9. See the beginning of the next chapter for Jonas's statement on ancient ontology.

4. Ancient and Modern Categories of Thought

1. I cite from an unpublished collection, "The Reorientation of Western Thought Circa 1100 A.D.: Four Talks by F. Edward Cranz," distributed at Connecticut College in 1985 in preparation for a symposium in honor of Professor Cranz's retirement. I use his own quite literal translations of the texts he cites.
2. Petrarch discusses it on a number of occasions, for example, in *De vita solitaria* (Petrarca 1955, p. 353) and *Invective contra medicum* (Petrarca 1950, p. 85).

5. Degeneration from Within

1. I have used Pfeiffer 1976 in summarizing the development of classical scholarship in the Renaissance.
2. See Billanovich 1951.
3. Camporeale 1972 provides a useful study of Valla's work.
4. See Lloyd-Jones 1982, p. 169. I have drawn for the most part on this work in surveying the classical revival in Germany.
5. The rediscovery of classical antiquity in the Renaissance and the classical revival in eighteenth-century Germany can both be seen, in part, at least, as a reaction against a previous "age of reason": the early humanists turned away from medieval scholasticism, the German Romantics from seventeenth-century rationalism.
6. See Lloyd-Jones 1982, pp. 33 and 48.
7. Turner 1981 provides a good account of the Greek revival in England.
8. See Lloyd-Jones 1982, p. 175.
9. See Lloyd-Jones 1982, pp. 172–75.
10. On the reception of *Altertumswissenschaft* in England, see Grafton, Spring 1983.
11. Kliebard 1984, pp. 11–15, shows that the concept of "mental discipline" was used as early as 1828 in America to defend the study of classics.
12. For a critique of Humboldt's philosophy of education as "human divinization," see Voegelin 1985, pp. 17–21.
13. On Sophoclean tragedy's acknowledgment of a cosmic moral order, see MacIntyre 1984, p. 143.
14. An article in a recent issue of *Science* devoted to psychotherapy points

out that "[a]s recently as 1957 only 13 percent of the [American] population had sought some kind of psychological counseling in their lifetimes. That number is now almost 30 percent—or 80 million people—at a cost of over $4 billion annually" (Meredith 1986, p. 31).

6. Change from Without

1. For the most part I have followed Anderson 1979, especially chapter 1, in summarizing the transition from feudalism to capitalism in Western Europe, the rise of the absolute monarchies, and the role which Roman law played in both of these phenomena.

2. "It is very rare, during the whole of the feudal era," Marc Bloch writes, "for anyone to speak of ownership, either of an estate or of an office; much rarer still—never perhaps except in Italy—for a lawsuit to turn on such ownership" (Bloch 1961, p. 115). Bloch goes on to observe that

> the word 'ownership', as applied to purely landed property, would have been almost meaningless. . . . For nearly all land and a great many human beings were burdened at this time with a multiplicity of obligations differing in their nature, but all apparently of equal importance. None implied that fixed proprietary exclusiveness which belonged to the conception of ownership in Roman law. The tenant who—from father to son, as a rule—ploughs the land and gathers in the crop; his immediate lord, to whom he pays dues and who, in certain circumstances, can resume possession of the land; the lord of the lord, and so on, right up the feudal scale—how many persons there are who can say, 'That is my field!' Even this is an understatement. For the ramifications extended horizontally as well as vertically an account should be taken of the village community, which normally recovered the use of the whole of its agricultural land as soon as it was cleared of crops; of the tenant's family, without whose consent the property could not be alienated; and of the families of successive lords. (Ibid., p. 115–16)

E. P. Thompson gives a graphic illustration of how a farmer in eighteenth-century England might experience the place he inherited "within the hierarchy of use-rights," and speaks of "the inherited grid of customs and controls within which that right was exercised" (Thompson 1978, p. 337). Duby 1968 describes other kinds of "rights," in addition to those directly associated with the land, typical of feudal society, such as a manorial lord's monopoly rights over wine sales, oil presses, and ovens (*banalités*), rights over lodgings (*droit de gîte*), and over fines in manorial courts.

3. In addition to Anderson 1979, see Tigar and Levy 1977 on the role that Roman law played in the rise of capitalism in Western Europe.

4. Witt 1982 describes this evolution and offers a good survey of the previous literature on the subject.

5. See Brucker 1979.

6. On the reception of the *studia humanitatis* in England, see Hay 1975.

7. See Hexter 1961, p. 50.

8. See Woodward 1967, p. 272.

9. See Hexter 1961, p. 66, n. 2.

10. See Baron 1966 for a full discussion of Bruni's political writings.

11. It is interesting to note, as Tigar and Levy (1977, p. 213) observe, that

as late as the last century civil-law lawyers, drawing on the tradition and terminology of Roman law, used the phrase *locatio conductio operarum*, "the hiring and renting of labor" (*locatio conductio* was the general Roman term for a bilateral contract of hiring) to describe the quintessentially capitalist relation of production, unknown to classical antiquity, whereby the industrial worker, having no tools, no means of production of his own, hires out his ability to work, his "labor power," for a certain portion of the day.

12. In thinking about the humanities in a social context, I have found the discussion of Weber in Nisbet 1966 particularly useful. Weber 1958 contains a good selection of Weber's writings on bureaucracy. Bendix 1974 has much of interest to say about the ideologies of management that come into being with industrialization, and how they are influenced by previously existing structures of authority.

13. Roland Mousnier, in his study of the absolute monarchy in France, speaks of what he calls "fealties," highly personal relationships between master and *fidèle*, and *proctecteur* and *créature,* characteristic of French society in the seventeenth and eighteenth centuries. Speaking of the gradual weakening of these relationships, Mousnier writes: "Perhaps Louis XIV contributed to this process during his personal government, before the philosophy of the Enlightenment turned men's hearts away from such relationships, while the spirit of capitalism, accustoming everyone to translate everything into figures, gradually dried them up" (Mousnier 1979, p. 107). Capitalism, in other words, entails the rationalization of the highly personal relationships which, according to Weber, are the substance of traditional society.

14. Finding alternatives to bureaucratic rationality may become a necessity for American business. See the Special Report "Management Discovers the Human Side of Automation," in *Business Week,* 29 September 1986, pp. 70–79.

15. See Taylor 1923. Braverman 1974 has a good discussion of scientific management.

16. Machiavelli's *Discourses* on the first ten books of Livy are a good example of how the Renaissance studied the past in order to think about politics in the present.

17. See Baron 1966.

18. On the relationship between fascism, nazism, and the study of classical antiquity, see Canfora 1980.

19. For a fuller discussion of our relationship to the past, see Lasch 1979 and Jameson 1983.

7. Lessons from the Renaissance

1. On the intellectual permissiveness underlying deconstructionism, see Veatch 1985. For discussion of the differences between the natural and the social sciences from the point of view of a pragmatic criterion of truth, see Hesse 1980, chap. 8.

2. Moral philosophy was one of the specific disciplines included in the Renaissance *studia humanitatis.* Leonardo Bruni, as we have seen, translated Aristotle's *Nichomachean Ethics,* and wrote an introduction to ethics, the *Isagogicon moralis disciplinae,* which marks an important stage in the beginning of humanist moral thought. For a survey of humanist writings on moral philosophy, see Kristeller 1965.

3. On the role of "justification in history" in the allegory of the *Divine Comedy*, see Singleton 1967, chap. 6.

4. On the concept of the "dark ages," first suggested by Petrarch, and the new division of the history of the West into two and eventually three periods, classical antiquity, the Middle Ages, and the Renaissance, see Mommsen 1959.

5. The definition of the humanities given in the bill creating the National Endowment for the Humanities was based on the definition suggested in the ACLS's Commission on the Humanities 1964 *Report* (Commission on the Humanities 1964, p. 10).

8. The Relevance of the Ancients

1. See Lasch 1979 for a description and analysis of this narcissism.

2. Thomas 1984, pp. 143–55, talks about the relationship between the humanities and the sciences, and the continuing influence of the nineteenth century's image of science.

3. For an interesting discussion of the effect of the new physics on traditionally theological questions, see Davies 1983. Zukav 1979 provides an informative exposition of the New Physics for the layman. Wilber 1984 is a collection of the writings of Heisenberg, Einstein, and other modern physicists on philosophical and theological questions.

4. On changing attitudes towards illness and disease, see the excellent article by Eric J. Cassell (Cassell 1986).

5. The leisure of the few in classical antiquity was made possible by the labor of many, often in the form of slavery. But the social and economic structures of domination upon which the ideal of *otium* was erected in no way call into question the value of the ideal itself. In our own time, as opposed to classical antiquity, we have the technological means to give everyone some of the leisure that was formerly reserved for only a few. And we certainly could accomplish much with this leisure. For example, a four-hour workday would not only help us to address a host of practical and economic problems, such as overemployment alongside of chronic unemployment, and the deterioration of the family because both parents work, but it also could be the first step in effecting a revolution in values by giving people the chance to replace a culture of consumption with a culture of contemplation. Most people who are employed in our society work too much. They come home from their often meaningless jobs too tired to think, so they watch television, drink, or take drugs. What leisure time they have on the weekends they spend shopping, often for things they really do not need. See Aronowitz 1986 on the four-hour workday.

6. Current discussions of "postmodernism," understood as the art and culture of the West which began roughly in the late fifties or early sixties, likewise call into question the very existence of the inner self we have been talking about. The "death of the subject" has become a fashionable theme in contemporary literary theory. See Jameson 1983, especially pp. 114–15.

7. On the moral classification of suicide according to Aristotle, Aquinas, and Dante, see Reade 1969, pp. 424–25.

8. In a June 1986 commencement address at Williams College, Zbigniew Brzezinski argued that as science gives us "the potential for overcoming our physical weaknesses, for transcending the finite boundaries of our bodies," it leads us to think about spirit:

By confronting us with the ultimate question, science may be encouraging us to look beyond science for some answers. The resulting debate will inevitably thus give new vitality and new salience also to the spiritual dimension of our life, to the role of the spiritual in defining what we are. Because the emerging issue involves the mysterious relationship between the spiritual and the physical, it portends a new and deeper role for the religious dimensions in our society. That does not necessarily mean institutionalized and formal religion as we have known it, but it does pose the prospect of renewed appreciation for the ultimate mystery of life and thus for life even beyond the physical life that we think we know." (Quoted in the *Christian Science Monitor*, 1 October 1986, pp. 21–22)

Michael Hooker, chancellor of the Baltimore County campus of the University of Maryland, believes that in preparing students for the world of the future, universities will have to address questions similar to the ones Brzezinski proposes. In a recent conference on universities in the twenty-first century he said:

The real challenge is to provide a metaphysics that adequately subtends our changing conception of the universe and our place in it, and our conception of the nature of life and the nature of persons. While these matters are inextricably linked to religion, they will be inescapable for universities in the next century.

Expanding on this point in a subsequent interview, Hooker argued that "we need to think about metaphysics. We need to confront questions on a broad scale that we have never confronted before—such as 'What makes life worth living? What makes it meaningful? What is its human purpose?' And these are, of course, religious questions" (quoted in the *Christian Science Monitor*, 1 October 1986, p. 17).

9. For an excellent discussion of levels of being, and science's reduction of reality to the lowest level, see Schumacher 1977.

9. A Curriculum for Today

1. MacIntyre writes:

I take it then that both the utilitarianism of the middle and late nineteenth century and the analytical moral philosophy of the middle and late twentieth century are alike unsuccessful attempts to rescue the autonomous moral agent from the predicament in which the failure of the Enlightenment project of providing him with a secular, rational justification for his moral allegiances had left him. I have already characterized that predicament as one in which the price paid for liberation from what appeared to be the external authority of traditional morality was the loss of any authoritative content from the would-be moral utterances of the newly autonomous agent. Each moral agent now spoke unconstrained by the externalities of divine law, natural teleology or hierarchical authority; but why should anyone else now listen to him? . . .

Contemporary moral experience as a consequence has a paradoxical character. For each of us is taught to see himself or herself as an autonomous moral agent; but each of us also becomes engaged by modes of practice, aesthetic or bureaucratic, which involve us in manipulative relationships with others. Seeking to protect the autonomy that we have learned to prize, we aspire ourselves *not* to be manipulated by others; seeking to incarnate our own principles and stand-point in the world of practice, we find no way open to us to do so except by directing towards others those very manipulative modes of relationship which each of us aspires to resist in our own case. . . . (MacIntyre 1984, p. 68)

2. Speaking about ecological science and ecological philosophy, Stephen Toulmin observes that

> once these are seen in their true relationship, it becomes clear that, far from being purely "factual" in their content, many of our central biological concepts are also by implication *ethical* concepts. The human species is directly involved in a great many ecological processes, often as their prime agent or even as their victim; so these processes cannot be treated as ethically indifferent "objects," for detached theoretical study alone. Nor can the associated questions about the mutual adaptation of human beings and other living things be regarded as purely theoretical questions for a detached spectator. Rather, the very concept of adaptation has an inescapable ethical component. The central biological question is not just "How are human beings (passively) adapted to the natural habitat?": it is, also, "How are we (actively) to adapt ourselves to that habitat?"

Toulmin goes on to point out that human beings have a responsibility to nature. This means that we must ask not only how we have coexisted with, for example, the horse, the snail darter, the smallpox virus in the past, but also "'How, on what conditions, and to what ends, ought the human species choose to continue coexisting with those other creatures?'" From the point of view of the humanities, to ask this question is to ask the human species to examine its understanding of its "self." Toulmin observes that "when we begin to ask what it is that scientific intelligence and moral discrimination, between them, demand of us in our relations with the rest of nature, the dreams of natural philosophy become both the concerns of natural religion and the responsibilities of public policy as well" (Toulmin 1982, pp. 267–68). This is the kind of thinking that begins to step out of the fragmentation and specialization of the modern disciplines, and approach the ancient unity of all areas of learning.

3. See Hirschman 1977 for a discussion of how seventeenth and eighteenth-century thinkers turned the vice of avarice into a virtue.

WORKS CITED

Ancient

Aristotle. *De anima*. Ed. W. D. Ross. Oxford: Clarendon, 1956.

Augustine, Aurelius. *De immortalitate animae. De trinitate. De vera religione*. In *Oeuvres*, ed. B. Roland-Gosselin et al., vols. 5, 15–16, and 8 respectively. Paris: Desclée, De Brouwer, 1947– .

Cicero, Marcus Tullius. *Cato maior de senectute. Laelius de amicitia*. Ed. K. Simbeck. 1917. Reprint. Stuttgart: Teubner, 1980.

———. *Cicero's Letters to Atticus*. Ed. D. R. Shackleton Bailey. Vol. 5. Cambridge: Cambridge University Press, 1966.

———. *De divinatione*. Ed. W. Ax. 1938. Reprint. Stuttgart: Teubner, 1977.

———. *De finibus bonorum et malorum*. Ed. Th. Schiche. 1915. Reprint. Stuttgart: Teubner, 1982.

———. *De legibus*. In *Scripta quae manserunt omnia*, ed. C. F. W. Mueller, part 4, vol. 2, pp. 380–450. Leipzig: Teubner, 1905.

———. *De natura deorum*. Ed. W. Ax. 1933. Reprint. Stuttgart: Teubner, 1980.

———. *De officiis*. Ed. C. Atzert. Leipzig: Teubner, 1940.

———. *De oratore*. Ed. Kazimierz F. Kumaniecki. Leipzig: Teubner, 1969.

———. *De re publica*. Ed. K. Ziegler. Leipzig: Teubner, 1929.

———. *Epistulae ad familiares*. Ed. D. R. Shackleton Bailey. Vol. 2. Cambridge: Cambridge University Press, 1977.

———. *Epistulae ad Quintum Fratrem et M. Brutum*. Ed. D. R. Shackleton Bailey. Cambridge: Cambridge University Press, 1980.

———. *Pro Archia*. In *M. Tulli Ciceronis Orationes*, ed. Albert Curtis Clark, vol. 6. 1911. Reprint. Oxford: Clarendon, 1964.

———. *Pro Murena*. In *M. Tulli Ciceronis Orationes*, ed. Albert Curtis Clark, vol. 1. 1905. Reprint. Oxford: Clarendon, 1961.

———. *Tusculanae disputationes*. Ed. M. Pohlenz. 1918. Reprint. Stuttgart: Teubner, 1982.

Digesta. Ed. Theodor Mommsen. Rev. Paul Krueger. In *Corpus Iuris Civilis*, vol. 1. Berlin: Weidmann, 1954.

Plotinus. *Ennéades*. Ed. Émile Brehier. 6 vols. Paris: Les Belles Lettres, 1924–38.

Plutarch. *Brutus*. In *Plutarch's Lives*, trans. Bernadotte Perrin, vol. 6, pp. 126–247. London: Heinemann, 1928.

Polybius. *The Histories*. Trans. W. R. Paton. Vol. 3. 1923. Reprint. London: Heinemann, 1972.

Seneca, Lucius Annaeus. *Epistulae morales*. Ed. Achille Beltrami. 2 vols. Rome: Typis Publicae Officinae Polygraphicae, 1949.

Valerius Maximus. *Factorum et dictorum memorabilium libri novem*. Ed. Karl Kempf. Stuttgart: Teubner, 1966.

Vergil. *The Aeneid*. Trans. Robert Fitzgerald. New York: Random House, 1983.

Modern

Abélard, Peter. *"Historia Calamitatum": The Story of My Misfortunes*. Trans. Henry Adams Bellows. Saint Paul: Boyd, 1922.

Adamson, John William. *English Education: 1789–1902*. Cambridge: Cambridge University Press, 1964.

Anderson, Perry. *Lineages of the Absolutist State*. London: Verso Editions, 1979.

Anselm. *Opera omnia*. Ed. Francis S. Schmitt. Vol. 1. Edinburgh: Thomas Nelson & Sons, 1946.

Arnold, Matthew. *Culture and Anarchy*. Ed. J. Dover Wilson. Cambridge: Cambridge University Press, 1966.

Aronowitz, Stanley. "The Myth of Full Employment." *Nation* 242 (8 February 1986): 135–38.

Avesani, Rino. "La professione dell' 'umanista' nel çinquecento." *Italia Mediovale e Umanistica* 13 (1970): 205–32.

Bailey, D. R. Shackleton. *Cicero*. New York: Scribner's, 1971.

Balsdon, J. P. V. D. "*Auctoritas, Dignitas, Otium.*" *Classical Quarterly*, n.s. 10 (1960): 43–50.

Baron, Hans. *The Crisis of the Early Italian Renaissance: Civic Humanism and Republican Liberty in an Age of Classicism and Tyranny*. Rev. ed. Princeton: Princeton University Press, 1966.

———. *Petrarch's* Secretum: *Its Making and Its Meaning*. Cambridge, Mass.: The Medieval Academy of America, 1985.

Becker, Ernest. *Angel in Armor: A Post-Freudian Perspective on the Nature of Man*. New York: Free Press, 1969.

———. *The Birth and Death of Meaning: An Interdisciplinary Perspective on the Problem of Man*. 2nd ed. New York: The Free Press, 1971.

———. *The Denial of Death*. New York: Free Press, 1973.

Bellah, Robert N., Richard Madsen, William M. Sullivan, Ann Swidler, and Steven M. Tipton. *Habits of the Heart: Individualism and Commitment in American Life*. Reprint. New York: Harper & Row, 1986.

Bendix, Reinhard. *Work and Authority in Industry: Ideologies of Management in the Course of Industrialization*. Berkeley: University of California Press, 1974.

Bennett, William J. "'To Reclaim a Legacy': Text of Report on the Humanities in Education." *Chronicle of Higher Education* 29 (28 November 1984): 16–21.

Berman, Marshall. *All That Is Solid Melts Into Air: The Experience of Modernity*. New York: Simon & Schuster, 1982.

Bertalot, Ludwig. *Studien zum italienischen und deutschen Humanismus*. Ed. P. O. Kristeller, vol. 2, pp. 430–31. Rome: Edizioni di Storia e Letteratura, 1985.

Billanovich, Giuseppe. "Petrarch and the Textual Tradition of Livy." *Journal of the Warburg and Courtauld Institutes* 14 (1951): 137–208.

Bloch, Marc. *Feudal Society*. Trans. L. A. Manyon. Vol. 1. Chicago: University of Chicago Press, 1961.

Bloom, Allan. *The Closing of the American Mind: How Higher Education Has Failed Democracy and Impoverished the Souls of Today's Students*. New York: Simon & Schuster, 1987.

Boccaccio, Giovanni. *Opere latine minori*. Ed. Aldo Francesco Massèra. Bari: Laterza, 1928.

Boyer, Ernest L. *College: The Undergraduate Experience in America*. New York: Harper & Row, 1987.

Bracciolini, Pioggio. *Opera omnia*. Ed. Riccardo Fubini. Vol. 2. Torino: Bottega d'Erasmo, 1966.

Braverman, Harry. *Labor and Monopoly Capital: The Degradation of Work in the Twentieth Century.* New York: Monthly Review Press, 1974.

Brucker, Gene. "Humanism, Politics and the Social Order in Early Renaissance Florence." In *Florence and Venice: Comparisons and Relations.* Acts of Two Conferences at Villa I Tatti in September 1976 and September 1977, Organized by Sergio Bertelli, N. Rubinstein, and C. H. Smyth. Vol. 1, *Quattrocento,* pp. 3–11. Florence: La Nuova Italia, 1979.

Bruni, Leonardo. *Ad Petrum Paulum Histrum dialogus.* In *Prosatori latini del Quattrocento,* ed. Eugenio Garin, pp. 44–99. Milan: Ricciardi, 1952.

———. *Humanistisch-philosophische Schriften.* Ed. Hans Baron. 1928. Reprint. Wiesbaden: Sädig, 1969.

———. "Leonardus Nicolao Strozae S." In *La disputa delle arti nel Quattrocento,* ed. Eugenio Garin, pp. 7–8. Florence: Vallecchi, 1947.

Bullock, Alan. *The Humanist Tradition in the West.* New York: W. W. Norton, 1985.

Campana, Augusto. "The Origin of the Word 'Humanist.'" *Journal of the Warburg and Courtauld Institutes* 9 (1946): 60–73.

Camporeale, Salvatore I. *Lorenzo Valla: Umanesimo e teologia.* Florence: Istituto Nazionale di Studi sul Rinascimento, 1972.

———. "Lorenzo Valla tra medievo e rinascimento: 'Encomion s. Thomae - 1457.'" *Memorie Domenicane,* n.s. 7 (1976): 3–190.

Canfora, Luciano. *Ideologie del classicismo.* Turin: Einaudi, 1980.

Carson, Rachel L. *Silent Spring.* Boston: Houghton Mifflin, 1962.

Cassell, Eric J. "Ideas in Conflict: The Rise and Fall (and Rise and Fall) of New Views of Disease." *Daedalus* 115 (Spring 1986): 19–41.

Cassirer, Ernst, Paul Oskar Kristeller, and John Herman Randall, Jr., eds. *The Renaissance Philosophy of Man.* Chicago and London: University of Chicago Press, 1948.

Commission on the Humanities. *Report.* New York, 1964.

Commission on the Humanities (Founded 1978). *The Humanities in American Life.* Berkeley and Los Angeles: University of California Press, 1980.

Connolly, Cyril. *Enemies of Promise.* 2nd ed. New York: Macmillan, 1948.

Courtenay, William J. "The Early Stages in the Introduction of Oxford Logic in Italy." In *English Logic in Italy in the 14th and 15th Centuries.* Acts of the 5th European Symposium on Medieval Logic and Semantics, Rome, 10–14 November 1980, ed. Alfonso Maierù, pp. 13–32. Naples: Bibliopolis, 1982.

Cranz, F. Edward. "The Reorientation of Western Thought Circa 1100 A.D.: Four Talks." Unpublished papers. New London, [1985].

D'Amico, John F. "The Progress of Renaissance Latin Prose: The Case of Apuleianism." *Renaissance Quarterly* 37 (Autumn 1984): 351–92.

Dante Alighieri. *The Divine Comedy.* Trans. C. S. Singleton. 6 vols. Princeton: Princeton University Press, 1970–75.

Davies, Paul. *God and the New Physics.* New York: Simon & Schuster, 1983.

Duby, Georges. *Rural Economy and Country Life in the Medieval West.* Trans. Cynthia Postan. Columbia, S.C.: University of South Carolina Press, 1968.

Dumont, Louis. *Homo Hierarchicus: The Caste System and Its Implications.* Trans. Mark Sainsbury, Louis Dumont, and Basia Gulati. Complete Revised English Edition. Chicago: University of Chicago Press, 1980.

Elyot, Sir Thomas. *The Book named The Governor.* Ed. S. E. Lehmberg. London: Dent, 1962.

Farrar, F. W., ed. *Essays on a Liberal Education.* 2nd ed. London: Macmillan, 1868.

Fuchs, Harald. "Enkyklios Paideia." *Reallexikon für Antike und Christentum.* Vol. 5, pp. 365–98 (1962).

Galileo Galilei. *Dialogue Concerning the Two Chief World Systems—Ptolemaic & Copernican.* Trans. Stillman Drake. Berkeley & Los Angeles: University of California Press, 1967.

Garin, Eugenio, ed. *L'educazione in Europa 1400/1600.* Bari: Laterza, 1976.

———. *Il pensiero pedagogico dello umanesimo.* Florence: Giuntina/Sansoni, 1958.

Geertz, Clifford. "'From the Native's Point of View': On the Nature of Anthropological Understanding." In *Meaning in Anthropology.* Ed. Keith H. Basso and Henry A. Selby, pp. 221–37. Albuquerque: University of New Mexico Press, 1976.

Giddens, Anthony. *Sociology: A Brief but Critical Introduction.* 2nd ed. New York: Harcourt Brace Jovanovich, 1987.

Gilbert, Neal W. "Richard de Bury and the 'Quires of Yesterday's Sophisms.'". In *Philosophy and Humanism: Renaissance Essays in Honor of Paul Oskar Kristeller,* ed. Edward P. Mahoney, pp. 229–57. New York: Columbia University Press, 1976.

Giustiniani, Vito R. "Homo, Humanus, and the Meanings of 'Humanism.'" *Journal of the History of Ideas* 46 (April–June 1985): 167–95.

Gleick, James. "Stephen Jay Gould: Breaking Tradition with Darwin." *New York Times Magazine,* 20 November 1983.

Grafton, Anthony. *Joseph Scaliger: A Study in the History of Classical Scholarship.* Vol. 1, *Textual Criticism and Exegesis.* Oxford: Clarendon, 1983.

———. "Mark Pattison." *American Scholar* 52 (Spring 1983): 229–36.

———, and Lisa Jardine. *From Humanism to the Humanities: Education and the Liberal Arts in Fifteenth- and Sixteenth-Century Europe.* Cambridge, Mass.: Harvard University Press, 1986.

Green, Arthur. "Jewish Studies and the Jewish Faith." *Tikkun* 1, no. 1 (1986): 84–90.

Greene, Thomas M. *The Light in Troy: Imitation and Discovery in Renaissance Poetry.* New Haven and London: Yale University Press, 1982.

Guarino Guarini. *Epistolario di Guarino Veronese.* Ed. Remigio Sabbadini. Vol. 1. 1915. Reprint. Turin: Bottega d'Erasmo, 1959.

Hartman, Geoffrey H. *Criticism in the Wilderness: The Study of Literature Today.* New Haven and London: Yale University Press, 1980.

Hawley, Richard A. *The Purpose of Pleasure: A Reflection on Youth and Drugs.* Wellesley Hills, Mass.: Independent School Press, 1983.

Hay, Denys. "England and the Humanities in the Fifteenth Century." In Oberman 1975, pp. 305–67.

Heilbroner, Robert L. *The Nature and Logic of Capitalism.* New York: Norton, 1985.

Hesse, Mary. *Revolutions and Reconstructions in the Philosophy of Science.* Bloomington and London: Indiana University Press, 1980.

Hexter, J. H. *Reappraisals in History.* London: Longmans, 1961.

Hirschman, Albert O. *The Passions and the Interests: Political Arguments for Capitalism before Its Triumph.* Princeton: Princeton University Press, 1977.

Humboldt, Wilhelm von. *Humanist without Portfolio: An Anthology of the Writings of Wilhelm von Humboldt.* Trans. Marianne Cowan. Detroit: Wayne State University Press, 1963.

———. *The Limits of State Action.* Trans. J. C. Coulthard. Rev. J. W. Burrow. Cambridge: Cambridge University Press, 1969.

Hume, David. *A Treatise of Human Nature.* Ed. L. A. Selby-Bigge. Oxford: Clarendon Press, 1928.

Jaeger, Werner. *Paideia: The Ideals of Greek Culture.* Vol. 1. *Archaic Greece: The Mind of Athens.* Trans. Gilbert Highet. 2nd ed. 1945. Reprint. New York: Oxford University Press, 1970.

Jaki, Stanley L. *The Relevance of Physics.* Chicago: University of Chicago Press, 1966.

Jameson, Fredric. "Postmodernism and Consumer Society." In *The Anti-Aesthetic: Essays on Postmodern Culture,* ed. Hal Foster, pp. 111–25. Port Townsend, Washington: Bay Press, 1983.

Jonas, Hans. *The Gnostic Religion.* 2nd ed. rev. Boston: Beacon Press, 1963.

Jones, Howard Mumford. *One Great Society: Humane Learning in the United States.* New York: Harcourt, Brace & Co., 1959.

Kelley, Donald R. *Foundations of Modern Historical Scholarship: Language, Law, and History in the French Renaissance.* New York: Columbia University Press, 1970.

————. Rev. of *Joseph Scaliger: A Study in the History of Classical Scholarship.* Vol. 1, *Textual Criticism and Exegesis,* by Anthony Grafton. *History and Theory* 24 (1985): 79–87.

Kerenyi, Carl. *The Religion of the Greeks and the Romans.* Trans. Christopher Holme. New York: Dutton, 1962.

Kliebard, Herbert M. "The Decline of Humanistic Studies in the American School Curriculum." In *The Humanities in Precollegiate Education.* Eighty-third Yearbook of the National Society for the Study of Education, part 2, ed. Benjamin Ladner, pp. 7–30. Chicago: University of Chicago Press, 1984.

Kramer, Hilton. Rev. of *The Humanities in American Life,* by the Commission on the Humanities, and *The Ministry of Culture: Connections among Art, Money and Politics* by Michael Macdonald Mooney. *New York Times Book Review,* 28 December 1980.

Kristeller, Paul Oskar. "Humanism and Scholasticism in the Italian Renaissance." In *Renaissance Thought and Its Sources,* ed. Michael Mooney, pp. 85–105. New York: Columbia University Press, 1979.

————. "The Moral Thought of Renaissance Humanism." In *Renaissance Thought II: Papers on Humanism and the Arts,* pp. 20–68. New York: Harper & Row, 1965.

Kuhn, Thomas S. *The Structure of Scientific Revolutions.* 2nd ed. Chicago: University of Chicago Press, 1970.

Lasch, Christopher. *The Culture of Narcissism: American Life in an Age of Diminishing Expectations.* New York: Warner, 1979.

Leff, Gordon. *William of Ockham: The Metamorphosis of Scholastic Discourse.* Totowa, N.J.: Rowan and Littlefield; Manchester: Manchester University Press, 1975.

Leontief, Wassily. "Academic Economics." Letter. *Science,* n.s. 217 (9 July 1982): 104 and 107.

Levi, Albert William. *Philosophy in the Modern World.* Bloomington: Indiana University Press, 1959.

Lloyd-Jones, Hugh. *Blood for the Ghosts: Classical Influences in the Nineteenth and Twentieth Centuries.* London: Duckworth, 1982.

McCloskey, Donald M. *The Rhetoric of Economics.* Madison, Wis.: University of Wisconsin Press, 1985.

MacIntyre, Alasdair. *After Virtue: A Study in Moral Theory*. 2nd ed. Notre Dame: University of Notre Dame Press, 1984.

Macpherson, C. B. *The Political Theory of Possessive Individualism: Hobbes to Locke*. London: Oxford University Press, 1962.

Mann, Nicholas. "Petrarch and Humanism: The Paradox of Posterity." In *Francesco Petrarch Citizen of the World*. Proceedings of the World Petrarch Congress, Washington D.C., April 6–13, 1974, ed. Aldo S. Bernardo, pp. 287–99. Albany: University of New York Press; Padua: Antenore, 1980.

Marx, Karl, and Friedrich Engels. *The Communist Manifesto*. New York: Monthly Review Press, 1968.

Menander. *Plays and Fragments*. Trans. Philip Vellacott. Harmondsworth: Penguin Books, 1967.

Meredith, Nikki. "Testing the Talking Cure." *Science 86* 7 (June 1986): 31–37.

Mommsen, Theodor E. "Petrarch's Conception of the 'Dark Ages.'" In *Medieval and Renaissance Studies,* ed. Eugene F. Rice, Jr., pp. 106–29. Ithaca: Cornell University Press, 1959.

Mousnier, Roland. *The Institutions of France under the Absolute Monarchy, 1598–1789*. Vol. 1, *Society and the State*. Trans. Brian Pearce. Chicago: University of Chicago Press, 1979.

Nietzsche, Friedrich. *Einleitung in das Studium der classischen Philologie*. In *Gesammelte Werke: Musarionausgabe,* ed. R. Oehler, M. Oehler, and F. Wurzbach, vol. 2, pp. 337–65. Munich: Musarion, 1920.

———. "Nietzsche on Classics and Classicists." Trans. William Arrowsmith. *Arion* 2 (Spring 1963): 5–18.

———. "Nietzsche on Classics and Classicists (Part II)." Trans. William Arrowsmith. *Arion* 2 (Summer 1963): 5–27.

———. *On the Future of Our Educational Institutions. Homer and Classical Philology*. Trans. J. M. Kennedy. New York: Macmillan, 1924.

Nisbet, Robert A. *The Sociological Tradition*. New York: Basic Books, 1966.

Oberman, Heiko A., and Thomas A. Brady, Jr., eds. *Itinerarium Italicum: The Profile of the Italian Renaissance in the Mirror of Its European Transformations*. Leiden: Brill, 1975.

O'Malley, John. "Erasmus and Luther, Continuity and Discontinuity as Key to Their Conflict." *Sixteenth Century Journal* 5 (1974): 47–65.

Panofsky, Erwin. *Renaissance and Renascences in Western Art*. New York: Harper & Row, 1972.

Parker, Harold T. *The Cult of Antiquity and the French Revolutionaries: A Study in the Development of the Revolutionary Spirit*. 1937. Reprint. New York: Octagon Books, 1965.

Parker, William Riley. "The Future of the 'Modern Humanities.'" In *The Future of the Modern Humanities*. Papers Delivered at the Jubilee Congress of the Modern Humanities Research Association in August 1968, ed. J. C. Laidlaw, pp. 106–26. Oxford [?]: The Modern Humanities Research Association, 1969.

Percival, W. Keith. "Renaissance Grammar: Rebellion or Evolution?" In *Interrogatvi dell'umanesimo*. Vol. II: Atti del X convegno internazionale di studi umanistici montepulciano - Palazzo Tarugi - 1973, ed. Giovannangiola Tarugi, pp. 73–90. Florence: Olschki, 1976.

Perreiah, Alan. "Humanistic Critiques of Scholastic Dialectic." *Sixteenth Century Journal* 13 (1982): 3–22.

Petrarca, Francesco. *De sui ipsius et multorum ignorantia*. Ed. L. M. Capelli. Paris: Champion, 1906.

———. *Le familiari*. 4 vols. Ed. Vittorio Rossi and Umberto Bosco. Florence: Sansoni, 1933–1942.

———. *Invective contra medicum*. Ed. Pier Giorgio Ricci. Rome: Edizioni di Storia e Letteratura, 1950.

———. *Opera omnia*. 4 vols. Basel, 1554. Reprint. Ridgewood, N.J.: Gregg Press, 1965.

———. *Physicke Against Fortune*. Trans. Thomas Twyne. 1579. Reprint. Delmar, N.Y.: Scholars' Facsimiles & Reprints, 1980.

———. *Prose*. Ed. G. Martellotti, P. G. Ricci, E. Carrara, and E. Bianchi. Milan and Naples: Ricciardi, 1955.

Pfeiffer, Rudolf. *History of Classical Scholarship from 1300 to 1850*. Oxford: Clarendon, 1976.

Pico della Mirandola, Giovanni. *De hominis dignitate, Heptaplus, De ente et uno, e scritti vari*. Ed. Eugenio Garin. Florence: Vallecchi, 1942.

Piérart, Marcel. "La 'liberté des anciens' et la 'liberté des modernes': Réflexions sur deux formes d'humanisme." *Les Études Classiques* 54 (1986): 111–34.

Plumb, J. H. *The Death of the Past*. London: Macmillan, 1969.

Quint, David. "Humanism and Modernity: A Reconsideration of Bruni's *Dialogues*." *Renaissance Quarterly* 38 (Autumn 1985): 423–45.

Ramage, Edwin S. "Early Roman Urbanity." *American Journal of Philology* 81 (1960): 65–72.

———. "*Urbanitas*: Cicero and Quintilian, A Contrast in Attitudes." *American Journal of Philology* 84 (1963): 390–414.

Reade, W. H. V. *The Moral System of Dante's Inferno*. 1909. Reprint. Port Washington, N.Y.: Kennikat Press, 1969.

Rico, Francisco. *Vida u obra de Petrarca*. Vol. 1, *Lectura del "Secretum."* Padua: Ente Nazionale Francesco Petrarca, 1974.

Rieff, Philip. *The Triumph of the Therapeutic: Uses of Faith After Freud*. New York: Harper & Row, 1966.

Rose, Phyllis. *Parallel Lives: Five Victorian Marriages*. New York: Knopf, 1983.

Sabbadini, Remigio. *La scuola e gli studi di Guarino Veronese*. 1896. Reprinted in *Guariniania*, ed. Mario Sancipriano. Turin: Bottega d'Erasmo, 1964.

Salutati, Coluccio. *Epistolario di Coluccio Salutati*. Ed. Francesco Novati. 4 vols. Rome: Istituto Storico Italiano, 1891–1911.

Sandys, Sir John Edwin. *A History of Classical Scholarship*. 8 vols. 1921. Reprint. New York: Hafner, 1967.

Schadewaldt, Wolfgang. "Humanitas Romana." In *Aufsteig und Niedergang der römischen Welt: Geschichte und Kultur Roms im Spiegel der neueren Forschung*, ed. Hildegard Temporini, part 1, vol. 4, pp. 43–62. Berlin and New York: De Gruyter, 1973.

Schumacher, E. F. *Good Work*. New York: Harper & Row, 1979.

———. *A Guide for the Perplexed*. New York: Harper & Row, 1977.

Schwartz, Barry. *The Battle for Human Nature: Science, Morality, and Modern Life*. 1st ed. New York: Norton, 1986.

Seigel, Jerrold E. *Rhetoric and Philosophy in Renaissance Humanism*. Princeton: Princeton University Press, 1968.

Silk, Leonard, and David Vogel. *Ethics and Profits: The Crisis of Confidence in American Business.* New York: Simon & Schuster, 1976.

Singleton, Charles S. *Dante Studies 2: Journey to Beatrice.* 1958. Reprint. Cambridge, Mass.: Harvard University Press, 1967.

——. *An Essay on the Vita Nuova.* Cambridge, Mass.: Harvard University Press, 1958.

Smith, Adam. *Supermoney.* New York: Random House, 1972.

Snell, Bruno. *The Discovery of the Mind: The Greek Origins of European Thought.* Trans. T. G. Rosenmeyer. 1953. Reprint. New York: Harper & Row, 1960.

Sommers, Christina Hoff. "Ethics Without Virtue: Moral Education in America." *American Scholar* 53 (Summer 1984): 381–89.

Stockman, David A. *The Triumph of Politics: Why the Reagan Revolution Failed.* New York: Harper & Row, 1986.

Sweezy, Paul M. *Four Lectures on Marxism.* New York: Monthly Review Press, 1981.

Taylor, Charles. *Hegel.* Cambridge: Cambridge University Press, 1975.

Taylor, Frederick Winslow. *The Principles of Scientific Management.* New York: Harper & Brothers, 1923.

Thomas Aquinas. *Summa theologica.* Vol. 12, *Human Intelligence,* ed. Paul T. Durbin. Cambridge: Blackfriars, 1968.

Thomas, Lewis. *Late Night Thoughts on Listening to Mahler's Ninth Symphony.* New York: Bantam, 1984.

Thompson, E. P. "The Grid of Inheritance: A Comment." In *Family and Inheritance: Rural Society in Western Europe 1200–1800.* Ed. Jack Goody, Joan Thirsk, and E. P. Thompson, pp. 328–60. Cambridge: Cambridge University Press, 1978.

Tigar, Michael E., and Madeleine R. Levy. *Law and the Rise of Capitalism.* New York: Monthly Review Press, 1977.

Toulmin, Stephen. *The Return to Cosmology: Postmodern Science and the Theology of Nature.* Berkeley and Los Angeles: University of California Press, 1982.

Trilling, Lionel. *Beyond Culture: Essays on Literature and Learning.* New York: Viking Press, 1965.

——. *Sincerity and Authenticity.* Cambridge, Mass.: Harvard University Press, 1972.

——. "The Uncertain Future of the Humanistic Educational Ideal." In *The Last Decade: Essays and Reviews, 1965–75,* ed. Diana Trilling, pp. 160–76. Oxford: Oxford University Press, 1982.

Trinkaus, Charles. "Humanism, Religion, Society: Concepts and Motivations of Some Recent Studies." *Renaissance Quarterly* 29 (Winter 1976): 676–713.

——. *In Our Image and Likeness: Humanity and Divinity in Italian Renaissance Thought.* 2 vols. Chicago: University of Chicago Press, 1970.

——. *The Scope of Renaissance Humanism.* Ann Arbor: University of Michigan Press, 1983.

Turner, Frank M. *The Greek Heritage in Victorian Britain.* New Haven: Yale University Press, 1981.

Valla, Lorenzo. *Elegantiarium libri.* In *Prosatori latini del quattrocento,* ed. Eugenio Garin, pp. 504–631. Milan: Ricciardi, 1952.

——. *Encomium S. Thomae.* In *Opera omnia,* vol. 2, pp. 346–52. Turin: Bottega d'Erasmo, 1962.

Veatch, Henry. "Deconstruction in Philosophy: Has Rorty Made It the Denouement of Contemporary Analytical Philosophy?" *Review of Metaphysics* 39 (December 1985): 303–20.

Veysey, Laurence R. *The Emergence of the American University*. Chicago: University of Chicago Press, 1965.

Voegelin, Eric. "The German University and the Order of German Society: A Reconsideration of the Nazi Era." *Intercollegiate Review* 20 (Spring/Summer 1985): 7–27.

Wagner, David L. "The Seven Liberal Arts and Classical Scholarship." In *The Seven Liberal Arts in the Middle Ages*, ed. David L. Wagner, pp. 1–31. Bloomington: Indiana University Press, 1983.

Weber, Max. *From Max Weber: Essays in Sociology*. Ed. H. H. Gerth and C. Wright Mills. New York: Oxford University Press, 1958.

Weisinger, Herbert. "Who Began the Revival of Learning? The Renaissance Point of View." *Papers of the Michigan Academy of Science and Letters* 30 (1940): 625–38.

West, Andrew F., ed. *Value of the Classics*. Princeton: Princeton University Press, 1917.

Whitehead, Alfred North. *Dialogues of Alfred North Whitehead, As Recorded by Lucien Price*. Boston: Little, Brown, 1954.

Wilamowitz-Moellendorff, U. von. *History of Classical Scholarship*. Trans. Alan Harris. Baltimore: Johns Hopkins University Press, 1982.

Wilber, Ken, ed. *Quantum Questions: Mystical Writings of the World's Great Physicists*. Boulder: Shambhala Publications, 1984.

Wilcox, Donald J. *The Development of Florentine Humanist Historiography in the Fifteenth Century*. Cambridge, Mass.: Harvard University Press, 1969.

Wilkins, Ernest H. *Petrarch's Correspondence*. Padua: Antenore, 1960.

Williams, Dyfri. "Ajax, Odysseus and the Arms of Achilles." *Antike Kunst* 23, no. 2 (1980): 137–45.

Witt, Ronald. "Medieval 'Ars Dictaminis' and the Beginnings of Humanism: A New Construction of the Problem." *Renaissance Quarterly* 35 (Spring 1982): 1–35.

Wolfe, Alan. "The Return of Values." *Tikkun* 1, no. 2 (1986): 59–64.

Woodward, W. H. *Studies in Education during the Age of the Renaissance*. 1906. Reprint. New York: Teachers College Press, 1967.

———. *Vittorino da Feltre and Other Humanist Educators*. 1897. Reprint. New York: Teachers College Press, 1963.

Zukav, Gary. *The Dancing Wu Li Masters: An Overview of the New Physics*. New York: Bantam, 1979.

INDEX

Abélard, Peter, 146, 214
Absolute monarchies: and Roman law,
    122, 123; described, 124–25
Accursio, Mainardo, 30, 34
Acid rain, 159
Adamson, John William, 98, 99, 100, 110
Adler, Alfred, 116
Aesop, 42, 126
African humanities, 189
Agricola, Rudolph, 25–26
Alexander of Macedonia, 48
Allen, William P., 101
Altertumswissenschaft, 92, 95, 98, 118. *See
    also* Philology
Amazon rain forests, 159
American Council of Learned Societies,
    154
Amnesia, 163, 174, 191, 196
Anachronism, 8, 154
Ancients. *See* Greeks and Romans
Anderson, Perry, 122
Anselm, Saint: proof for existence of
    God, 79–80; mentioned, 150, 180, 189
Anthropology, 49, 72–73, 154, 167, 211
Antony, Mark, 69–70
Aquinas, Thomas, 38, 46, 164
Archaeology, 8, 154, 155
Aristocrats, education of, 127
Aristotelianism: scholastic, xxv, 22, 38,
    148; and modernity, 187–88; men-
    tioned, 189. *See also* Scholasticism
Aristotle: on the circle of the moon,
    xxvi; Bruni on, 3, 9, 11; in Middle
    Ages, 8; Petrarch on, 45, 149, 187; his
    De anima, 78; his theory of the virtues,
    131, 149, 165; his *Nichomachaean Ethics,*
    161, 187–88, 211, 218; his definition of
    man, 164; mentioned, 10, 94, 192, 213
Aristophanes, 126
Arnold, Matthew: on Humboldt, 104–105;
    his *Culture and Anarchy,* 105, 107, 153;
    and *Bildung,* 106, 108, 110, 113, 115;
    mentioned, 92, 109, 179
Arrowsmith, William, 95
Artes humanitatis, 19–20, 21, 168
Artes liberales, 212, 213–14
Asian humanities, 188
Association of American Colleges, 194
Astura, 59, 72, 166
Athens, 116, 124, 150
Atom bomb, 159
Atticus, T. Pomponius, 59–72 *passim,* 166
Auctoritas, 50, 51–52, 207

Augustine, Saint: Bruni on, 4, 5, 9, 10; on
    liberal arts, 20; and Petrarch, 82–83;
    mentioned, 26, 46
—Works: *De immortalitate animae,* 79; *De
    Trinitate,* 78–79; *De vera religione,* 81,
    82, 178, 179
Augustus Caesar, 48, 153

Bach, Johann Sebastian, 160
Barbaro, Ermolao, 90
Basel, University of, 103
Basil, Saint, 5
Bateson, Gregory, 159
Battista di Montefeltro, 4–12 *passim,* 46,
    127, 147, 171
Beatrice Portinari, 59–60, 153–54
Becker, Ernest: his *The Denial of Death,*
    33, 167; on human condition, 167; on
    obsession with technique, 203
Beethoven, Ludwig van, 160
Bellah, Robert: his *Habits of the Heart,*
    149, 153, 163, 164, 192
Bennett, William J.: on humanities, xxiii,
    144–45, 190–92; his "To Reclaim a
    Legacy," 7, 105, 190–92
Berlin, University of, 103–104
Berman, Marshall, 137
Beroaldo, Filippo, 90
Bhopal, 159
Bible, 8, 46, 89, 90, 163, 189, 192, 193
Bildung, xxvii, 104–17 *passim. See also*
    Self, the: shaping of
Black Death, 27–29, 40–41
Bloch, Marc, 122, 209
Bloom, Allan, 144
Boccaccio, Giovanni: and Petrarch, 25, 26,
    44; his *Decameron,* 111
Boethius, 10, 44
Bologna, xxiv, 102, 121, 130
Botstein, Leon, 132
Boyer, Ernest L., 193–95
Brown, William L., 134
Brunelleschi, xxiv
Bruni, Leonardo: his definition of *studia
    humanitatis,* xxvii, 3, 10, 12, 14; his let-
    ter to N. Strozzi, 3–4, 10–12; his career,
    4, 123, 129; on Latin, 4–5, 46; on an-
    cient historians, 10, 135; and the self,
    12, 49, 110, 115; and Cicero, 19–20, 49,
    76; on Petrarch, 25; his letter to Duke
    Humphrey, 127–28; on Florence, 127,
    150; writings, 203, 210; mentioned,
    xxvi, 89, 90, 91, 126, 147

—Works: *De studiis et litteris,* 4–6, 8–12, 127, 171, 179; *Laudatio Florentinae Urbis,* 124; *Historia Florentini populi,* 203; *Isagogicon moralis disciplinae,* 203, 210

Brutus, Marcus, 61, 70, 166

Brzezinski, Zbigniew, 211–12

Budé, Guillaume, 90

Bullock, Alan, 204

Bureaucratic rationality, 131–34

Caesar, Julius, 61

Cambridge, 125, 176

Capitalism, xiii, 121, 122, 137–39, 163, 184–85, 192, 210

Carnegie Foundation for the Advancement of Teaching, 193

Carson, Rachel: her *Silent Spring,* 159

Carthage, destruction of, 205

Cato the Censor, 67

Catullus, 77

Change: in sublunar world, xxvi, 37; Petrarch's awareness of, xxvii, 35, 43, 178, 206; in capitalism, 138, 139; historical, 154; and science, 206

Chernobyl, 159

Choice: obsession with, 195–97

Christianity, 189

Chrysippus of Soli, 18

Cicero, Marcus Tullius: on perfection, xxvi, 17–20; on cosmos, xxvi, 17–20, 49, 76, 79, 109; Bruni on, 3, 5, 10, 11; contrasted with Bruni, 19–20, 49, 76; his letters, 27; on circle of the moon, 37, 66; his Latin, 42, 44, 45, 46, 82, 177–78; on Marius, 49–52; on the Decii, 53–56, 74; on Romans, 56; contrasted with Dante and Petrarch, 59–60, 76, 82–83; and death of Tullia, 59–63; his philosophical writings, 62–63; on philosophy, 65; on wisdom, 66, 200; on gladiators, 69; his death, 69–70; on "seeing with the mind," 81, 82; in curriculum, 63, 177–78, 187; use of *humanitas,* 199, 205–206; letter to Quintus, 205; as a Roman, 207; mentioned, xxiv, xxvi, xxvii, 20, 26, 38, 58–74 *passim,* 127, 150, 166, 169

—Works: *Academica,* 63; *Cato maior de senectute,* xxvi, 53, 63; *Consolatio,* 63; *De divinatione,* 53, 54–55, 63; *De facto,* 63; *De finibus,* 53, 55, 63, 171; *De legibus,* 18; *De natura deorum,* xxvi, 16–18, 63, 160, 177–78, 182; *De officiis,* 63, 129–30, 166, 187, 190, 198, 199; *De optimo genere oratorum,* 63; *De oratore,* 15–

16; *De re publica,* 19, 21, 37, 66; *Laelius de amicitia,* 60, 63, 65–66; *Paradoxica Stoicorum,* 63; *Pro Archia,* 14–16, 21, 88, 177, 178, 205–206; *Pro Murena,* 15; *Tusculanae disputationes,* 20, 44, 49–72 *passim* 81, 82, 160, 177–78, 198, 208

Circle of the moon, xxvi, 36–37; 38, 39, 43, 66, 68, 71, 83, 103, 206–207

Citizen, etymology of, 164

City-state, classical. *See* Polis

Civic virtue, 166, 169, 188

Civil Rights Movement, 145

Civitas, 109, 150

Clarendon Commission, 100

Classical antiquity: and Renaissance, 5, 134–35, 145, 151, 208; and ourselves, 8, 136, 145, 174–75; study of, 113; and fascism and nazism, 135, 210; language and culture of, 143, 188; its concept of the past, 153–54; community in, 166; unity of learning in, 172; and democracy, 190; in eighteenth-century Germany, 208; no capitalism in, 210; leisure in, 211; slavery in, 211; mentioned, 97, 101, 102, 103, 104, 155, 156, 161, 176, 184, 187, 189, 191

Classical education: spread of, xxiv; described by Nietzsche, xxiv; as new curriculum, xxiv; demise of, xxviii, 113, 118, 144, 173; as *studia humanitatis,* 6; and mental discipline, 101; and concept of the self, 103; in Germany, 103; in Renaissance, 124–25; has not been replaced, 143–44; and ruling classes, 189–90; tradition of, 193; turns ancients into enemies, 197. *See also* Humanities, *Studia humanitatis*

Classical humanities, ix, 7

Classical languages. *See* Greek and Latin

Classical tradition, 189

Classics: in education in the West, 8; Greek and Latin, xxiii, xxiv, xxvi, 39, 130, 134, 190

Colonna, Giacomo, 29

Colonna, Giovanni, 27, 29, 31, 32, 44, 52

Commission on the Humanities (founded 1978) xxiii

Commission on the Humanities, 211

Community, 58, 61, 68, 71, 148–53, 162–66 *passim,* 187, 190, 193, 199, 207

Comte, Auguste, 183

Conference Board, 138

Connecticut College: humanities program in international studies, 205–10

Connolly, Cyril, 96–97

Conrad, Joseph, 71, 113–14

Consumption, culture of, 162
Contemplation, 71, 76, 109, 161–62, 168, 194, 206
Contemporary culture, 7–8, 196. *See also* Modernity
Contingency: for Petrarch, xxvii, 35, 39, 40, 43, 129; in Middle Ages, 36–38
Corinth, conquest of, 205
Corpus iuris civilis, 121
Cosmology, 159, 178
Cosmos, 20, 37, 44, 49, 67, 68, 69, 76, 78, 79, 109, 114, 132, 150, 178, 181
Cournot, Antoine Augustin, 100
Cranz, F. Edward, 77–83, 109, 180, 184, 189, 206
Crassus, Marcus Licinius, 48
Cristiani, Luca, 30, 34
Cultural relativity, 154, 203–204
Culture: Matthew Arnold on, 105, 107, 108
Curriculum: contemporary, xxiv, xxvi, 21, 110, 130–31, 144, 145, 172, 196, 198; of original humanities, ix, xxiv, 10, 13, 63, 83; of liberal arts, 143, 144, 173, 175; proposals for, 175–76, 190–95; science in, 180–81; humanities in, 188; exercise of choice in, 195–97; application of author's approach, xv, 205–10
Curtius, Rufus, 10

Dante, xxvi, xxvii, 25, 37, 38, 42, 59–60, 119, 153–54, 164, 184, 192, 193
Dark Ages: as concept, 211
Death: Petrarch on, 27–36, 43, 81–82; Becker on, 33; ancient and modern experiences of, 77
Decii, the, 52–56, 58, 74
Deconstructionism, xxv, 112, 147, 210
Democracy, 135, 190
Democritus, 103
Descartes, René, 23, 160, 180, 184
Dialectic. *See* Logic
Dickens, Charles, 96, 97, 197
Dictatores, 123–24
Diderot, Denis, 71, 113
Dodds, E. R., 95
Donatello, xxiv
Dryden, John, 119–20
Duby, Georges, 209
Dumont, Louis, 184
Durkheim, Émile, 183

Ecology, 159, 160, 178, 213
Education: content vs. skills, xiii; current conditions, xv–xvii; and classics, 8; pre-professional, 10, 172; Renaissance, 23–

24; discussions of, 129; and humanities, 170–76; democratization of, 189–90
Einstein, Albert, 211
Eliot, T. S., 190
Elyot, Richard, 125–26
Elyot, Sir Thomas, 125–27, 128
Engels, Friedrich, 137
England: critiques of classical education in, 98–99; Renaissance humanities in, 125
English: literature, 106–108, 110; as literary language, 119–20
Enlightenment, 149, 175, 183, 212
Epicurus, 9, 55, 103
Erasmus, Desiderius, 25, 46, 89–91, 95, 96, 102, 125, 134
Essays on a Liberal Education. See Farrar, F. W.
Eton, 96
Exempla, xxvii, 12–13, 47–48

Faculty psychology, 11–101, 108
Farrar, F. W.: his *Essays on a Liberal Education,* 98, 101, 110, 119, 137
Fascism, 135, 210
Fathers of the Church, 4–5, 8, 9, 26, 46, 89, 90
Faulkner, William, 190
Ferrara, xxiv, 129
Feudalism, 121, 122, 127, 133, 183, 184, 209, 210
First National Bank of Boston, 134
First World War, 92
Florence, 124, 125, 127, 135, 150, 203
Forster, E. M., 185
Fortune, xxvi, xxvii, 34, 35, 43, 58, 76, 103, 129, 130. *See also* Contingency
Franceschino degli Albizzi, 27, 30, 34–35, 48
French Revolution, 135, 137, 174, 182, 183
Freud: and Petrarch, 83, 151; his theory of psychoanalysis, 113–14; attraction of, 116; and Cicero, 160; influence of, 160; mentioned, 71, 101, 152
Friendship, virtue of, 165–66

Gadamer, Hans-Georg, x
Galen, 8
Galileo, xxvii, 23, 36, 80, 180, 206–207
Geertz, Clifford, 72–74
Gellius, Aulus, 204
Germany: classical studies in, 91–92, 103, 208
Giddens, Anthony, 183
Gilbert, Humphrey, 127
Giovanni dell'Incisa, 30

Giustiniani, Vito R., 204–205
Goethe, Johann Wolfgang von, 91, 92
Gould, John Jay, xxviii
Graff, Gerald, xi
Grafton, Anthony, 88, 90–91
Grandgent, C. H., 7
Great Books programs, xi, 192–93
Greece: ancient, 87, 103
Greece and Rome. *See* Classical antiquity
Greed, 163, 192, 197
Greek and Latin: decline of, 96, 97, 98,
    101, 105, 110, 119, 134, 136; rhetorical
    training in, 120; uses of, 121; value of,
    143–44; in high school, 197–98; men-
    tioned, 143, 148. *See also* Classical edu-
    cation
Greek antiquity, 94, 95
Greek language, 89, 90, 104, 121, 177
Greeks: Arnold and Humboldt on, 104–
    109 *passim;* on nature, 159, 162; on hu-
    man, 168; and Roman *virtus,* 205
Greeks and Romans: disappearance of,
    xxiv, 8, 99, 145; and Petrarch, 33, 103;
    their concept of the human, 75, 168,
    174, 175, 182; on the soul, 66–67; as
    school subjects, 96, 98, 118; as models,
    108, 153, 175, 194; and original humani-
    ties, 110, 131; in Western tradition, 156;
    and religion, 162, 169; and community,
    164; need for today, 173; and moral edu-
    cation, 186–87; mentioned, xxviii, 155,
    160, 166, 175, 185, 187, 188, 193
Green, Arthur, 167
Greene, Thomas M., 154
Greenhouse effect, 159
Gregory Nazianzen, Saint, 5
Guarino Guarini, 129–30
Guidi, Count Roberto, 33

Habits of the Heart. See Bellah
Hales, J. W., 98, 99, 119, 120
Hamlet, 71, 110, 198
Hannibal, 48
Hawley, Richard A., 198
Hegel, G. W. F.: his *The Phenomenology of
    the Mind,* 113–14; mentioned, 87, 101,
    175, 180
Heidegger, Martin, 204
Heilbroner, Robert L., 138
Heisenberg, Werner, 159, 211
Henry VII, King of England, 125
Henry VIII, King of England, 125
Herder, Johann Gottfried von, 91
Hermann, Gottfried, 91
Hesse, Mary, 158
High schools: science in, 180–81, 198; hu-
    manities in, 197–98

History: discipline of, 8, 10, 153–54, 203;
    Petrarch on, 135, 151; consciousness of,
    150, 153, 155, 175, 183, 187, 188, 196,
    207; mentioned, xxiv, xxviii, 128, 129,
    130, 155
Hitler, Adolf, 135
Hobbes, Thomas, 165, 186
Homer, xxiv, 8, 10, 48, 91–92, 97, 126,
    154, 190, 192
Homo, 50–51, 67
Hooker, Michael, 212
Horace, 44, 45, 96–97, 126, 187
Howald, Ernst, 95
Humanist, etymology of, 6–7
Humanista, 6–7, 14, 123, 204
Humanists: Renaissance, xxiv, xxv, 5, 8,
    149, 150, 155, 173, 175; nineteenth-
    century, 101
Humanitas, xxvi, 14–16, 168, 199, 200,
    204–206
Humanities: current discussions of, xxiii,
    5–6, 98, 120, 143–44; definition of, ix,
    xxiii, 7, 13, 143, 145, 154–55, 191, 211;
    and science, xxiii, 21, 23–24, 159, 207;
    demise of, xxiv, xxviii, 33, 92–93, 96,
    102, 120, 134, 143–45, 154; Renaissance,
    x, xxvi, 48, 76, 83, 110, 114, 118, 194;
    and curriculum, xxvi, 134, 175–90,
    195, 198, 205–10; and contingency,
    xxvii, 129; and moral education, 3, 9,
    175, 185–88, 198; classical, 7; etymol-
    ogy of, 7, 188; reports on, 7, 87, 190–
    91; and antiquity, 8; and the self, 79,
    103, 131, 173–74; history of, 87; 155,
    173, 191, 192–93, 199; and psychother-
    apy, 116; as a tradition, 118, 132, 145,
    174–83 *passim,* 188, 193, 195; relevance
    of, 134, 188, 197; and technique, 148,
    172; provide community, 162; and re-
    publican tradition, 164; and liberal arts,
    170–76; and preprofessional training,
    172; and social sciences, 183–86; and
    minorities, 188; and women, 188; Asian,
    188–89; and non-Western cultures, 188–
    89; African, 189; and Judeo-Christian
    tradition, 189; in translation, 197; and
    ecology, 213; mentioned, 99, 130, 147.
    See also Classical education; *Studia hu-
    manitatis*
Humboldt, Wilhelm von: his educa-
    tional reforms, 103–104; and *Bildung,*
    106, 107;
—Works: *The Eighteenth Century,* 104;
    *History of the Fall and Decline of the
    Greek City States,* 104; *The Limits of
    State Action,* 104; mentioned, 91, 109,
    113, 115

Hume, David, 186, 194
Humphrey of Gloucester, 127

Illness, popular attitudes toward, 160
Indeterminacy, Heisenberg's principle
   of, 159
Individualism, 149, 156, 163–64, 165, 187,
   192, 193
Industrial Revolution, 137, 167, 174, 182,
   183
Industrial Society, 136, 161, 163, 174, 183.
   See also Modernity
Irnerius, 121
Italy, xxiv, 120, 123, 133

Jaeger, Werner, 204
Jaki, Stanley L., 180–81
Javanese: their concept of person, 73–74
Jerome, Saint, 4, 5, 10, 46, 89
Jerusalem, 116
John Chrysostom, Saint, 5
Jonas, Hans, 69, 76–77, 164–65
Judeo-Christian tradition, 189
Jung, Carl Gustav, 116
Justin, 127
Justinian, 8, 121

Kant, Immanuel, 175, 186
Kelley, Donald R., 90–91, 203
Kempen, Ludwig van, 27, 30, 32–33,
   34, 40
Kerenyi, Carl, 77, 162, 169
Kimball, Bruce A., x
Kramer, Hilton, 144
Kristeller, Paul Oskar, 10
Kuhn, Thomas S., 157

Lactantius, Caelius Firmianus, 4, 5, 10
Laertes, 71, 192
Lannoy, Ghillebert de, 127
La Noue, François de, 127
Laplace, Marquis de, 160
Latin: classical, xxiv, 5, 8, 42, 45–46, 90,
   96–97, 98–99, 123, 128, 134, 177–78;
   medieval, xxiv, 5, 6, 42, 45–46; re-
   placed by vernacular, 119–21
Laura, 27
Lausus, 74–75, 166
Law: Bruni on, 3–4; Roman, 121, 122,
   123, 128, 209, 210; mentioned, 8, 22, 155
Lawrence, D. H., 116
Learning: and goodness, 45, 93, 128; pro-
   fessionalization of, 148
Leisure, 20, 161, 162, 211
Leo X, Pope, 90
Leontief, Wassily, xxv
Le Play, Pierre, 183

Lessing, Gotthold Ephraim, 91
Levi, Albert William, 191
Liberal Arts: arguments for, 9–10, 105–
   106, 110, 120, 171–72; ancient, 16, 20,
   21, 194; debate on, 98, 143, 170; and
   mental discipline, 101, 102; and curricu-
   lum, 143, 144, 173, 175, 193–94, 205–
   10; and humanities, 171–90, 195, 199;
   and choice, 195–97; and high schools,
   197
Liège, 88
Linacre, Thomas, 126
Literary theory, 97, 112, 147
Literature: classical, xxviii, 109–10; study
   of, 99, 106, 112; modern, 113, 136
Livy: his *History of Rome,* 88–89, 207;
   mentioned, xxiv, 5, 10
Lloyd-Jones, Hugh, 95
Locke, John, 186
Logic: medieval, xxv, 8, 22, 38, 39, 147;
   Petrarch on, xxv, 102–103, 171–72; hu-
   manists on, 5, 10, 46, 89
Love Canal, 159
Lucan, 127
Lucian, 126
Luther, Martin, 90, 91

McCloskey, Donald N., 183
Machiavelli, Niccolò, 210
MacIntyre, Alasdaire, 131, 132, 133, 149,
   165, 174, 187–88
Macpherson, C. B., 182
Malatesta, Carlo, 127
Mamertus, Claudianus, 20
Management, science of, 130, 133, 134
Manager, the, 130–34 *passim*
Mantua, xxiv
Many and the One, 75, 82, 161, 178
Marius, Caius, 47–52, 56, 65, 74
Marnix, Phillippe de, 127
Marseilles, 33
Marx, Karl: his *The Communist Manifesto,*
   137; on capital, 137–38; his *Critique of
   Political Economy,* 185; mentioned, 101,
   103, 180, 183, 184
Menander, 162
Mental discipline, 99–101, 102, 106, 110,
   112, 171
Merton, Thomas, xii
Messina, Tommaso da, 42–43
Metaphysics, xxv, 8, 10, 22, 38, 46, 89,
   147, 167, 212
Methodology. *See* Technique
Mezentius, 74–75
Michelangelo, xxiv
Middle Ages: and classics, 8; culture of,
   36–38, 191; community in, 152; con-

cept of the past in, 153–54; and sociology, 184; as concept, 211
Mill, John Stuart, 14, 186
Minorities, study of, 188
Modern humanism, 98, 99, 110
Modern humanities, 7
Modern Humanities Research Association, 7
Modern languages and literatures, 99, 103, 110, 143
Modernity: problems of, 137, 157–87 passim; and science, 167–68; revolts against, 180; and social sciences, 182; and curriculum, 192, 195, 196; emphasis on skills over content, xiii
Molière, 71
Money, 138–39, 156, 166
Montaigne, Michel Eyquem de, 127
Moral education, 149, 171–88 passim
Moral philosophy, xxiv, xxviii, 9, 10, 128, 129, 130, 132, 155, 171, 175, 176, 186–88, 198, 199, 210, 212–13
More, Saint Thomas, 46, 102, 126
Mousnier, Roland, 210
Multiculturalism, xi–xii, xiv
Mussolini, Benito, 135

Naples, 31–32
Napoleon I, 135
Narcissism, 151–57 passim, 163, 169, 173
National Endowment of the Humanities (NEH), xxiii, 13, 105, 154–55, 191, 211
Natural science: and social sciences, 148; mentioned, 8, 10, 22, 158
Nature: theology of, 161, 178; and mind, 166, 175, 184, 188; objectification of, 176, 179, 181; mentioned, 24, 157, 159, 169, 174, 175, 178, 213
Nazism, 210
New Criticism, xxv
New physics, 158, 159, 211
Newtonian physics, 157
Nicholas V, Pope, 10
Nietzsche, Friedrich, Wilhelm, xxiv, 71, 91–103 passim, 118, 179
—Works: "Introduction to Philology," 93, 95; On the Future of Our Educational Institutions, 94, 97; On the Genealogy of Morals, 93; The Birth of Tragedy, 95; We Philologists, 93–94, 95
Nisbet, Robert A., 131–32, 182, 184
Nominalism, 39
Non-Western cultures, 72, 143, 188

Ockham, William of, 39, 46
Orosius, Paulus, 127
Otium. See Leisure

Ovid, 126
Oxford, 39, 116, 125, 176

Paideia, 204–205
Paris, xxiv, 39, 102, 116
Parker, Harold T., 135
Parker, William Riley, 7
Parma, 34
Past, the: and industrial society, 137; and capitalism, 137–39; death of, 137–39, 174; authority of, 151, 152; use of, 144, 148, 163; classical, 144, 164, 188, 199; in antiquity and Middle Ages, 153–54; mentioned, 8, 156, 164, 183, 184, 196
Pattison, Mark, 104
Paul, Saint, 90, 189
Penna, Luca da, 42
Perfection: participation in, xxvi, 109; Bruni on, 3, 11–12, 19–20, 49; Cicero on, 16–20, 49, 79, 187; Humboldt on, 104; Arnold on, 105, 108; of the shelf, 108, 110, 112–13, 173
Perturbations of the soul, 64–65
Petrarca, Gerardo, 36
Petrarch: on scholastic theology, xxv, 38–39; on logic, xxv, 102–103, 171–72; and circle of the moon, xxvi–xxvii, 36–37; his use of ancients, xxvii, 12–13, 41–56 passim, 109, 129, 149, 150–51, 207; on contingency, xxvii, 43; on study of nature, 22–23; and Galileo, 23, 206–207; early humanists on, 25–26; on own historical importance, 26; and learning, 26, 46, 48, 89, 128, 171; his works, 27; on Black Death, 27–28, 40–41; on own literary style, 28–29; and death of friends, 28–29; and grief, 29, 59, 76; on dangers in own life, 32–33; on death, 32–33, 36, 81–82; and change, 35–36, 205; and Dante, 38; on reading, 42–45 passim, 82; on classical Latin, 42, 45, 187; his depressions, 42–43; on Aristotle, 45, 149, 187; on spiritual battles, 47, 129; discovers works by Cicero, 88, and the self, 115, 162, 174; studied law, 121, 123; on Rome, 135; on history, 135, 151, 154; relevance of, 146; meaning of his humanism, 149–50; and Freud, 151; on own times, 151; on human condition, 151–52; his letters to ancients, 154; on humanities verses liberal arts, 171–73; and will power, 179; and "dark ages," 211; mentioned, xxiv, 25–58 passim, 83, 89, 90, 91, 95, 96, 102, 126, 129, 148, 152–53, 155, 180
—Works: Africa, 89, 119; De otio religioso, 40; De remediis utriusque fortunae, xvii,

43–44, 150–51; *De sui ipsius et multorum ignorantia,* 22–23, 45, 177, 178; *De viris illustribus,* 89; *De vita solitaria,* 40, 208; *Familiares,* 27–52 *passim; Invective contra medicum,* 208; *Posteritati,* 151; *Secretum,* 40, 43, 48, 82, 177, 178, 179, 198
Pfeiffer, Rudolf, 88
Philip of Macedonia, 48
Philology: and humanist scholarship, 8; early practice of, 88; becomes *Alttertumswissenschaft,* 92; Nietzsche on, 93–95, 97; mentioned, 91, 101, 103, 110, 147, 154, 155
Philosophy: Cicero on, 65; modern, 174, 179
Pico della Mirandola, Giovanni, 13, 24
Piérart, Marcel, 143–44
Pipher, Mary, xiii
Pizzinga, Jacopo, 25
Plague. *See* Black Death
Plato: his *Apology,* 164; mentioned, 10, 21, 64, 97, 168, 178, 189, 192, 205
Plotinus, 78
Plumb, J. H., 136–37
Plutarch, 61
Polis, 109, 149, 150, 164, 165
Politics, etymology of, 164
Poliziano, Angelo, 90
Polonius, 71, 192
Polybius, 56–58, 152, 153, 166
Porter, Noah, 101
Portia, wife of Brutus, 61
Postmodernism, 211
Premodern societies, 184, 210
Present, the: tyranny of, 137, 144, 148; mentioned, 154, 174, 183, 196
Price, Lucien, 200
Private property, 122
Progress, myth of, 162, 163
Prosper of Aquitaine, 42
Psychoanalysis, 113, 116–17, 152
Psychotherapy, 115, 116, 208–209
Public service, 156, 166, 190
Pydna, Battle of, 205
Pythagoras, 64

Quantification, xxv, 130, 136, 147–48, 210
Quantum mechanics, 157, 159

Reason: ancient, 78–79, 180; modern, 79–80, 132, 158, 169, 180, 184, 195
Reformation, the, 89
Reich, Wilhelm, 116
Relativity, theory of, 157
Religion: Greek and Roman, 162, 169; study and teaching of, 9, 167, 169; questions of, 167, 212; natural, 213

Renaissance: created by humanists, xxiv; and ourselves, xxviii, 8, 144, 145, 146, 155, 164, 173, 188, 199; and antiquity, xxviii, 92, 96, 135, 145, 156, 174, 175, 176–79, 188, 189, 197, 208; emphasis on oratory, x–xi; and Petrarch, 26; and the self, 44, 48–49, 109, 178; and Cicero, 63; and humanities, 87, 111, 114, 116, 178, 193; in Italy, 116, 124, 167; leaders, 130, 131, 133–34; on the past, 135, 154; and community, 152, 153; individualism, 156; as concept, 211; mentioned, 20, 109, 120, 132, 155
Republican tradition, 149, 153, 164, 192
Rhetoric, 9, 10, 120, 149, 155
Rieff, Philip, 115–17, 152, 182
Riemer, Friedrich Wilhelm, 91
Romans: Petrarch on, xxvii, 46, 109; and Greek classics, 8, their self, 24, 71, 74, 192; on mourning, 60–61; and deeds, 70; virtues of, 205
Romantics, German, 180
Rome: Petrarch on, 42, 135; community in, 52, 55, 150, 166; as a source of courage, 52, 56; funerals in, 56–58; and Cicero, 59, 62, 177; and Renaissance cities, 124, 127, 135; and United States, 135; Dante on, 153; mentioned, 119, 127, 150
Rose, Phyllis, 111, 112
Ruling classes, 119, 133, 189–90
Russian formalism, xxv

Salerno, Gian Nicola, 130
Sallust, 5, 10, 127
Salutati, Coluccio, xxvi, 4, 33, 46, 88, 93, 127, 129
Sandys, Sir John Edwin, 88
Scaevola, Quintus Mucius, 60
Scaliger, Joseph, 88, 91
Schadewaldt, Wolfgang, 205–206
Scheler, Max, 77
Scholarship: humanist, 8; Petrarch's, 26; classical, 88–96 *passim,* 104; contemporary, 147, 148. *See also* Philology; Technique
Scholasticism, 22, 38, 39, 79, 93, 148, 171. *See also* Aristotelianism; Theology
Schulpforta, 92
Schumacher, E. F., 161–62
Schwartz, Barry, 183
Science: and humanities, xxiii, 23–24, 143, 206–207; limits of, 157–59, 167–68, 181; and nature, 157, 158, 159; history of, 157, 179, 180–81; future of, 158; postmodern, 159–60; teaching of, 179, 180–81, 198; as superstition, 180;

and social sciences, 182, 210; and
    change, 206–207; and the spiritual,
    211–12; mentioned, 143, 174, 176, 178
Scientific Revolution, xxvii, 10, 23, 167,
    175
Scipio Aemilianus, 37, 60, 66, 205
Scipio Africanus, 37, 89
Self, the: modern, passim; ancient, 21, 78,
    109, 153, 173, 177, 181, 184, 197, 198,
    206, 208; changing concept of, 103;
    Arnold on, 107; and psychoanalysis,
    114–15; and nature, 174, 213; and social
    sciences, 182; shaping of, xxvii–xxviii,
    12, 13, 19–20, 24, 56, 100, 103, 105–106,
    108, 109, 111, 114, 115, 118, 129, 151,
    153. See also Bildung
Seneca, Lucius Annaeus, 10, 37, 45, 46,
    53–56, 60–61, 74, 187
Sette, Guido, 36
Seveso, 159
Shakespeare: his Hamlet, 71, 114, 198; his
    Troilus and Cressida, 109, 119, 147, 192,
    193
Sidgwick, Henry, 96–108 passim, 128, 136
Silk, Leonard, 138
Simmel, Georg, 183
Sixties, protests of, 145, 180
Slavery in classical antiquity, 211
Snell, Bruno, 168
Snow, C. P., 180
Social sciences: qualification in, xxv, 147–
    48; as moral theories, 175, 176, 182;
    contrasted with natural sciences, 182,
    210; and humanities; 183–86; and tradi-
    tion, 185–86; mentioned, 131, 143, 167,
    174, 175, 179, 182, 183
Sociology: quantification in, xxv; moral
    concerns of, xxv, 183, 185; history of,
    183; and modernity; 184, mentioned,
    167
Socrates, 164
Sommers, Christina Hoff, 186
Sophocles, 110, 190
Sound of words: and Petrarch, 42, 43–
    44, 46
Statistics, xxv, 136, 148
Stockman, David A., 136
Stoicism, 16–18, 51, 102, 171, 205
Strozzi, Niccolò, 3, 4, 10–12, 195
Structuralism, xxv
Studia humanitatis: in Renaissance, xxiv,
    xxvi, xxvii, 10, 11, 16, 19–20, 114, 154,
    155, 194; as new pedagogy, xxiv, xxvi,
    56, 123–29 passim, on technique, xxv;
    and the self, xxvii, xxviii, 111, 129; de-
    mise of, 7, 87, 90; as used by Cicero,
    14–16, 63, 88, 178, 204–206; and Scien-

tific Revolution, 23; and Petrarch, 25–
    26, 83; today, 109; and psychoanalysis,
    115–17; and humanista, 123; and classi-
    cal moral thought, 132; and liberal arts,
    172; mentioned, 8, 49, 102, 108, 126,
    128, 134. See also Classical education
Sweezy, Paul M., 185
Swift, Jonathan, 105

Tacitus, Publius Cornelius, 10, 97
Tauton Commission, 100
Taylor, Charles, 180
Taylor, Frederick Winslow, 134
Teaching: and the demise of humanities,
    96–99, 101
Technique, obsession with, xxiv–xxv, 39,
    97, 102, 144, 146–49, 184, 190, 203
Technology, xxiii, 159, 179
Textual criticism, 89–90. See also
    Philology
Theology, scholastic: xxv, 4–5, 9, 38–39,
    46, 90, 147, 148, 167
Thomas, Lewis, 180
Thompson, E. P., 209
Thoreau, Henry David, 163
Three Mile Island, 159
Tocqueville, Alexis de, 183
Tolstoy, Leo, 192, 193
Toulmin, Stephen, 159–60, 182, 213
Tradition: deterioration of, 87; authority
    of, 132; biblical and republican, 164; of
    humanities, xiv, 114, 118, 129, 143, 144,
    145, 156, 188, 193; humanities and so-
    cial sciences on, 185–86
Trilling, Lionel: his Sincerity and Authentic-
    ity, 70–71, 109; on Bildung, xxvii, 106–
    12 passim
Trinkaus, Charles, 26, 167, 203–204
Tullia, Cicero's daughter, 59, 70, 150, 166
Turner, Frank M., 135
Turner, Frederick Jackson, 101
Turnus, 74
Tusculanum, 59

Ulpian, 123, 128
Ulysses, 33, 35–36
Unconscious, Freud's theory of, 114
United States: psychotherapy in, 116, 216–
    17; education of leaders in, 131; and
    Roman Republic, 135; politicians in,
    136; debate on education in, 143; repub-
    lican tradition, 149; secondary lan-
    guages of, 149, 163–64; cult of indi-
    vidualism in, 163; middle-class mores
    in, 163; fear of aging and death in, 165;
    forms of instruction in, 176
Universities: medieval, xxiv, 6, 22, 46,

102, 146; nineteenth-century, 103, 147;
contemporary, xxiii, xxv, 132, 146–47,
179, 212; development in U.S., 204–205

Valerius Maximus, 53–56, 74, 127
Valla, Lorenzo, 45–46, 89, 90, 91, 147, 148
Varro, Marcus Terentius, 20
Vergil: his *Aeneid,* 74–75, 166; mentioned,
   xxiv, 5, 10, 44, 74, 82, 96–97, 126,
   153–54
Verona, 88
Veysey, Lawrence R. 100–101
Vico, Giambattista, ix–x
Vienna, 116
Vietnam War, 145
Vir, 50–52, 67–74 *passim*
Virtue, 18, 128, 132, 133, 149, 153, 166,
   171, 186, 187, 188, 190, 192
Virtus, 68, 70, 73, 132, 205
Vogel, David, 138

Weber, Max: his *The Theory of Social and
   Economic Organization,* 131; mentioned,
   132, 134, 183, 210
West, the: history of, xxviii, 116, 189,

192, 211; and classics, 8; and Freud, 116;
and humanities, 87, 188–89; and
Greeks and Romans, 144, 156; ob-
jectification of nature in, 179, 181
Whitehead, Alfred North, 156, 157, 200–
201
Whyte, William H., 133
Wilamowitz-Moellendorff, Ulrich von,
   88, 92, 95
Winckelman, Johann Joachim, 91
Wisdom: and eloquence, 10; Cicero on,
   19, 72, 200; and virtue, 126, 128–29,
   131, 147, 149, 150, 151, 172–88 *passim,*
   195, 199, 200; of the ancients, 160; as
   goal of learning, 196
Wolf, Friedrich August, 91, 94
Wolfe, Alan, 185
Wolsey, Thomas, 126
Women, study of: and the humanities, 188
Work ethic, 162

Xenophon, 205

Yankelovich, Daniel, 148
Zeno of Citium, 9